Building Party Systems in Developing Democracies

This book addresses the question of why a party system with a modest number of nationally oriented political parties emerges in some democracies but not others. The number of parties and nationalization are the product of coordination between voters, candidates, and party leaders within local electoral districts and coordination among candidates and elites across districts. Candidates and voters can and do coordinate locally in response to electoral incentives, but coordination across districts, or aggregation, often fails in developing democracies. A key contribution of this book is the development and testing of a theory of aggregation incentives that focuses on the payoff to being a large party and the probability of capturing that payoff. The book relies on in-depth case studies of Thailand and the Philippines, and on large-N analysis to establish its arguments.

Allen Hicken is an Associate Professor of Political Science at the University of Michigan, a Faculty Associate at the Center for Southeast Asian Studies, and a Research Associate Professor at the Center for Political Studies. He studies elections, parties, and party systems in developing democracies, with a particular focus on Southeast Asia. He has carried out research and held research positions in Thailand, the Philippines, Singapore, and Cambodia. He is the recipient of a Fulbright Award and, with Ken Kollman, an NSF grant. His publications include articles in the *American Journal of Political Science*, the *Journal of Politics*, *Electoral Studies*, the *Journal of East Asian Studies*, and *Taiwan Journal of Democracy*.

Building Party Systems in Developing Democracies

ALLEN HICKEN
University of Michigan

CAMBRIDGE UNIVERSITY PRESS
Cambridge, New York, Melbourne, Madrid, Cape Town,
Singapore, São Paulo, Delhi, Mexico City

Cambridge University Press
32 Avenue of the Americas, New York, NY 10013-2473, USA

www.cambridge.org
Information on this title: www.cambridge.org/9780521885348

© Allen Hicken 2009

This publication is in copyright. Subject to statutory exception
and to the provisions of relevant collective licensing agreements,
no reproduction of any part may take place without the written
permission of Cambridge University Press.

First published 2009
Reprinted 2012

A catalog record for this publication is available from the British Library.

Library of Congress Cataloging in Publication Data

Hicken, Allen, 1969–
  Building party systems in developing democracies / Allen Hicken.
    p. cm.
  Includes bibliographical references and index.
  ISBN 978-0-521-88534-8 (hardback)
  1. Political parties – Thailand. 2. Political parties – Philippines.
  3. Thailand – Politics and government – 1986– 4. Philippines – Politics and
  government – 1986– I. Title.
  JQ1749.A795H53 2009
  324.2´04–dc22   2008021940

ISBN 978-0-521-88534-8 Hardback

Cambridge University Press has no responsibility for the persistence or accuracy of URLs
for external or third-party Internet Web sites referred to in this publication and does not
guarantee that any content on such Web sites is, or will remain, accurate or appropriate.

For BALANCER

Contents

Acknowledgments		*page* ix
1	Introduction	1
2	A Theory of Aggregation Incentives	26
3	Testing the Theory	47
4	Aggregation, Nationalization, and the Number of Parties in Thailand	86
5	Explaining Aggregation in Thailand	116
6	Term Limits, Aggregation Incentives, and the Number of Parties in the Philippines	149
7	Conclusion	180
References		187
Index		205

Acknowledgments

Completing this book, I have incurred debts to many people that I will never be able to adequately repay. Numerous friends and colleagues have commented on all or parts of this work, and I thank them each for their input. All errors and omissions are my own. As a graduate student at the University of California, San Diego, I was fortunate to be the recipient of intellectual and professional mentoring from Gary Cox, Andrew MacIntyre, Peter Gourevitch, Stephan Haggard, and Matthew Shugart. Their counsel and constant questioning (and patience) helped give the original dissertation shape, and they have continued to encourage me as I've worked on this book. I find it difficult to imagine a more ideal committee for any student. Thanks, too, to Matt Baum (for his example and a quick answer to a midnight email), Lorelei Moosbruger (for making me think), and Andrew MacIntyre, a wonderful mentor and an even better friend.

At Michigan, I received valuable feedback from my colleagues in the junior faculty workshop. Mary Gallagher, Orit Kedar, Mika LaVaque-Manty, and Rob Mickey have been wonderful colleagues in all senses of the word. I am still amazed that my colleagues Anna Grzymala-Busse, Skip Lupia, Ken Kollman, and Scott Page consented to read and discuss an early version of this manuscript. Their detailed and difficult feedback greatly improved the manuscript. Special thanks to Anna for being the consummate public goods provider. Finally, this book is better than it might have been due to the research assistance of Joel Simmons; thanks Joel. Outside of Michigan, I owe debts of gratitude to several people

ix

who read parts of the book and offered useful feedback. These include Pradeep Chhibber, Rick Doner, Mark Jones, and Ben Reilly.

My work in Thailand and the Philippines was made easier by people's willingness to speak with me about confusing, complex, and sometimes controversial issues. I was fortunate to be affiliated with the Asian Institute of Management in Makati during my stay in 2004 and made grateful use of the resources of that fine institution. During my trips to the Philippines, the following individuals were among those who shared helpful insights with me: Anthony Abat, Jose Almonte, Manuel Perez Aquino, Rommel Banlaoi, Enrico Basilio, Father Joaquin Bernas, Resurreccion Borra, Felix Berto Bustos, Venus Cajucom, Consuelo Callangan, Clarita Carlos, Emmanuel de Dios, Robert de Ocampo, Benjamin Diokno, Raul Fabella, James Faustino, Willibold Frehner, Vicente Gambito, Crisanta Legaspi, Victor Lim, Felipe Medalla, Amado Mendoza, Filipe Miranda, Romulo Neri, Rogelio Paglomutan, Epictetus Patalinghug, Joel Rocamora, Chito Salazar, Meliton Salazar, and Gwen Tecson. A special thanks to Josie and Bebe Paren at IDE for their help and generous hospitality. Bobby de Ocampo proved an insightful guide to Philippine politics and a wonderful friend and host. My family and I will always be grateful.

In Thailand, Michael Nelson's knowledge and friendship and healthy skepticism were extremely helpful. Others willing to sit down with me (often more than once) include Abhisit Vellajivva, Ammar Siamwalla, Amorn Chandara-Somboon, Anek Laothamatas, Anusorn Limanee, Areepong Bhoocha-oom, Chris Baker, Peter Brimble, Trevor Bull, Chaowana Traimas, Charoen Kanthawongs, Chinawut Naressaenee, Scott Christensen, Gothom Arya, Hatasakdi Na Pombejra, Kanok Wongtrangan, Dan King, Kraisak Choonhavan, Kramol Thongthamachart, Simon Leary, Likhit Dhiravegin, Manop Sangiambut, Medhi Krongkaew, Pallapa Runagrong, Pasuk Phongpaichit, Patcharee Siriros, Phipat Thairry, Phongthep Thepkanjana, Pornsak Phongpaew, Piyasnast Amranand, Serirat Prasutanond, Jeremy Price, Sombat Chantornvong, Terana Settasompop, Uwe Solinger, Thiti Kumnerddee, Suchit Bongbongkorn, Varathep Ratanakorn, Vichai Tunsiri, and Vuthipong Priebjrivat. I am grateful to Ajarn Suchit Bongbongkorn for inviting me to be a visitor at the Institute for Security and International Studies at Chulalongkorn during my dissertation fieldwork. During a subsequent visit to Thailand, the Thailand Development and Research Institute was

Acknowledgments

my intellectual home away from home. Thanks to Dr. Chalongphob Sussangkarn for extending the invitation and to Ajarn Ammar Siamwalla for stimulating discussions about parties, political economy, and the $M + 1$ rule.

The research for this book would not have been possible without the financial support of several institutions. Part of the original dissertation research was supported by a Dissertation Research Fellowship from the Institute on Global Conflict and Cooperation. Subsequent research was made possible by a Fulbright Fellowship, which funded more time in Thailand and the Philippines. Finally, a good portion of the book manuscript was completed while I was a visiting researcher at the Asian Research Institute and the National University of Singapore. I am grateful to Tony Reid for his vision of an interdisciplinary community of scholars and for inviting me to be a part of that community. While I was thankful for the time to write, the proximity of so many interesting colleagues sometimes made that a challenge. The debates and conversations with Erik Kuhonta, K. S. Jomo, Michael Montesano, Suzaina Kadir, and Tony Reid were a highlight of my time there.

Foremost among my creditors is my wife Alisa. Without her patience, editorial eye, and skills as wife and mother, this would not have been possible. She amazes me. I also owe a debt to my children, Camille, Bethany, Nathan, Laura, Emma, and Rachel, for long hours spent at the office that took time away from them. Their tolerance and good humor (my daughter one day exasperatedly asked, "Just how long *is* this book anyway?"), and daily reminders that I needed to finish helped spur me on. I also enjoyed commiserating with my brother, Bret, who, as I was writing the dissertation from which this book draws, was going through his own Ph.D. program. I refuse to say who finished first. Finally, I am grateful to my parents for their support and encouragement and for teaching (or trying to teach) me how to work.

Building Party Systems in Developing Democracies

1

Introduction

> Political parties created democracy.... [M]odern democracy is unthinkable save in terms of the parties.
>
> E. E. Schattschneider (1942)
>
> Political parties are the weakest link in the system.
>
> Thai politician (1999)

1.1 INTRODUCTION

This book answers the question of why a party system with a modest number of nationally oriented political parties emerges in some democracies but not others. This question is of considerable importance given the staggering number of countries struggling with democratic consolidation in the wake of the so-called third wave of democratization. The question of how and why certain party systems emerge is equally relevant for a number of older democracies where perceived weaknesses in existing party systems have generated proposals for political-institutional reform (e.g. Great Britain, Italy, and Japan). As E. E. Schattschneider argued more than sixty years ago, the party system is in many ways the keystone of any effort to construct a well-functioning democracy (1942). Yet among the numerous tasks involved in the transition to and consolidation of democracy, the building of an effective and supportive party system has arguably proved the most difficult and elusive. Indeed, the sentiment of the Thai politician quoted above would resonate in many democracies across the globe, whether developing or developed (see Carothers 2006).

If an enduring and effective party system is a necessary condition for an enduring and effective democracy, it is essential that we understand how and why such party systems develop (or fail to develop). This is a challenging task, in part because party systems can be studied along multiple dimensions. These include, but are not limited to, the extent of ideological polarization within the party system (Sartori 1976), the level of party system institutionalization (Mainwaring and Scully 1995), the number of parties (Duverger 1954; Taagepera and Shugart 1989; Cox 1997), the degree of intra-party cohesion (Cox and McCubbins 2001; Hicken 2002), and the degree of party system nationalization (Chhibber and Kollman 1998, 2004).[1] Rather than attempting to address all of these dimensions simultaneously, I focus in this book on two features of the party system: (1) the degree of party system nationalization and (2) the size of the party system or the number of parties.

I argue that both party system size and nationalization are a function of aggregation, defined as the extent to which electoral competitors from different districts come together under a common party banner.[2] Where aggregation is poor, that is where candidates fail to coordinate with other candidates across districts, the number of political parties proliferates, and those parties tend to have less than national constituencies. Conversely, high levels of aggregation are associated with fewer, more nationally oriented political parties. The central task of this book is to explore the factors that affect candidates' incentives to coordinate or aggregate across districts.

Obviously aggregation is not the only factor that affects nationalization and the number of parties. It is, however, among the most neglected in the existing literature. Of course, the presence of this "gap" in the literature is not sufficient justification for focusing on aggregation (most topics are neglected by the literature for good reason). Instead, one must demonstrate that by including aggregation in our analyses, we can substantially improve our understanding of party systems. I endeavor

---

[1] These dimensions need not be mutually exclusive. For example, party system nationalization is a component of Mainwaring and Scully's definition of institutionalization.

[2] The extent to which competitors from different districts join together to form regional or national political parties has been labeled "linkage" by Cox (1997, 1999) and "aggregation" by Chhibber and Kollman (1998, 2004). The terms are interchangeable but for the sake of consistency I will mainly rely on Chhibber and Kollman's terminology.

Introduction

to do this throughout the book by, first, highlighting the theoretical contributions of a focus on aggregation incentives; second, showing how aggregation and aggregation incentives have shaped the party systems in two developing democracies (Thailand and the Philippines); and, third, examining the dynamics of aggregation across a sample of 280 elections in 46 countries.

When studying party systems, it is important to recognize that there is no consensus about what an ideal party system should look like. For example, even though we may agree that hyper-inflated party systems are unworkable and that a one-party system calls into question the reality of democracy, beyond this there is considerable disagreement over the optimal number of political parties, or whether such an ideal even exists. This reflects the fact that institutions necessarily involve trade-offs between competing objectives (see Powell 2000). For example, fewer parties can come at the cost of less correspondence between voter and party positions (Powell and Vanberg 2000). Likewise, larger, more national parties may undermine the links between politicians and local constituencies. For this reason, I avoid language that casts greater or lesser aggregation, fewer or more parties, or more or less nationalization as a straightforward normative choice.

The remainder of this chapter proceeds as follows. In the next section, I briefly review arguments for why voters, candidates, and legislators might derive benefits from the formation of political parties. I then discuss the two features of the party system at issue here – nationalization and the number of parties – in more detail. The core of this chapter is a brief summary of the arguments in this book and a discussion of how a focus on aggregation and aggregation incentives improves our understanding of why party systems develop as they do. I then talk about the use of Thailand and Philippines as cases with which to evaluate the theory. The final section outlines the contents of the remainder of the book.

1.2 WHY PARTIES?

Throughout this book, I define a *political party* as any group of candidates that contests an election under a common party label (Epstein 1967; Cox 1999).[3] A *party system* is an enduring pattern of intra-party

---

[3] I recognize parties can be much more than this as well.

organization and inter-party electoral competition (Chhibber and Kollman 2004, 4). We know that parties and party systems have real and important consequences for a variety of outcomes that we care about. This list includes the health of democratic government (Mainwaring and Scully 1995), the nature and quality of democratic representation (Lijphart 1999; Powell 2000), government stability (Sartori 1976; Laver and Schofield 1990; Mainwaring and Shugart 1997), and the nature of the policymaking environment and policy outcomes (Alesina, Roubini, and Cohen 1997; Persson and Tabellini 2000; Franzese 2002; Hicken 2002; MacIntyre 2002; Chhibber and Nooruddin 2004; Hicken and Simmons 2008). It is understandable then that scholars focus so much attention on political parties and party systems. It is also no surprise that constitutional architects and political reformers (in democracies old and new) often have the party system in mind when (re)designing political rules and institutions. By adopting certain institutions, they hope, among other things, to produce a certain type of party system.

This emphasis on political parties and party systems by both political scientists and political practitioners reflects the central role for political parties in modern democratic government. Why and how parties emerge as the core institutions of modern democracy is the subject of much discussion in the literature. One way to parse this literature is to separate it based on the unit of analysis – voters (citizens), candidates, or legislators (Chhibber and Kollman 2004, 67). Voter-focused approaches view political parties as the natural outgrowth of shared preferences among subsets of voters (social cleavages) (Lipset and Rokkan 1967; Rose 1974; Caramani 2004).[4] These parties endure as long as those preferences remain stable. However, fundamental changes in those preferences, whether from demographic shifts, industrialization, postmodernization, or some other source, generate opportunities for new parties to form (Key 1949; Schattschneider 1960; LeDuc 1985; Ingelhart 1997).[5]

A second portion of the literature emphasizes the incentives for candidates to join with other candidates under a common party banner. To be elected, candidates must grapple with two collective

---

[4] For critiques of this literature see Kitschelt (1989) and Bartolini (2000).
[5] The effect of changes in underlying social preferences is mediated through electoral institutions (Amorim-Neto and Cox 1997; Ordeshook and Shvetsova 1994; Hug 2001; Clark and Golder 2006).

action problems among their potential supporters (Aldrich 1995). Given the negligible impact of a single vote on the outcome, why should potential voters (a) pay the cost of educating themselves about the available choices (Downs 1957) and (b) bother to vote at all (Downs 1957; Riker and Ordeshook 1968)? Candidates have strong incentives to help potential supporters overcome these obstacles, and a party can be an effective tool toward that end. Consider the case of the candidate who seeks office merely for the perks and rewards that come with the position. (I will consider in a moment candidates who have policy preferences they wish to see adopted.) Parties offer two advantages to office-seeking candidates. First, party affiliation can aid candidates in establishing a reputation – a "brand name" – in the eyes of voters. Party labels, in other words, can serve as useful information shortcuts, reducing the information costs to voters and providing candidates with a core of likely supporters (Campbell et al. 1960; Lupia and McCubbins 1998). Second, candidates can recognize economies of scale through coordinating with other candidates under a common party label. For example, if the party were to invest in voter education or work to increase the turnout of likely party supporters, all candidates on the party's ticket would potentially benefit.

Gains from economies of scale also play an important role in explanations of party formation that focus on legislators' incentives. Legislators often face tasks that require the help of a large number of legislators (Cox 1997). Whether it is implementing a policy agenda, blocking proposals to change the status quo, or gaining access to the resources of government, large groups are often better able to accomplish these tasks than smaller groups. More generally, parties help solve collective action dilemmas for legislators by enabling legislators to enforce agreements to support each others' bills (and avoid cycling among various policy proposals) (Aldrich 1995; Jackson and Moselle 2002) and by providing a mechanism for protecting the party's collective reputation and long term interests (Kiewit and McCubbins 1991; Cox and McCubbins 1993).

To summarize, during elections, political parties provide a means of aggregating, organizing, and coordinating voters, candidates, and donors (Chhibber and Kollman 2004, 4). Within the legislature, parties are vehicles for solving collective action problems and coordinating the behavior of legislative and executive actors (ibid.). Political parties also provide a means for balancing local concerns with national interests and long-term priorities with short-term political demands.

In new and developing democracies, parties do all these things and more. Political parties are often the most immediate and potent symbols of democracy to voters in new democracies and can either bolster support for democratic norms and institutions or undermine their legitimacy. Parties are also important for managing the conflict and upheaval that are an unavoidable part of democratic transitions and economic development. Finally, political parties are also key to creating viable organizational alternatives to military cliques. Without strong parties and an effective party system, it is more difficult to drive the military back to the barracks and keep them there. In short, the progress of democratic consolidation can very much hinge on the kind of party system that emerges in developing democracies (Sartori 1976, 1986, 1994; Mainwaring and Scully 1995).

1.3 NATIONALIZATION AND THE NUMBER OF PARTIES

Even though party systems have many important features, the chief focus of this book is on two of those features – the degree of party system nationalization and the number of political parties. I define *nationalization* as the extent to which parties have broad, national constituencies as opposed to constituencies that are primarily regional, local, or parochial in nature. With respect to the number of parties in a party system, they can be "counted" in a variety of ways.[6] For the purposes of this book, I employ the definition used in much of the parties and elections literature by calculating the "effective number of parties" (ENP) (Laakso and Taagepera 1979), while recognizing the limitations involved with this measure (see Dunleavy and Boucek 2003). ENP is defined as 1 divided by the sum of the weighted values for each party. This measure weights parties according to their size – parties with large vote shares are weighted more than parties with small shares.[7] If one party captures all of the votes, then ENP = 1. If n parties have equal vote shares then

---

[6] For example, in the 1995 Thai election, there were 20 registered political parties, 14 of which actually fielded candidates, 11 of which actually won seats in the National Assembly.

[7] The weighted values are calculated by squaring each party's vote share (v_j): ENP = $1/(\sum v_j^2)$.

ENP = n.[8] I discuss both the number of parties and nationalization in turn, starting with the number of parties.

The Number of Parties

We know that the number of political parties in a party system has a variety of important consequences. The number of political parties affects such things as coalition stability, government decisiveness, government credibility, and the likelihood that voters will be able to vote for a party that is close to their ideal point (Laver and Schofield 1990; Colomer 2001; MacIntyre 2002). Obviously what is considered an optimal number of political parties will vary from country to country, expert to expert, depending on which governance goals we wish to privilege. Some advocate a multiparty system for its representational advantages (Lijphart 1977; Powell 2000; Colomer 2001), whereas others argue that a two-party (or even a single-party) system has advantage in terms of accountability, decisiveness, and incentives for moderation (Horowitz 1985; Shugart and Carey 1992; Reilly 2001).

Within this debate, however, there is considerable consensus that either extreme in party system size is inimical to effective democratic governance. Where a single party dominates, we may justifiably wonder whether the system is truly democratic and question the degree to which elections are free and fair. Likewise, the problematic nature of a hyper-inflated party system is a common theme in the comparative politics literature, although again definitions of what constitutes "too many" parties may differ.[9] An inflated party system can give rise to a gulf

---

[8] One can calculate ENP using either the vote share of a particular party or its seat share. Using votes yields the effective number of electoral parties, whereas the seat share gives the effective number of legislative parties. I use vote shares unless otherwise noted.

[9] Quotes like these are common in discussions of developing democracies:

Romania: "The large number of political parties often renders the democratic workings of government immobile. A certain instability has thus become the hallmark of the government." (Lovatt 2000)
Kosovo: "There are too many political parties in the Balkans as it is; we have enough of them for export." (Quemail Morina, quoted in ERP KiM Newsletters 2004)
Brazil: "The fact is that there are simply too many parties to allow an effective government to be set up and implement consistent policies based on the national interest." (Fitzpatrick 2006)
Gambia: "One of the hard truths of the 2001 elections is that there existed too many political parties." (Ceesay 2005)

between visible and invisible politics (especially when combined with ideological polarization (Sartori 1976)), undermine cabinet/government stability (e.g., Laver and Schofield 1990) and make it difficult for governments to pass needed policies in a timely manner (e.g., Tsebelis 1995, 2002; Mainwaring and Shugart 1997; Cox and McCubbins 2001; Franzese 2002). Perhaps, then, it is not surprising that institutional reforms in existing democracies are often aimed at reducing the number of parties in the party system (Shugart 2001; Shugart and Wattenberg 2001; Reilly 2006).

Nationalization

A growing number of scholars are focusing on the causes and consequences of party system nationalization (Cox 1997, 1999; Chhibber and Kollman 1998, 2004; Jones and Mainwaring 2003; Caramani 2004; Morgenstern and Swindle 2005). The degree of party system nationalization matters for a large number of issues that interest political scientists. The degree of nationalization communicates important information about the nature of political parties' and politicians' constituency.[10] The more nationalized the party system, the larger or broader the constituency is likely to be, ceteris paribus. In other words, the nature of the groups and interests to whom parties respond very much depends on the extent to which parties garner votes nationally (across a country's various electoral districts and geographic regions) or draw support from narrow subnational constituencies.

Whether or not more or less nationalization is preferable is not my focus here. However, it is worth noting that, like the number of parties, nationalization embodies a trade-off between competing objectives. If the goal is to maximize the incentives for political actors to respond to, promote, and protect broad national interests or to create or maintain a national identity, then more nationalization is preferable to less, all else equal. For example, a number of scholars have argued that democratic

---

Vanuatu: "We have to stop the disorganization caused by too many political parties." (Saribo 2003)

[10] The degree of nationalization is also related to the kinds of electoral strategies candidates and parties employ as well as the types of appeals to which voters respond (Schattschneider 1960; Hicken 2002; Jones and Mainwaring 2003).

Introduction

consolidation in divided societies is more likely where parties compete for nationwide votes as opposed to votes from a narrow group or region (Horowitz 1985, 1991; Diamond 1988; Reynolds 1999; Reilly 2001). On the other hand, if the priority is a party system that preserves and protects the preferences of small, subnational constituencies (e.g., regions or geographically concentrated ethnic/religious groups), then less nationalization is better. From this perspective, nationalized party systems are more likely to under-represent the interests of potentially powerful subnational groups leading to diminished democratic responsiveness (Lijphart 1977; Powell 2000).

1.4 ARGUMENTS OF THE BOOK: A QUESTION OF COORDINATION

What explains the type of party systems that emerge in democracies? To answer this question, it is useful to think of the party system as the outcome of various coordination opportunities. Voters and candidates may successfully coordinate on a small number of parties, or such coordination may fail, leading to a proliferation of parties. Candidates may choose to coordinate across districts to form large national parties, or they may eschew such cross-district coordination.

In the chapters that follow, I explore the coordination successes and failures at the heart of democratic party systems. Specifically, I examine factors that encourage and discourage greater coordination between voters, candidates, and parties. I argue that coordination incentives are often not conducive to a party system with a modest number of national parties – especially in developing democracies. In the case study analyses, I discuss how various historical and societal factors helped shape the development of the party system. However, the focus of the argument is on the role of institutional factors. Rules and institutions such as the electoral system, the manner of selecting the chief executive, and the distribution of power between different branches of government have profound and predictable impacts on the development of parties and party systems.

The features of the party system of interest in this study – the number of parties and nationalization – are the product of coordination (or coordination failures) among voters, candidates, and party leaders *within* electoral districts (intra-district coordination) and *across* districts (inter-district coordination or aggregation). I argue that coordination failures at the district level are not the primary explanation for why party systems in many democracies often diverge from expectations. Though there are certainly exceptions (see Backer and Kollman 2003; Chhibber and Kollman 2004), voters, candidates, and parties can and do coordinate locally in response to electoral incentives, even in new democracies (Clark and Golder 2006 and Chapters 4 and 6 in this study). Cross-district coordination, however, is another matter. Cross-district coordination requires that political elites from many localities cooperate by, for example, forging an electoral alliance (a party) and compromising on a set of policy goals and priorities. It is these cross-district attempts at coordination or aggregation that often fail, particularly in developing democracies, with two consequences. First, where aggregation failures regularly occur, national parties do not develop. Second, poor aggregation is associated with the inflation of the number of political parties.

By way of a brief illustration, consider the relationship between coordination (within and across districts) and the size of the party system. (I will discuss this in more detail later in Chapter 2). The bulk of the existing work on the determinants of the number of parties focuses on the electoral system – specifically the electoral formula (e.g., plurality versus proportional representation) and the number of seats open for competition (district magnitude) (Duverger 1954; Taagepera and Shugart 1989; Cox 1997). Cox's $M + 1$ rule is useful as a generalized statement of the relationship between the electoral system and the number of political parties. M equals the number of seats in a district, and the $M + 1$ rule predicts that no more than $M + 1$ candidates or parties are viable in any single seat districts ($M = 1$), and that no more than $M + 1$ parties are viable in multiseat districts ($M > 1$). In other words, as the number of seats in a district increases, we expect more parties, ceteris paribus.[11]

Often lost in discussions of electoral systems is the fact that although these institutions allow predictions about the number of parties in each individual electoral district, they do not enable one to anticipate the number of parties that will arise nationally. Electoral rules directly affect the nature of coordination *within* electoral districts. Why

---

[11] The $M + 1$ rule is an upper limit on the number of political parties. Whether a party system is at or below the $M + 1$ threshold is a function of the degree of social heterogeneity (Amorim-Neto and Cox 1997; Clark and Golder 2006).

candidates might (fail to) coordinate *across* districts is a separate, but equally important question. Despite observations by numerous scholars that the size of the national party system can diverge quite sharply from what we observe in individual districts (see, for example, Riker 1982; Sartori 1986; Kim and Ohn 1992), the issue of cross-district coordination or aggregation has received relatively little attention.[12] Yet, understanding aggregation is crucial if we are to explain why party systems look as they do.

Imagine two countries, A and B in Figure 1.1. The result of within-district coordination in each country is numerous district-level party systems each with its own effective number of parties. In this case, the electoral system induces coordination on two parties within each electoral district. Thus the average effective number of parties locally (ENP$_{avg}$) is 2 in both country A and B.[13] How, though, do these numerous local party systems map onto the national party system? Does a unique set of parties run in each district or are the same few parties the frontrunners in most districts? Countries A and B differ in the degree of aggregation – that is, the extent to which candidates coordinate across districts under a common party label. In country A, each electoral district contains a different set of parties – Yellow and Green in district 1, Purple and Blue in district 2, and Red and Orange in district 3. At the other extreme, the same two parties – Yellow and Green – are the frontrunners in all the districts in country B. The difference in the level of aggregation between the two countries has profound implications for the national party system. In country A, the effective number of parties nationally (ENP$_{nat}$) is 6 – much larger than the average effective number of parties at the district level (ENP$_{avg}$). By contrast, the national effective number of parties in country B equals 2 – reflecting exactly what we see in each of the districts.

Now consider a third country, country C. Here a permissive electoral system allows for a large number of parties in each district (ENP$_{avg}$ = 6). However, coordination across districts is extensive such that when we

---

[12] Riker (1982) notes that single-member district plurality systems may not generate two national parties when third parties nationally are continually one of two parties locally. Sartori (1986) and Kim and Ohn (1992) also argue that single-member district plurality systems will not lead to a two-party system if the electorate is comprised of geographically concentrated minorities.

[13] Assuming the two parties split the vote equally.

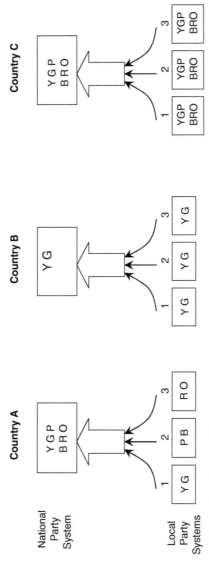

FIGURE 1.1. Comparing Aggregation

Introduction

aggregate to the national level, the national party system mirrors the local party systems in both size and composition ($ENP_{nat} = 6$).

As these examples make clear, a country's party system may be large or inflated due to (1) a large number of parties winning seats in each district (country C), (2) poor aggregation across districts (country A), or (3) a combination of 1 and 2. Looking at the national effective number of parties in isolation tells us nothing about whether party system inflation is due to coordination failures within districts, across districts, or both. Instead, it is necessary to compare the size of the national party system to the local party system in order to separate out aggregation from district level processes.

Table 1.1 displays the information on the size of the local party systems (ENP_{avg}) and national party systems (ENP_{nat}) in 16 countries from around the world.[14] The difference between the effective number of parties nationally (ENP_{nat}) and the average effective number of parties in the district (ENP_{avg}) is a measure of the extent of aggregation across districts ($D = ENP_{nat} - ENP_{avg}$). Higher differences reflect worse aggregation. One useful way to capture the extent of aggregation is to convert this difference into a percentage measure of how much larger the national party system is than the average district-level party system. This party system inflation measure (I) is computed by dividing the difference between ENP_{nat} and ENP_{avg} (D) by ENP_{nat} and then multiplying by 100 (Cox 1999:17). $I = 100(ENP_{nat} - ENP_{avg})/ENP_{nat}$. The resulting inflation score tells us what portion of the size of the national party system is due to poor aggregation, and what percentage reflects the extent of coordination within districts. Based on this calculation, if I is 10, then 10% of the size of the national party system can be attributed to different parties garnering votes in different parts of the country (poor aggregation), with the other 90% ascribable to the average number of parties at the district level. The larger the inflation score, the poorer the aggregation. Note that in Table 1.1, for the countries with a large number of parties, poor aggregation is responsible for one-third or more of party system inflation.[15] In short, in

---

[14] These 16 countries were chosen from a sample of 46 countries used in Chapter 3. The list of all 46 countries and their inflation scores is available in Chapter 3.
[15] In addition, electoral rules and institutions appear to be having the expected effect on the coordination within districts. In almost all of the countries listed in Table 1.1, ENP_{avg} is within the range we would expect given the average number of seats in each district. The only exceptions are some of the single-member-district cases (e.g., India,

TABLE 1.1. *The Size of the Local and National Party System Compared*

Country	ENP$_{avg}$	ENP$_{nat}$	Inflation
Ecuador (1979–88)	3.5	8.3	58
Thailand (1986–2001)	3.1	6.6	53
Belgium (1971–99)	4.1	8.0	49
India (1971–99)	2.4	4.7	49
Switzerland (1971–95)	4.0	6.4	38
Philippines (1992–98)	2.3	3.6	36
Brazil (1986–2002)	5.4	7.8	31
South Korea (1988–2000)	2.8	3.9	28
Germany (1972–98)	2.5	3.2	22
Canada (1972–2000)	2.6	3.3	21
Argentina (1983–99)	2.7	3.2	16
United Kingdom (1970–97)	2.5	3.0	17
Botswana (1994–99)	2.1	2.4	13
United States (1972–2000)	1.8	2.0	10
Venezuela (1973–83)	2.9	3.1	6
Denmark (1971–98)	5.1	5.2	2

Notes: ENP$_{avg}$ is the average effective number of parties in each district. ENP$_{nat}$ is the effective number of parties nationally (as measured by a party's vote share). Both terms are averaged across all elections within the specified time period.
Source: Author's calculation.

many countries, the lack of coordination across districts accounts for a substantial share of the party system's size, in some cases the lion's share.

Understanding the role aggregation plays in shaping a country's party system is crucial not just because of its effect on the number of parties. The degree of aggregation also communicates important information about the nature of parties in a given party system. Where aggregation is good, parties will tend to have larger, broader, more national constituencies than where aggregation is poor. The fact that aggregation is extremely poor in a place like Thailand, for example, supplies important clues about the interests and orientation of Thai parties (and their members).

Given the role aggregation plays in shaping the party system, ignoring aggregation carries considerable theoretical and practical risks. The failure to take aggregation into account might lead one to misinterpret the results of hypothesis tests (for example, concluding

the Philippines, and Canada) where there is slightly more than the expected two parties. For more on violations of Duverger's law and the $M + 1$ rule in single-seat districts, see Backer and Kollman (2003).

erroneously that electoral rules failed to produce the predicted number of parties). The neglect of aggregation might also lead to a misdiagnosis of the causes of an inflated party system and the subsequent prescription of an ineffective or inappropriate remedy.

Explaining Aggregation

Thanks to the rich literature in comparative electoral studies, we know a good deal about what shapes intra-district coordination (Duverger 1954; Taagepera and Shugart 1989; Lijphart 1994; Cox 1997, 1999; Clark and Golder 2006). We know much less about the factors that influence cross-district coordination or aggregation. A key contribution of this book is the development and testing of a theory of aggregation incentives.

Even though there is a lack of theorizing about aggregation, some students of comparative elections have acknowledged its role in shaping the national party system. Maurice Duverger, for example, considered the question of how local two-party systems become a national two party system, stating:

[T]he increased centralization of organization within the parties and the consequent tendency to see political problems from the wider, national standpoint tend of themselves to project on to the entire country the localized two-party system brought about by the ballot procedure. (1954, 228)

In a similar vein, Giovanni Sartori argues that the plurality rule will have no effect beyond the district until parties have both nationwide organizations and party labels that command a habitual following in the electorate (1968, 281, 293). However, if what we are trying to explain is aggregation, then both Duverger and Sartori beg the question.[16] How and why does the establishment of nationwide organizations occur? What incentives do parties have to become more centralized and nationally oriented? How does the local party system come to "project" on to the national party system?

Recently a few scholars have begun to explore these questions, chief among them Cox (1997, 1999) and Chhibber and Kollman (1998, 2004). Chhibber and Kollman single out for attention the degree of economic and political authority wielded by national governments

---

[16] See also Leys 1959.

relative to subnational governments. They find that more centralization of authority at the national level is positively associated with aggregation. In other words, the more power and resources the central government controls, the stronger the incentives of voters and candidates to cooperate across districts to form large national parties.

This centralization of power within the national government (what I dub vertical centralization) is certainly an important variable; however, I argue that by itself vertical centralization is not enough to produce strong aggregation incentives. Two other institutional variables play key roles. (These are discussed in greater depth in Chapter 2.) First, the degree of *horizontal centralization* – the degree to which power is concentrated *within* the national government – also influences incentives to aggregate across districts. Horizontal centralization interacts with vertical centralization to determine the payoff to being the largest legislative party. The larger this aggregation payoff is, the stronger the incentives will be for candidates to coordinate across districts to form national parties. What kinds of variables affect the degree of horizontal centralization in a political system? I focus on three: (1) the presence of a second chamber in the legislature, (2) the degree of internal party cohesion, and (3) the presence of reserve domains.[17] The latter are institutional or policy domains controlled by actors who are not directly accountable to elected officials (Valenzuela 1992). Where there is a second legislative chamber, parties are highly factionalized, and significant reserve domains exist, the likelihood of significant checks on the power of the largest legislative party reduces the payoff to aggregation.

The second variable that shapes aggregation incentives is the probability that the largest legislative party will actually be able to capture the aggregation payoff. A large payoff has little effect on candidate incentives if there is only a small chance that the largest party will capture that prize. The dynamics of this probability variable are different in parliamentary and presidential regimes, as I explore in Chapter 2. In parliamentary regimes, the key question is whether or not the leader of the largest party automatically captures the premiership. If the answer is yes, then aggregation incentives are

---

[17] The number of parties is another variable that can effect the horizontal distribution of power. However, as I will demonstrate in Chapter 2, the number of political parties itself is partially endogenous to the level of aggregation.

stronger than if there is a good chance that someone other than the leader of the largest party will become prime minister. In presidential regimes, the probability of capturing the aggregation payoff is a function of the proximity of the presidential and legislative elections and the number of presidential candidates. The probability that the largest legislative party will also control the presidency is the greatest where legislative and presidential elections are proximate and where there is a small number of presidential contenders. (The latter is contingent on electoral rules and rules governing presidential reelection.)

In short, I argue that aggregation incentives are a product of two factors: (a) the payoff to being the largest party at the national level, which itself is a product of vertical and horizontal centralization, and (b) the probability that the largest party will be able to capture that payoff. Taken together these two variables yield the expected utility of aggregating to form the largest national party.

This theory of aggregation incentives helps explain why in developing democracies coordination on a small number of national political parties often fails to emerge. The political environments in some developing democracies are inimical to such coordination. First, where state capacity is lacking and the central government bureaucracy is weak and ineffective (as is frequently the case in developing democracies), de jure or de facto control of power and resources may rest with subnational actors. Second, given the authoritarian pasts of many developing democracies, there is often an understandable desire to avoid concentrating too much power in the hands of the executive. Instead, democratic reformers attempt to disperse political authority both vertically and horizontally throughout the political system – providing for a series of checks and balances on arbitrary behavior by government actors. This is a laudable goal to be sure but institutions embody trade-offs. The diffusion/decentralization of political authority comes at the cost of reducing the incentives for aggregation. Third, authoritarian legacies can sometimes extend a good way into the democratic period. These legacies or reserve domains in the form of certain institutions (e.g., appointed or reserved seats in the legislature) or unwritten norms (e.g., restrictions on who can serve in certain positions) undermine the incentives to coordinate across districts to form large national parties.

I test this theory of aggregation incentives in several ways. First, I use the theory to derive a set of hypotheses, which I test using a dataset of nearly 280 elections in 46 countries. The results from these tests support the theory. Second, I also draw on data from two developing democracies – Thailand and the Philippines – to make three sets of comparisons. First, I analyze the extent to which the theory can account for the differences between the party systems of Thailand and the Philippines in terms of aggregation (and by extension the number of parties and nationalization). Second, within both country cases, I draw comparisons across time. In both Thailand and the Philippines, the degree of aggregation varies significantly over time. To what extent can the theory account for this variation? Various institutional reforms in each country allow me to make use of comparative statics tests. Finally, I compare across space within a single case – comparing coordination within and between various regions and provinces in Thailand.

1.5 CASE SELECTION

Much of this book focuses on the party systems in Thailand and the Philippines. This case selection has both a theoretical and methodological rationale. To begin with, Thailand and the Philippines provide ample variation on the dependent variable – aggregation – and by extension variation in terms of the two-party system features of interest – the number of parties and nationalization. Looking across the cases, aggregation has historically been much more extensive in the Philippines than it has been in Thailand, and the result has been a smaller, more nationalized party system. In recent years however, this pattern has reversed itself with Thailand experiencing much better aggregation than the Philippines. This change reflects the fact that within each country there is also substantial variation across time in the degree of aggregation and hence the size and nationalization of the party system. In the Philippines, cross-district coordination was extensive in the pre-Marcos democratic period but deteriorated sharply after the (re)transition to democracy in 1986. Thailand has traditionally been characterized by very poor aggregation, but this changed in the 2001 and 2005 elections. There is also variation (again both cross-country and within-country) on the independent variable side of the equation. Specifically, the institutional arrangements that centralize or disperse power as well as the rules and the norms that govern the chance that the largest party will capture the chief executive position vary across time and across countries. In part, this variation arises from the fact that Thailand is a parliamentary system, whereas the system in the Philippines is presidential.

Even though Thailand and the Philippines vary in ways that are of interest for the theory, they also have much in common, which allows me to control for other competing explanations. To begin with, apart from the size and degree of nationalization, the party systems in Thailand and the Philippines are very similar. The level of party system institutionalization in both countries is very low (Mainwaring and Scully 1995). In both countries, parties typically do not differ much in terms of ideology. In fact, it is impossible to align most Thai and Filipino parties along any coherent ideological dimension.[18] Political parties in each country have generally been fleeting alliances of convenience rather than stable unions of like-minded politicians. Party switching abounds, and parties are factionalized or atomized rather than cohesive unitary actors. These similarities along multiple dimensions of the party system allowed me to hold these features of the party system more or less constant while focusing my attention on the number of parties and nationalization.

Thailand and the Philippines also share other similarities. As members of the same region, they share certain similarities in terms of history (though less so than the countries of Latin America for example). They are of similar size geographically, demographically, and economically (both middle-income countries). Both countries began their transition (or retransition in the case of the Philippines) to democracy in the 1980s. Institutionally, they both use (primarily) majoritarian electoral systems which privilege candidate-centered over party-centered electoral strategies (Hicken 2002). The Thai and Philippine publics also share similar views toward democracy generally, and more specifically their political parties and party system. Large majorities of respondents in both countries profess a belief in democratic norms and consider democratic rules and procedures to be the only legitimate way of choosing and removing political leaders (Mangahas 1998; WVS 2000; Albritton and Thawilwadee 2002; SWS 2002). Yet their opinions of political parties – these keystones of modern democracy – border on contempt. For example, out

---

[18] In both countries, parties on the Left have been absent or electorally irrelevant in virtually all posttransition elections.

of 23 possibilities, political parties ranked next to last in a Thai survey designed to assess the public's trust in various institutions (KPI 2003).[19] Political parties were viewed as less trustworthy than the media, civil servants, and police (KPI 2003). Philippine respondents report similar disenchantment with that country's political parties (WVS 2004).

Thailand, the Philippines, and the Study of Comparative Politics

For students of comparative politics and comparative elections/parties, Thailand and the Philippines are valuable but relatively untapped resources. At the most basic level, the sheer size of Thailand and the Philippines makes them difficult to ignore. Both are among the 20 most populous countries in the world. Of the states in Latin America and the former communist bloc, only Brazil, Mexico, and Russia are larger. More important though, is what these cases can contribute to our understanding of democratic party systems, especially those in developing democracies. A growing community of scholars has begun to examine party systems in developing democracies. There are studies that draw on the experience of developing democracies in Latin America (Dix 1992; Mainwaring and Scully 1995; Schedler 1995; Coppedge 1998; Mainwaring 1999; Wallis 2003), Eastern Europe/former Soviet Union (Kischelt et al. 1999; Moser 2001; Stoner-Weiss 2001; Bielasiak 2002; Grzymala-Busse 2002), and Africa (Kuezni and Lambright 2001). However, to date very few of these studies have included cases from democratizing Asia.[20] An even smaller number consider party system cases from Southeast Asia. Apart from the literature on dominant party systems – which sometimes includes the cases of Singapore and Malaysia – only a handful of scholars have addressed the issue of party system development within Southeast Asian democracies.[21]

At one level, the experiences of the Philippines and Thailand look familiar to students of the developing world. The nineteenth and early twentieth centuries in Southeast Asia were eras of Western colonialism

---

[19] Only nongovernmental organizations (NGOs) scored lower.
[20] Chhibber's (1998) examination of India's party system is a notable exception. See also Stockton's (2001) comparison between party systems in Latin American with those Taiwan and South Korea.
[21] Paige Johnson Tan's work on party system institutionalization in Indonesia is one example (Tan 2002) as is Croissant and John (2002). See Hicken (2008) for a review of the Southeast Asia-focused political parties literature.

Introduction

and imperialism. World War II hastened the end of colonialism in Southeast Asia, and, in its wake, Thailand and the Philippines embarked on a period of democratic government, like many other countries around the globe. As in so much of the rest of the world, democratic governments eventually gave way to authoritarian regimes, with democracy staging a comeback during the 1980s. Yet, a closer look at these two states reveals interesting differences from the Latin American or Eastern European experiences, with potentially important theoretical implications. For example, the Thai and Philippine experiences with colonialism are distinct from those of most other countries/regions – Thailand was never colonized, and the Philippines was one of the few countries colonized by the United States – and neither country was home to the type of strong nationalist movements that gave rise to postindependence political parties elsewhere. Thus consideration of these two countries can help delineate the limits of existing theories of party and party system development in the democratizing world.

A second example of the way in which Thailand and the Philippines diverge from many other democracies is the role ideology plays in the political system. In Western Europe and parts of Latin America and Eastern Europe, it is a fairly simple task to array political parties along an ideological – usually Left–Right – spectrum. Ideology and ideological distance thus become important features of the party system – affecting everything from interest representation to democratic stability (Blondel 1968; Sartori 1976). However, as mentioned previously, it is nearly impossible to line up Thai and Filipino parties along an ideological dimension.[22] Thailand and the Philippines are certainly not unique in this regard. There are other developing democracies, including those in the rest of noncommunist East/Southeast Asia, for which applying ideologically based descriptive or analytical tools is problematic. An examination of the Thai and Philippine cases can help improve our understanding of how party systems develop in such nonideological environments.

Finally, the paring of Thailand and the Philippines also provides us with a degree of institutional variation that is sometimes lacking in comparative studies of party systems. Party systems research often focuses on a single case or a single region in which national-level executive institutions do not vary. Studies of party systems in Latin

---

[22] The 1973–6 period in Thailand is a partial exception.

America, for example, are by necessity studies of presidential party systems. Likewise, work on Western European party systems is predominantly based on the experience of parliamentary (or hybrid) democracies. By comparing the Philippines presidential system with Thailand's parliamentary government, we can consider whether the nature of executive institutions affects the development of the party system. At the same time, we can maintain the advantages of staying within a single region (e.g., the commonalities of history and level of economy development, as discussed previously). Since much of existing work on developing democracy party systems focuses on presidential or hybrid democracies, the case of parliamentary Thailand is especially valuable.

The experiences of Thailand and the Philippines can help us develop, test, and refine our ideas of how the world works, but the theories and approaches of political science also have something to offer in return. Specifically, the application of the theory developed in this book to the cases of Thailand and the Philippines allows me to address a number of interesting and unresolved empirical puzzles. First, what accounts for the large party system size and relative lack of nationalization in each country? Second, why were there historically more parties in Thailand than in the Philippines? Third, to what do we ascribe the sharp drop in the number of parties in Thailand in the 2000s? Finally, how do we explain the increase in the number of parties and the demise of the Philippine two-party system since the return of democracy in 1986?

Using the theory to help answer these questions, I demonstrate that differences in the extent of aggregation in the Philippines and Thailand help explain why the Thai party system has more parties than its Philippine counterpart. I also establish that the deterioration of the two-party system in the Philippines after the fall of Marcos is primarily due to aggregation failures – an explanation that outperforms existing theories of why this change occurred. I also show that the fall in the number of parties since 2000 in Thailand is almost completely a function of improved aggregation. Finally, I demonstrate that the variation of aggregation over time and cross-nationally is consistent with the theory of aggregation incentives outlined earlier.

In investigating these empirical puzzles, I consider and reject two opposing lines of argument about the relationship between the electoral

Introduction

and party systems. First, to some the presence of multiple parties in two countries using majoritarian/first-past-the-post electoral systems might suggest that theories linking the number of parties to the type of electoral system are at worse, wrong, or, at best, not applicable to developing democracies like Thailand and the Philippines. Those who ascribe to the latter view argue that the assumptions underlying electoral system theories are problematic in many developing democracies. In countries like Thailand and the Philippines, poor education and a lack of access to media raise information costs, while vote buying or the dominance of traditional social networks (e.g., patron-client relationships) limits voter behavior. Thus voters and candidates do not act in the ways the theories predict, and we do not see the coordination on a small number of parties that we see in developed democracies with similar electoral systems. As plausible as this argument may sound, it does not stand up to scrutiny in the Thai and Philippine cases. Using data from Thai and Philippine elections, I demonstrate that coordination by voters and candidates, and the resulting number of parties, is generally consistent with theoretical expectations. In so doing, I present a novel analysis of the way in which the block vote electoral system (used by Thailand) operates to shape the coordination incentives of candidates and voters.

A second line of argument, rather than dismissing the electoral system as unimportant, takes the opposite position. Namely, the number of political parties is primarily a function of the type of electoral system a country employs.[23] As discussed earlier, I argue that even though electoral systems do shape behavior in significant ways they are only a part of the story. The number of parties nationally is also a function of coordination by candidates and parties across districts. The analysis of election results from Thailand and the Philippines demonstrates that aggregation (or aggregation failure) is a crucial determinant of the number of parties and the degree of nationalization – more important in some cases than the electoral system. This finding supports growing evidence that very large party systems are large not because of district level failures but because of aggregation failures.

---

[23] More accurately, it is a function of the interaction between the electoral system and underlying social cleavages (Powell 1982; Ordeshook and Shvetsova 1994; Amorim-Neto and Cox 1997; Clark and Golder 2006).

Party Systems and Consequences of Institutional Reform

A focus on the Thai and Philippines party systems also allows me to address the issue of the (unintended) consequences of institutional reform. I focus on one set of institutional reforms in each country – the 1987 Philippine constitution and the 1997 Thai constitution. I argue that institutional reform has indeed produced changes in the party system, but not always in the way reformers anticipated or intended.

After the fall of Ferdinand Marcos in 1986, a new democratic constitution was adopted. It largely reestablished the rules and institutions that had existed during the 26 years before the Marcos regime, but with at least one important exception. The constitution placed a new single-term limit on the president, a reaction to the Marcos dictatorship, which proved to have profound, though unintended, consequences for the party system. Specifically, I show how the introduction of presidential term limits undermined aggregation incentives and prevented the return of the two-party system. I demonstrate that this account of party system change in the Philippines logically and empirically outperforms existing explanations of the demise of the two-party system.

In 1997 Thailand also adopted a new constitution. Among the goals of the constitutional drafters was a major reform of the party system. Specifically, they hoped the reforms would lead to fewer, more nationalized political parties. As a result of the reforms, nationalization did improve and the number of political parties did in fact fall dramatically in the first post-1997 election. Even though this was consistent with the drafters' goals, I argue that the reduction came about largely for the reasons they did not anticipate. The decrease in the number of parties had more to do with new, stronger incentives for cross-district coordination, an unintended consequence of constitutional reform, than it did with deliberate changes to the electoral system.

1.6 PLAN OF THE BOOK

The remainder of the book is organized into six chapters – a theoretical chapter, a large-N comparative chapter, three country-focused comparative chapters, and a conclusion. In Chapter 2, I develop and discuss the theory of aggregation incentives to be used throughout the rest of the book. In Chapter 3, I derive a set of hypotheses from the theory outlined in

Introduction

Chapter 2, discuss strategies for operationalizing the various dependant, explanatory (and control) variables of interest, and test those hypotheses using a dataset of 280 elections in 46 countries. Chapter 4 is the first of two chapters grappling with the Thai case. I first examine within-district coordination in Thailand and demonstrate that the large number of parties and lack of nationalization that defined Thailand's party system cannot be explained by coordination failures at the district level. In fact, the prevalence of patron-client links, poorly educated voters, and cultural differences from Western democracies has not significantly hindered intra-district coordination as some may have supposed. Thailand uses an unusual type of majoritarian electoral system that has rarely been studied – the block vote system. As a result, I first derive a set of hypotheses regarding the nature of intra-district coordination in Thailand and test those hypotheses using data from Thai elections. I then demonstrate that poor aggregation is chiefly responsible for the large number of parties and lack of nationalization in Thailand.

In Chapter 5, having established that coordination failures are more prevalent across districts than within them in Thailand, I use the theory outlined in Chapter 2 to explain the poor aggregation in pre-1997 Thailand. I then focus on the way in which constitutional reform altered the aggregation incentives for Thai politicians resulting in fewer, more national parties. I also discuss the way in which the improvement in aggregation incentives contributed to the rise of Thaksin Shinawatra and his Thai Rak Thai Party. Finally, I analyze the way in which the 2007 Constitution reforms, adopted in the wake of the 2006 coup, should alter aggregation incentives moving forward.

Chapter 6 shifts the focus to the case of the Philippines and one of the most interesting questions in the study of Philippine parties and elections – the demise of the two-party system in the post-Marcos era. I also draw on theory to explain an unusual electoral pattern the Philippines – namely, that there are fewer parties in midterm legislative elections than when legislative elections are concurrent with presidential elections. I dub this the counter-currency effect and note that it is precisely the opposite pattern than that observed in many other presidential democracies (Shugart 1995). The chapter ends with an analysis of the differences between the Thai and Philippine party systems. The concluding chapter summarizes the major findings and offers some directions for further research.

2

A Theory of Aggregation Incentives

2.1 INTRODUCTION

Imagine you are a political entrepreneur seeking political power in pursuit of some goal. This could include everything from pursuing personal enrichment, to protecting or advancing the interests of a certain group, to implementing your preferred set of programmatic policies. As discussed in the last chapter, there are many reasons why, in a modern democracy, a political party would most likely be your vehicle for seeking political power in pursuit of that goal. But what factors dictate the *kind* of party you choose to join or organize? Specifically, when would you want to join or form a large, national party, and when might you be content with belonging to a smaller organization? These are the questions I seek to answer in this chapter.

To answer these questions, I focus on the incentives of two types of actors – first, political entrepreneurs or nascent party leaders, and second, candidates for the national legislature.[1] Political entrepreneurs

---

[1] In order to keep the exposition simple I generally treat voters as passive actors – responding to the incentives in the political environment and the actions of candidates and political parties. However, as Chhibber and Kollman (2004) show, assigning a more active role to voters would likely generate similar conclusions since voters respond to many of the same incentives to which the other actors in my story respond. Specifically, Chhibber and Kollman demonstrate that where political power and control of resources are concentrated at the national level of government, voters respond by voting for nationally oriented parties in a position to compete for that power. Conversely, where subnational actors control significant power and resources, voters are more likely to support smaller local or regional parties.

A Theory of Aggregation Incentives

can come of in a variety of types – they might be the leader of the political group or faction, the leader of a small or medium-sized political party, or a notable figure looking to enter politics. The distinguishing feature of these entrepreneurs is their goal to capture some share of national executive authority via their position as head of a political party. I assume legislative candidates, whether in pursuit of personal, parochial, or policy goals, seek to win a seat in the legislature and thereafter gain access to the power and resources of government. Candidates may operate as individuals, or, as in many countries, as part of political groups, factions, or clans. We can think of these groups as proto-parties, the building blocks of organized political parties large or small. Individual candidates must decide with what kind of political party to ally, and groups of candidates face a decision about whether to compete as a small, stand-alone party or to ally with other groups of candidates to form a larger party.

What factors shape the incentives of these two types of actors to coordinate across districts in national legislative elections?[2] This is an important question. In Chapter 1, I demonstrated that the degree of cross-district coordination has consequences for a variety of outcomes we care about. This is because cross-district coordination, or aggregation, helps determine the number of political parties and the degree of party system nationalization. In this chapter, I present a theory of aggregation incentives.

In one of the few existing studies of this subject Chhibber and Kollman (1998, 2004) demonstrate that actors respond to the concentration of power and resources at the national level of government (relative to subnational units). Specifically, aggregation incentives are positively related to the concentration of power and resources. I label this *vertical centralization*. I recognize that the degree of vertical centralization may shape actors' incentives to link across districts under a common party label; however, I argue that a high degree of vertical concentration is not enough to induce aggregation. Two other factors play key roles. First, the degree of *horizontal centralization* – that is, the concentration or dispersion of power *within* the national

---

[2] When there are two legislative chambers, I focus on the competition for the lower, primary chamber. I discuss the implications of bicameralism for lower chamber electoral coordination later.

government – also influences aggregation incentives. Specifically, horizontal and vertical centralization interact to determine the payoff to being the largest party at the national level: the larger the payoff (the greater the horizontal and vertical centralization), the stronger the incentives for entrepreneurs to organize large national parties, and for candidates to link across districts, ceteris paribus. Second, the *probability* that the largest party will be able to capture the reins of government is another variable that helps shape aggregation incentives. Indeed, a large potential payoff may do little to induce aggregation absent some reasonable expectation that those actors who successfully coordinate will receive that payoff. In short, I argue that aggregation incentives are a product of two factors: (a) the payoff to being the largest party at the national level (which itself is a product of vertical and horizontal concentration), and (b) the probability that the largest party will be able to capture that payoff.

The chapter proceeds as follows. In the next section, I develop a theory of aggregation incentives and explain why the addition of the horizontal centralization variable offers an improvement on existing models that focus exclusively on vertical centralization. I then explore the way in which the probability variable (the probability that the largest party will capture executive power) plays out differently in parliamentary and presidential systems. In parliamentary systems, the question is whether the largest party gets the chance to form the government and capture the prime minister's office, while in presidential systems the timing of elections, the number of presidential candidates, and the president's eligibility for reelection are key. The final section concludes.

2.2 A THEORY OF AGGREGATION INCENTIVES

One way to think of elections is as a series of coordination problems (Cox 1999). In most elections, there are fewer seats to be filled than there are potential candidates who would like to fill them. Coordination refers to the process by which electoral competitors and voters act together to limit the number of competitors. Potential competitors can coordinate to reduce the number of actual competitors (e.g., via candidates withdrawing from the race or party mergers) and/or voters can coordinate to limit the number of candidates for which they actually vote. Thanks to the rich literature in comparative electoral studies, we know a good deal

A Theory of Aggregation Incentives

about what shapes coordination within electoral districts where district magnitude and degree of social heterogeneity are key. However, coordination opportunities do not end at the boundary of an electoral district. Candidates must decide whether to coordinate with candidates from other districts to form regional or national parties. The leaders of small parties or factions must decide whether or not to ally with other groups or parties. Political entrepreneurs in pursuit of executive office must decide to what extent they will pursue a nationwide campaign and organizational strategy. The scope and size of a country's party system is the joint product of both coordination within districts and these decisions about coordination across districts.

Unfortunately, unlike intra-district coordination, we know relatively little about the factors that shape cross-district coordination or aggregation. What factors aid or impede the incentives and ability of actors to coordinate across districts? When would actors choose to join a larger national party over a smaller party and vice versa? To begin with, candidates, faction leaders, and entrepreneurs might be driven by a concern over the potential risks and rewards associated with an aggregation strategy or its alternatives. If they join with a larger party, they will increase the joint probability of getting into power, but at the risk of having to share that power with other actors within the party. For example, a political entrepreneur who successfully organizes a large national party may find his or her power checked by rival factional leaders from within the party. Intra-party factional conflict is often a recipe for party, cabinet, and government instability (Chambers 2003; Druckman 1996; Laver and Shepsle 1990). On the other hand, if candidates or factions decide to go it alone, a candidate as an independent and the faction as a small party, they trade off greater intra-organization unity with a smaller (though nonzero) chance of getting into power.[3] A variety of factors might conceivably affect actors' calculations about the risks and rewards associated with each of these strategies. These include first, the size of the prize to be divided among potential copartisans/faction leaders. The smaller the prize at stake the smaller the share any one actor is likely to receive, ceteris paribus, and the weaker the incentives to cooperate with others to try and capture that prize. Second, if

---

[3] These two options represent the extremes. Actors can and do choose strategies between these two extremes by forming mid-sized parties.

combining with other actors to form a large national party does not significantly increase the joint probability of capturing the prize of government – for example if the largest party does not always capture the executive office – then the expectation of rewards for coordination may not be enough to outweigh the potential risks.

One reason that politicians from different districts might link together under a common party label is that they face some task that requires the help of a large number of legislators (Cox 1997). In other words, for some political tasks, there are economies of scale – large groups are better able to accomplish those tasks than smaller groups. A group trying to accomplish one of these tasks will seek to induce candidates from many different constituencies to link or aggregate within a larger organization – in this case a political party. One of these tasks is gaining control of national-level power and resources – either as an end in itself or as a means to pursuing other goals. It stands to reason that the more substantial the power and resources available at the national level, the stronger the incentives for coordinating to try and capture that prize. In addition, aggregation incentives will be shaped by actors' assessment of the chance of gaining control of national-level power and resources should they succeed at coordinating to form a large national party.

In short, whether we think of candidates, faction leaders, and entrepreneurs as motivated by their calculations of the risks and rewards of coordination or by a desire to pursue goals that require the cooperation of multiple actors, two key determinants of aggregation incentives are the perception of the benefits to such coordination and the probability that coordinating will enable the party members to enjoy those benefits.

To flesh this argument out further, and highlight the nested nature of the argument, imagine a politician with a power base in one district. (Let us assume for simplicity that this politician is the head of a regional party.) The decision he must make is whether to coordinate across districts (i.e., become part of a large party) or to not do so (i.e., be part of a small party).[4] His decision is based on a comparison of the expected

---

[4] A mid-range option could be to form a pre-electoral coalition with other parties. See Sona Golder's recent work for a systematic treatment of the causes and consequences of pre-electoral coalition formation (2006).

A Theory of Aggregation Incentives

utility of being part of a large party and the expected utility of being part of a small party. Given that cross-district coordination does not offer a *guarantee* of becoming the largest party in the legislature, the expected utility of coordinating is as follows:

$$EU_{large} = p(EPL) + (1-p)(EP{\sim}L) - C \qquad (1)$$

where p is the probability that cross-district coordination produces the largest party, and $1-p$ is the probability coordination falls short of producing the largest party, EPL is the expected payoff for being the largest party, and EP$\sim$L is the expected payoff for not being the largest party. C is the cost of coordinating across districts. These costs might be the real resources that must be expended for such coordination, or we might think of the cost as the things our politician must give up to become part of a larger party (i.e., the opportunity cost of coordination).[5] The relevant comparison is the expected utility of coordination (EU$_{large}$) versus the expected utility of remaining a small party (EU$_{small}$). The bigger EU$_{large}$ is relative to EU$_{small}$, the stronger the incentives to coordination across districts will be.

Equation 1, however, begs the question, what shapes our politician's expectations of the payoff of being the largest party (EPL)? I argue the following:

$$EPL = q(L) + (1-q)(F) \qquad (2)$$

Where q equals the probability that the largest legislative party also gains control of the chief executive office, L is the payoff for becoming the largest legislative party, and $1-q(F)$ is the expected payoff to the largest party if it fails to capture the executive.

Substituting Equation 2 into 1 we get the following:

$$EU_{large} = p(q(L) + (1-q)(F)) + (1-p)(EP{\sim}L) - C \qquad (3)$$

Equation 3 yields several comparative statics. Our politician's expected utility of coordinating to try to form a large party is decreasing in C (the cost of coordination)[6] and EU$_{small}$ while increasing in

---

[5] For example, joining a larger party means some loss of control of the party label and party program and loss of control of overall campaign strategy.
[6] In Chapter 3, I will consider some factors that may affect the cost of coordination such as the number of electoral districts and the level of ethnic heterogeneity.

- The probability that cross-district coordination produces the largest party (p)
- The payoff if the party is not the largest party (EP$\sim$L)
- The probability that the largest legislative party controls the executive (q)
- The payoff to becoming the largest party (the aggregation payoff) (L)
- The payoff associated with the largest legislative party not capturing the executive (F)

This simple formalization suggests several possible hypotheses. For example, aggregation is likely to be more appealing in countries where the largest party, in the event of not gaining the chief executive, is at least assured of gaining other important ministries (such as the finance ministry) than it would be in countries where this is not assured. In other words, aggregation is more likely where the rewards are still substantial for coming in second. Likewise aggregation is likely to be less appealing in countries where small regional parties anticipate that they will be needed to form a coalition government (and the expected utility of remaining small is thus relatively high) than it would be in countries where small regional parties are unlikely to be needed to form a coalition.

The focus of this book, however, is on the two hypotheses related to the expected payoff of becoming the largest party (EPL): namely, that aggregation incentives increase with (1) the payoff to being the largest party (the aggregation payoff) and (2) the probability that the largest legislative will actually capture that payoff.[7] Again, together these two factors yield the expected payoff, or expected utility of being the largest legislative party. The larger this expected utility, the stronger the incentives to coordinate across districts, ceteris paribus. I discuss the factors that affect the size and the probability of capturing the payoff in detail in the next section. Let me conclude this section, however, with a brief discussion of one other explanation for the degree aggregation across and within democracies – the level of social heterogeneity.

---

[7] Cox discusses some of these factors in his analysis of when district bipartism is reproduced at the national level in both presidential and parliamentary systems (1997, 189–91).

A Theory of Aggregation Incentives

One branch of the literature might ascribe aggregation (or the lack thereof) to preference heterogeneity across geographic regions. This heterogeneity often arises from societal cleavages (e.g., ethnicity, religion, class) and hinders aggregation, especially where cleavage groups are geographically concentrated (Lipset and Rokkan 1967; Riker 1982; Kim and Onh 1992; Ordeshook and Shvetsova 1994; Amorim-Neto and Cox 1997; Cox 1999; Morelli 2001; and Brancati 2003). (In terms of Equation 3, we might think of high levels of social heterogeneity as raising the costs of cross-district coordination.) However, by themselves societal cleavages are neither necessary nor sufficient to produce poor aggregation. Countries with similar cleavage structures can have very different national party systems. For example, Thailand and Venezuela have very similar levels of ethnic fractionalization yet aggregation in Venezuela is much better than in Thailand (see Table 1.1).[8] Likewise, a country with fewer/less pronounced social cleavages can have worse aggregation than a very divided country (e.g., Ecuador, with less heterogeneity than India, has worse aggregation). In addition, since cleavage structures change very slowly they usually cannot adequately account for intra-country variation in aggregation over time. I argue that the influence of social cleavages on cross-district coordination can be understood in much the same way as their influence on intra-district coordination. Namely, societal cleavages interact with other (largely institutional) variables to shape the incentives and ability of candidates to coordinate.[9] I turn my attention now to these other variables, beginning with the payoff for aggregation.

2.2.1 Aggregation Payoff: Concentration of Power and the Prize of Government

Consistent with existing studies that explicitly consider the issue of aggregation (Chhibber and Kollman 1998, 2004), I argue that the degree of political and economic centralization can influence aggregation incentives. The logic of the argument is straightforward. If power is concentrated at the center, a group wishing to wield that power has an

---

[8] Thailand and Venezuela have a fractionalization score of .43 and .48, respectively, on Fearon's ethnic fractionalization measure (Fearon 2003).
[9] Specifically, for a given level of social heterogeneity the expected utility of becoming the largest party should be positively correlated with aggregation.

incentive to induce candidates from multiple districts to participate in a larger organization to compete for that power (see Cox 1997). Aggregation is positively related to economic and political concentration – greater concentrations of power lead to stronger cross-district coordination incentives. However, existing studies focus solely on the distribution of power and resources between the central government and subnational units – what I term *vertical centralization*. Distinct from these previous studies, I argue that vertical centralization is only one of two important components of the centralization equation.[10] Both components need to be present to produce a maximal aggregation payoff. Specifically, aggregation incentives are strongest when (a) power is concentrated at the national level (*vertical centralization*) and (b) power is concentrated within the national government (*horizontal centralization*). If either component is absent, the incentives to form large, nationwide parties will be diminished. In other words, this centralization equation is interactive in nature – any one component is not enough by itself to produce a maximal aggregation payoff.

Vertical Centralization

Those who have previously studied aggregation find that the extent to which power and control of resources is in the hands of the central versus subnational governments to be a key variable that accounts for aggregation (Chhibber and Kollman 1998, 2004; Samuels 1998). In Brazil, where state governments are extremely powerful vis-à-vis the national government, aggregation is poor (Samuels 1998). Chhibber and Kollman find that aggregation has varied along with changes in the national government's share of total spending in their four country cases (1998, 2004).[11] Where power is concentrated at the national level, voters tend to privilege national issues and vote for national parties. In contrast, where subnational governments control substantial resources, voters tend to vote for regional or subnational parties. Chhibber and Kollman focus on voters' incentives and behavior; however, it is not difficult to imagine a companion story that focuses on the incentives of candidates and nascent party leaders. Where power is concentrated at the national

---

[10] Another difference between Chhibber and Kollman's work and this study is that I focus on the incentives and behavior of candidates and party leaders while Chhibber and Kollman focus on the incentives and the behavior of voters.

[11] These are the United States, India, Canada, and the United Kingdom.

level, these actors have an incentive to coordinate across districts nationally in a bid to capture that prize. By contrast, where subnational governments control substantial resources, candidates and party leaders may focus their attention on winning these prizes and eschew cross-district coordination on a national scale.[12] Ultimately, however, vertical centralization is not sufficient to produce strong aggregation incentives. The other component of the centralization equation is also important.

Horizontal Centralization

Aggregation incentives are greatest where political power is concentrated not only vertically but horizontally (within the national government) as well. To assess the degree to which power is horizontally centralized, we want to consider the extent to which the largest legislative party controls all the reins of government. Where power and control of resources are concentrated horizontally, a party that successfully coordinates can expect to face relatively few checks on its exercise of national power. However, where power is dispersed at the national level, the largest legislative party may still find it is unable to fully control or direct the resources of government. The greater is the degree of horizontal centralization, the stronger are the incentives for actors to coordinate across districts to try to win control of government.

A variety of factors affect the degree to which power is horizontally centralized. Here I focus on three: (a) the separation of power – specifically the presence of a second legislative chamber; (b) the degree of party cohesion; and (c) the existence of reserve domains. Note that the number of parties or partisan veto players is missing from this list. At first blush this may seem an oversight – the addition of another partisan veto player other than the largest party would certainly represent a potential check on that party's authority. However, the distinction between partisan veto players and veto gates is crucial in this context. Veto *gates* are the points in the policy process where approval must be granted in order to change the status quo (cf. Tsebelis's institutional veto points – Tsebelis 1995). Veto *players* are those actors, single or collective, who sit at each veto gate. I assume that, for most elections, candidates, party leaders, and voters treat the number of veto gates at the national level as exogenous.

---

[12] With reference to the model, a high degree of vertical decentralization raises the expected utility of remaining a small, subnational party, ceteris paribus.

Ultimately we know that institutions are at least partially endogenous to the configurations of power at their inception but most elections do not occur during founding institutional moments and so it seems reasonable to assume that actors generally take the formal, institutional distribution of veto authority as given. The same assumption cannot be made about the number of partisan veto players. The number of partisan veto players is partially endogenous to aggregation. Control of government by a single elected veto player (e.g., a majority party) is itself likely evidence of successful cross-district coordination. Likewise, multiple partisan veto players (as in coalition governments) may reflect poor aggregation across districts.[13] It is inaccurate, therefore, to treat the number of veto players as an exogenous explanatory variable.

Separation of Power – Bicameralism

Where there is a separation of power and authority at the national level (e.g., where power is spread among multiple veto gates), there is always a risk that the largest legislative party will have to share control of government with other actors. Given this risk, aggregation incentives should be negatively correlated with the number of veto gates within the national government, ceteris paribus. The diffusion of power can arise from a variety of institutional sources, including the division of the legislature into two chambers. Where there is an upper chamber with veto authority, the party with a lower chamber majority may still not control all the points of power. The upper chamber is most likely to represent a check on the largest party in the lower chamber where district boundaries for the lower and upper chamber are not the same, where upper and lower chamber elections are not concurrent, and where upper chamber support is required to pass new legislation.[14]

Diffusion of power may also result from the separation of executive and legislative power as occurs in presidential systems. However, the effects of presidentialism are conditional on the proximity of presidential and legislative elections, which is discussed later in more detail.[15]

---

[13] It may also reflect a permissive electoral system.

[14] For more on bicameralism and its effects, see Diermeier and Myerson (1999); Heller (2001); Druckman and Thies (2002); Rogers (2003); Tsebelis and Money (1997); and an excellent review by Cutrone and McCarty (n.d).

[15] The rules that govern interactions between different veto gates and veto players (e.g., agenda-setting powers, reversion points, veto powers) can also shape the degree of

A Theory of Aggregation Incentives

Party Cohesion

Party cohesion can also affect the degree of power concentration within the national government. Where parties are not cohesive (e.g., when parties are factionalized), the payoff to being the largest party in government is reduced. When the party is cohesive, it is, in effect, a hierarchical and unitary actor. Party leaders can be reasonably confident of the support and cooperation from the party's other members. However, when the party is more like a coalition of factions (Laver and Schofield 1990) than a cohesive political hierarchy, it ceases to be a unitary actor, and each party faction becomes a potential veto player. Thus even if the party controls all the reins of government, the power (and payoff) associated with control of government will have to be shared between various subparty factions. The head of a majority party might still find his or her power checked by rival internal party factions. All else equal then, party factionalism should discourage attempts at aggregation by would-be party leaders/chief executives.

I am assuming here that party cohesion is exogenous to aggregation. For example, party factionalism has been linked to the nature of the electoral system, specifically the presence of intra-party competition (Katz 1986; Shugart and Carey 1992; Lijphart 1994; Reed 1994; Hicken 2002). Rules that govern party leaders' ability to control backbenchers (and are exogenous to the parties themselves) such as rules about party switching or campaign finance regulations can also affect party cohesion. In short, to the extent that such systemic factors exist, it seems reasonable to expect that actors will treat party factionalism as exogenous – at least in the short term. However, I acknowledge that factionalism may be at least partially endogenous to aggregation. Stronger incentives to coordinate across districts may induce smaller groups/parties to ally under the

---

horizontal centralization and hence aggregation incentives, particularly the power of the chief executive relative to other actors at the national level. I do not explore the role presidential power plays in shaping aggregation incentives in this book for both theoretical and practical reasons. First, I expect that the effect of presidential powers is secondary to the influence presidentialism exerts through the timing of elections and the number of presidential candidates. Second, reliable comparable data on presidential powers are difficult to come by, though efforts are underway to try to collect such data by a number of scholars (e.g., Tsebelis and Aleman 2005; Tsebelis and Rizova 2007). As data become available, it is worth looking more closely the role presidential power plays in shaping aggregation incentives. See Hicken and Stoll (2006) for some initial work along these lines.

banner of a larger party. The net effect of this may be an increase in intra-party factionalism. I attempt to control for this potential endogeneity in the large-N tests in Chapter 3 by using the features of the electoral system as my proxy for party cohesion rather than a more direct measure.

Reserve Domains

Finally, in transitioning democracies, it is useful to keep in mind the possible effects of *reserve domains* – institutional or policy domains controlled by actors who are not directly accountable to elected officials (Valenzuela 1992). These might include appointed legislative seats (or chambers)[16] as well as cabinet positions or policy areas that are widely considered off limits to elected officials (e.g., control over military appointments and budgets). For example, in Thailand an appointed Senate was traditionally stacked with representatives of Thailand's military and bureaucracy – conservative forces often at odds with Thailand's elected representatives. The appointed Senate was not replaced with an elected body until 1997. In newly democratic Indonesia, large portions of the military's operations and budget are still considered, by custom and necessity, off limits to the country's elected leaders. Pinochet's 1980 Chilean constitution famously provided for nine non-elected senators (out of a total of 26) including eventually Senator-for-life Pinochet. It also denied the president the power to remove the commander in chief of the armed forces and chief of police. Though Pinochet lost a plebiscite and stepped down as president in 1988, these provisions remained in place until 2005. In short, by guaranteeing that even majority parties will face checks on their authority, the existence of reserve domains effectively reduces the payoff to being the largest party in government, and hence undermines aggregation incentives.

Reserve domains operate in concert with party cohesion and bicameralism to shape the size of the aggregation payoff. This payoff should be highest where party cohesion is high, reserve domains are absent, and the legislature is unicameral. The aggregation payoff should be smallest where reserve domains exist along side a bicameral legislature populated by factionalized political parties.

It is possible to imagine a counterargument to the theory as I have described it thus far – one that turns my hypothesis about the link

---

[16] Conditional, of course, on the specific appointment and removal procedures.

A Theory of Aggregation Incentives

between horizontal centralization and aggregation on its head. Rather than horizontal decentralization serving as a deterrent to coordination attempts, one might argue that horizontal decentralization should spur greater aggregation as parties endeavor to capture all of the relevant veto gates and obtain enough power to eliminate any lingering reserve domains. Even though this alternative hypothesis still does not address the issue of party cohesion, it would serve as falsifying evidence for this portion of the theory should I find that horizontal decentralization is associated with better rather than worse aggregation.

To summarize, I argue a chain of variables together determine the payoff to being the largest party in the legislature – the larger the payoff, the stronger the aggregation incentives. This payoff is greatest where the national government dominates subnational units (vertical centralization) and where power is concentrated within the national government (horizontal centralization). If there is a high degree of decentralization on either dimension, then the payoff to being the largest party in government is sharply reduced. For example, even if the largest national party could rule unchecked at the national level, national office would not be worth organizing for if the power and resources were really controlled by subnational units. Likewise, a national government with great power means little if other actors regularly block the largest party from exercising that power.

2.2.2 Probability of Capturing the Payoff

Even though a sufficiently large payoff is necessary to induce aggregation, it is not sufficient. There must also be a reasonable probability that the largest party will be able to capture that prize. Of chief concern is whether or not the largest legislative party is also able to win control of the executive office (Cox 1997). If the largest legislative party has no chance of capturing the reins of government, then even a potentially large payoff will not be enough to induce national coordination. In contrast, where the largest legislative party also captures executive power with a high degree of probability, the expected utility of coordinating to form a large party will be greater.

The relationship between legislative and executive power varies greatly from country to country, but the most fundamental distinction is between presidential and parliamentary regimes. In this section, I discuss the way in which the probability of capturing executive office operates in each.

Presidential Systems

In presidential systems, the probability that the largest legislative party will also win control of the chief executive office is a function of three variables: (a) whether or not presidential and legislative elections are held concurrently; (b) whether or not voters cast a single, fused vote for the executive and legislature;[17] and (c) the number of viable presidential candidates.[18] Because fused votes are relatively rare, I will focus on the remaining two variables.[19]

Where presidential and legislative elections are concurrent, the electoral stakes are magnified, and it is likely that the same parties will be the frontrunner in both presidential and legislative contests (Shugart 1995). In effect, when elections are concurrent, the presidential contest casts a shadow over legislative contests in the eyes of both voters and candidates (Shugart 1995; Cox 1997). The issues and parties that are in contention in the nationwide presidential race tend to migrate down the ballot and influence voter choices for legislative elections. In effect, voters use the presidential campaign as an information shortcut to help guide their choice of legislative candidates (Samuels 2003; Golder 2006). Candidates, for their part, recognize that voters will rely on the presidential contest as a cue in concurrent elections, and so face strong incentives to try to coordinate their campaigns with one of the front-running presidential candidates. There are also economies of scale to be had from such coordination (Samuels 2002; Golder 2006). Presidential campaigns typically involve strong, national campaign organizations and command the bulk of media and donor attention. By coordinating their campaign

---

[17] Under a fused vote, voters cast a single vote in the legislative contest, which is also counted as a vote for that party's presidential candidate. When fused votes occur, the probability that the largest party will capture both the legislature and the executive is virtually 100 percent. See Jones (2000) for more information on the fused vote.

[18] See Cox (1997, 190). My list differs from Cox's in one respect. He uses the "strength of the presidential election procedure" as his third variable; I instead use the number of viable presidential candidates.

[19] For work on the link between presidential elections and fewer legislative parties, see Shugart and Carey (1992), Jones (1994, 1999), Shugart (1995), Cox (1997), Mozzaffar, Scarritt, and Galaich (2003), Hicken (2005), and Golder (2006). For an opposing view see Filippov, Ordeshook, and Shvetsova (1999) and Coppedge (2002).

with the campaign of a leading presidential candidate (usually from the same party), legislative candidates expect to enhance their own electoral fortunes.

This rallying around the leading presidential contender occurs both within districts, leading to a smaller effective number of candidates/parties in each districts, and across districts, leading to better aggregation and fewer national political parties. In short, the more proximate the presidential and legislative elections are, the stronger the aggregation incentives will be, and the higher the probability that the largest legislative party will also be the party of the president.

However, the effect of concurrent elections is conditional on the number of viable presidential candidates. Where the presidential electoral system regularly produces two strong presidential contenders, candidates for the legislature are better able to distinguish between front-running and trailing candidates and thus able to aggregate strategically. The number of viable presidential candidates, then, is key to understanding aggregation incentives. Concurrent elections have their strongest effect when there are two clear frontrunners for the presidency. If distinguishing the frontrunners is difficult, then the probability that the largest legislative party will also capture the presidency is greatly reduced, and so are the incentives to coordinate across districts. This is true even when presidential and legislative elections are concurrent. A handful of recent studies find that a large number of presidential candidates can completely undermine the effect of concurrent elections on the number of parties (Amorim-Neto and Cox 1997; Chhibber and Kollman 2004; Golder 2006).

What types of factors affect the number of viable presidential candidates? The degree of social heterogeneity is one important factor – greater ethnic fractionalization, for example, puts upward pressure on the effective number of presidential candidates.[20] However, just as the social structure and electoral institutions interact to determine the number of parties at the district level, so to do these variables interact to shape the number of presidential candidates. Social heterogeneity only increases the effective number of candidates when combined with a permissive presidential electoral formula (Golder 2006). "Strong"

---

[20] The effective number of presidential candidates is calculated by dividing 1 by the sum of each candidate's squared vote share: $1/\Sigma v_i^2$.

formulas such as the plurality rule generally produce fewer viable candidates than more permissive arrangements (e.g., majority runoff), even in the face of social heterogeneity. Indeed, several scholars have found that more restrictive electoral rules produce fewer candidates than more permissive rules (Cox 1997; Jones 1997; Jones 1999; Jones 2004; Golder 2006). In short, consistent with Duverger's law, restrictive rules push the number of presidential candidates toward two, even where there is a high degree of social heterogeneity (Golder 2006).[21]

A second, but oft overlooked factor that helps shape the number of presidential candidates is the rule governing presidential reelection. Systems with term limits, particularly those that ban any reelection, should be associated with a higher number of viable presidential candidates compared to those that do not limit reelection (Jones 1999). Why would limits on reelection be associated with more viable presidential candidates? Assuming that presidential office has some value and that there is open contestation for the office, there will always be multiple possible presidential hopefuls. Yet often it is the case that all but two of those hopefuls drop out of the contest along the way, or never enter the race in the first place. Why? One factor, as discussed previously, is certainly the restrictiveness of the electoral formula. But another key factor that whittles down the field of candidates is the presence of an incumbent. In all democracies, the presence of an incumbent significantly raises the entry barrier for potential challengers. Incumbents generally have better name recognition than challengers and are able to bring the power, resources, and networks associated with political office to bear on the campaign. In addition, presidents (and presidential contenders) who are eligible for reelection have strong incentives to invest in building and maintaining an effective party organization and base of support – assets that can be mobilized for future presidential contests.[22] The net effect of incumbency is to encourage an incumbent's opponents to coordinate in

---

[21] Evidence about the direct effect of social heterogeneity on the effective number of presidential candidates is mixed (see, for example, Jones 1997; Jones 2004).

[22] Note that candidates facing a single term limit might still have reasons to party-build if the reelection ban applies only to consecutive reelection. The prospect of a future run for office can be enough to induce lame-duck incumbents to take a longer-term view. Lame-duck presidents may also have an incentive to party-build if their future career prospects are tied to the party.

A Theory of Aggregation Incentives

support of a single standard-bearer for the opposition in order to maximize their prospects at the ballot box.[23]

The lack of an incumbent, either by rule or the incumbent's choice, can dramatically reduce the entry barriers for presidential hopefuls.[24] Why, though, would not a strong electoral formula eventually push the effective number of presidential candidates down to 2, even if there are multiple candidates to begin with? Indeed, that is what we would expect given Duverger's law and Cox's $M + 1$ rule. In single-seat plurality contests, all but the two frontrunners should eventually withdraw from the race (strategic entry). Where trailing candidates fail to withdraw, voters should respond by voting strategically for their most preferred of the two frontrunners (strategic voting). The end result of this strategic behavior is an effective number of presidential candidates near 2.

However, recall that in order for Duverger's law and the $M + 1$ rule to work as predicted, certain assumptions must be met. One of these is that voters, candidates, donors, and the like must be able to clearly identify the two front-running candidates.[25] Where they cannot do so, the coordination on two candidates breaks down. Returning to the issue of incumbency, I argue that without an incumbent in the race it will be more difficult to identify the two frontrunners, ceteris paribus. Imagine, for example, a presidential contest in which there is one clear frontrunner among all challengers. Where there is an incumbent in the race, identifying the two frontrunners is relatively simple. If, however, there is not an incumbent, actors have good information about one of the frontrunners, but may have difficulty determining which of the remaining candidates is the other frontrunner. A more concrete example is the case of the 1992 Philippine presidential election, which will be discussed in more detail in Chapter 6. Due to a new prohibition on presidential reelection, the 1992 contest had no incumbent. Numerous challengers entered the race, but unlike previous elections in the months, weeks, and days before the poll no clear frontrunners ever emerged. The eventual winner, Fidel Ramos, was victorious with only 23.6 percent of the vote. Only nine percentage

---

[23] The strength of the incumbent will also influence the opposition's incentives to coordinate on a single candidate.
[24] Exactly how low that barrier is will depend in part on whether a clear, designated successor exists that can inherit many of the advantages of incumbency.
[25] See Chapter 4 for a discussion of each the assumptions.

points separated Ramos from the fourth place finisher. Less than two percentage points separated the second- and third-place candidates. These final results reflected the fact that voters, candidates, party leaders, and donors all had a difficult time distinguishing the frontrunners from the also-rans – a task made much more difficult without the presence of an incumbent in the race.

In summary, the lack of an incumbent lowers the barriers to entry for presidential contenders and undermines the incentives of presidents to invest in party building. The result should be an increase in the number of viable presidential candidates over elections where incumbents are present.

To conclude, the probability of capturing the prize of government in presidential systems depends jointly on the proximity of legislative and presidential elections and the effective number of presidential candidates. The more proximate the presidential and legislative contests are, the stronger the aggregation incentives will be. However, as the effective number of presidential candidates rises, the relationship between proximity and aggregation weakens. Aggregation incentives are strongest when presidential and legislative elections are concurrent and there are a small number of presidential candidates. The number of presidential candidates in turn is a function of social heterogeneity, the electoral formula, and the presence or lack of an incumbent.

Parliamentary Systems

In pure parliamentary systems, the executive and legislative elections are always concurrent, and the vote is always fused. As a result, the probability of capturing the aggregation payoff rests on the strength of the prime ministerial selection method. A strong method of selection is one in which the rules or norms of parliament are such that the leader of the largest party always has the first opportunity to form a government. If this is the case, and the leader usually succeeds, then the system looks like a plurality election – the leader of the party with the most support becomes the head of the government (Cox 1997). If, on the other hand, actors other than the leader of the largest party often form or get a chance to form the government, then there are weaker incentives to try to become the largest party. As a political entrepreneur with an eye on the premiership, the actor's willingness to go to the costly effort of

A Theory of Aggregation Incentives

attempting to organize a large party will be less if success will not guarantee the premiership. As a candidate or faction leader, uncertainty about whether a successful cross-district coordination effort will bring with it the rewards of government is a strong disincentive. In short, where there is a low probability that the leader of the largest party will capture the aggregation payoff, aggregation incentives are weak, and aggregation should be poor.

To summarize, aggregation incentives are a function of the payoff to being the largest party at the national level and the probability that the largest party will receive that payoff. Both are necessary to produce maximum aggregation incentives. A low probability can undermine cross-district coordination incentives, even if the potential payoff is large. Likewise, a guarantee that the largest legislative party will capture the reins of government will not produce strong aggregation incentives if being in power at the national level is not worth very much.

2.3 CONCLUSION

In this chapter I have presented a theory of aggregation incentives. A concentration of power within at the national-level of government may indeed be an important determinant of aggregation incentives, but I argue that by itself vertical centralization is not enough to produce aggregation. Two other variables play key roles. First, the degree of horizontal centralization – the degree to which power is concentrated *within* the national government – influences the incentives to aggregate across districts. Horizontal centralization interacts with vertical centralization to determine the payoff to being the largest legislative party. I argued that the presence of bicameralism, party factionalism, and reserve domains increase horizontal decentralization and so decrease the size of the aggregation payoff.

Second, the probability that the largest party will actually be able to capture the aggregation payoff also shapes coordination incentives. Where that probability is low, aggregation incentives will be weaker. In parliamentary systems, the probability of capturing that prize is a function of who typically becomes prime minister. In presidential systems, the effective number of presidential candidates and the proximity of legislative and presidential candidates shape the probability that the largest legislative party will also control the presidency.

In the next chapter, I use this theory to derive a series of testable hypotheses. I then discuss various strategies for operationalizing my dependent and explanatory variables and test my hypotheses on a large-N dataset. In Chapters 4–6 I draw on the theory to explain the dynamics of party system development and aggregation in Thailand and the Philippines.

3

Testing the Theory

3.1 INTRODUCTION

In Chapter 2 I developed a theory of aggregation incentives that stressed the interaction of the size of the aggregation payoff (itself a product of vertical and horizontal centralization) with the probability of capturing that prize. In this chapter, I turn to the task of testing some of the theory's hypotheses using a dataset of 280 elections in 46 countries. In Chapters 5 and 6, I conduct further tests of the theory using data from Thailand and the Philippines. The chapter proceeds as follows. In the next section, I discuss the operationalization and measurement of the dependent variable – party system aggregation. I then devote a section each examining the payoff to aggregation, the probability of capturing the payoff in parliamentary systems, the probability in presidential systems, and finally the effect of social heterogeneity on aggregation. In each of these sections, I derive a set of hypotheses from the theory outlined in Chapter 2, discuss my strategy for operationalizing the various explanatory (and control) variables of interest, describe the dataset used to test the hypotheses, and finally present the results of those tests. The final section concludes.

3.2 THE DEPENDENT VARIABLE: AGGREGATION AS INFLATION

As discussed in Chapter 1, the national party system is the product of two types of coordination – intra-district coordination and aggregation. Simply using the effective number of electoral parties in legislative elections is insufficient. The effective number of parties contains information about both the district-level party systems *and* the extent of coordination or aggregation across districts. To test the effect of various factors on aggregation, we need a way to separate the district and aggregation effects. One way to do this is to calculate the difference between the effective number of electoral parties nationally (ENP_{nat}) and the average effective number of parties in each district (ENP_{avg}) and to use this as a measure of the extent of aggregation from the local to national party system (see Chhibber and Kollman 1998). The larger the difference is, the poorer the aggregation.

$$D = ENP_{nat} - ENP_{avg} \qquad (1)$$

Cox uses this difference measure to calculate how much larger the national party system is than the average district-level party system in percentage terms. This measure, which he dubs the party system inflation measure (I) is computed by dividing the difference between ENP_{nat} and ENP_{avg} (D) by ENP_{nat} and multiplying by 100 (Cox 1999, 17).[1] Larger inflation scores correspond to poorer aggregation.

$$I = [(ENP_{nat} - ENP_{avg})/ENP_{nat}] * 100 \qquad (2)$$

The interpretation of this measure is straightforward. If I is 10, this suggests that only 10% of the size of the national party system can be attributed to different parties garnering votes in different parts of the country (poor aggregation), with the other 90% due to the average number of parties at the district level (ibid.). In short, aggregation is very good – the same parties are generally the frontrunners in most districts nationwide. On the other hand, if the inflation score is 60, we know that poor aggregation deserves most of the credit for producing a large number of parties nationally, while intra-district coordination can only account for 40% of the national party system's size. I use the inflation score as my aggregation measure throughout this chapter and the remainder of the book. Once again, higher inflation scores represent worse levels of aggregation (or the more severe the cross-district coordination failures).

To create the *inflation* measure, I collected district and national level election returns and calculated ENP_{nat} and ENP_{avg} for 280 elections in 46

---

[1] Cox multiplies this by one hundred to convert the decimal into a percentage.

Testing the Theory

countries. Over half of these countries (25) are developing democracies. I included only those elections where a country was minimally democratic (defined as a having a Polity2 score above 0).[2] These election return data were culled from various sources including Caramani (2000), Matt Golder's Democratic Electoral Systems Around the World dataset,[3] Scott Morgenstern's District-Level Electoral Dataset,[4] and the author's own work on elections in Southeast Asia (Hicken 2002).[5] Calculating both kinds of ENP can be complicated, particularly where party alliances are common, election results include large "other" categories, or there are large numbers of independent candidates. Fortunately, the percentage of votes cast for parties in the "other" category, or for independents is generally small, rarely more than 5% of total votes cast. Where I had information about the number of parties in the "other" category, or the number of independents I used this information to create an "average" score for all other parties/independents by dividing the total vote share for "others"/independents by the number of parties/candidates in that category.[6] Where I lacked this information, I was forced to treat "others" and independents as if they were single parties.[7] In the case of party alliances, to calculate both ENP_{avg} and ENP_{nat}, I used as my basic unit of analysis the entity for which voters actually cast their vote on election day. This means that the alliance is counted as a single party if the alliance by itself appears on the ballot and that is what voters vote for. If, on the other hand, parties may enter into an electoral alliance but individual party names still appear on the ballot separately, I count the votes for each individual party in the alliance.

Table 3.1 presents the average inflation scores for the 46 countries I use to test the theory. Since many of my key independent variables

---

[2] The Polity2 score is a combination of the autocratic and democratic variables in the Polity IV dataset (Marshall and Jaggers 2002).
[3] http://homepages.nyu.edu/%7Emrg217/elections.html. See also Golder (2005).
[4] http://www.duke.edu/~smorgens/componentsdata.html
[5] Special thanks also to Gary Cox and Ken Kollman for sharing their district-level data with me.
[6] For example, (Vote share for "others") / (# of parties in the "other" category).
[7] The actual difference in the ENP score using the two methods is actually quite small as long as the percentage of "others" or independents is not large (which is almost always the case for the set of elections used here). For example, in the 1983 Thai election independent candidates received 7.4% of the vote. If we divide that percentage by the number of independents (in effect treating each as a party of one), then ENP_{nat} is 5.9. If we, instead, count all independents together as a single "party," then ENP_{nat} is 5.7.

TABLE 3.1. *Average Inflation Scores*

Country	Inflation
Costa Rica	.00
Cyprus	.00
Honduras	.02
Austria	.02
Chile	.04
Denmark	.04
Sweden	.04
Jamaica	.04
Dominican Republic	.05
Greece	.05
Norway	.05
Ireland	.05
Iceland	.05
Netherlands	.06
Mexico	.07
Colombia	.07
Mauritius	.07
Venezuela	.08
New Zealand	.08
United States	.10
Italy	.10
Japan	.10
Taiwan	.12
Portugal	.12
Botswana	.13
Poland	.14
Spain	.15
United Kingdom	.15
Argentina	.16
Trinidad	.17
Zambia	.17
Australia	.17
Kenya	.18
Finland	.19
Canada	.20
Germany	.21
South Korea	.28
France	.29
Brazil	.29
Philippines	.32
Malawi	.32
Switzerland	.38
India	.47
Belgium	.48
Thailand	.50
Ecuador	.55

Testing the Theory

range from 0 to 1, I convert the inflation score to a variable that also ranges from 0 and 1.[8] This eases the interpretation of the results. Scores range from a low of .00 in Costa Rica to a high of .55 in Ecuador.

3.3 THE AGGREGATION PAYOFF (SIZE OF THE PRIZE)

Chapter 2 discussed a variety of factors that I argue should affect aggregation incentives. These can be broken down into two categories – those that affect the size of the payoff for being the largest legislative party and those that affect the probability that the largest party will capture that payoff. Starting with the payoff, I argued that the size of the prize is a function of both the degree of *vertical centralization* in the polity as well as the degree of *horizontal centralization*.

Vertical Centralization

If Chhibber and Kollman (2004) are correct, the more power and control of resources are devolved to subnational actors, the worse aggregation will be. This is summarized in the following hypothesis. (In all of the hypotheses that follow, I state the relationships in terms of the inflation score. Recall that higher inflation scores equate to poorer aggregation.)

Vertical Centralization Hypothesis: The degree of vertical centralization is negatively related to inflation.

To estimate the effects of vertical centralization I use two newly developed measures of fiscal decentralization created by the World Bank (World Bank n.d.). *Subrevgdp* measures subnational government revenues as a share of GDP, while *subexpengdp* does the same with subnational expenditures. The results are generally robust to the use of either measure so for the sake of consistency I report only the revenues measure in the following models, noting the few instances where the choice of one or the other makes a substantive difference.[9]

---

[8] This is done by simply taking the percentage difference in size between the national and local party system, without multiplying the result by 100: $I = (ENP_{nat} - ENP_{avg})/ENP_{nat}$.

[9] The World Bank also reports subnational revenues and spending as a percentage of total governmental spending, but I prefer the percent of GDP figures because they simultaneously capture the degree of fiscal (de)centralization along with the relative importance of government spending vis-à-vis the economy as whole. However, the results are not dependent on which measure I use.

Horizontal Centralization

In addition to vertical centralization the degree to which power is concentrated within the national government (horizontal centralization) also affects aggregation incentives. Specifically, I argued that in the presence of bicameralism, reserve domains, and party factionalism aggregation incentives should be weaker. Together these variables shape the degree of horizontal centralization. I also discussed a counterargument that links horizontal decentralization to increased aggregation. To summarize:

> **Bicameral Hypothesis**: Inflation will be higher in bicameral systems, relative to unicameral systems
> **Reserve Domain Hypothesis**: Where reserve domains exist inflation will be higher.
> **Party Factionalism Hypothesis**: The degree of party factionalism is positively related to inflation.
> **Horizontal Centralization Hypothesis**: The degree of horizontal centralization is negatively related to inflation.
> **Alternative Hypothesis**: The degree of horizontal centralization is positively related to inflation.

In an effort to capture the extent of horizontal centralization, I use several different measures created using data from the Database of Political Institutions (DPI) (Beck et al. 2001) and Matt Golder's Democratic Electoral Systems Around the World dataset (Golder 2005).[10] For bicameralism, I created a variable called *Senate* that equals 1 if there is an upper chamber in the legislature; 0 otherwise.[11] As a proxy for the presence of reserve domains, I use a measure of the military's involvement

---

[10] http://homepages.nyu.edu/%7Emrg217/elections.html. See also Golder (2005).
[11] As an alternative, I also used Henisz's measure of "an effective second legislative chamber" (*L2*), which takes on a value of 1 if the second chamber that is elected under a distinct electoral system has a substantial (i.e., not merely delaying) role in fiscal policymaking (2000). I prefer my simpler measure of bicameralism for two reasons. First, we know that upper chambers can affect policy even when they lack formal veto authority (as the Thai case will demonstrate in Chapters 4 and 5). Second, the Henisz measure excludes some important legislative powers that might constitute a check on executive authority (e.g., appointment and confirmation authority). Using *L2* rather than *Senate* yields similar results, though *L2* is always weaker than *Senate* and often falls below traditional levels of significance. Other variables in the models are substantively unaffected by the substitution of *L2*.

Testing the Theory

in politics. *Military5* equals 1 if the chief executive has been a member of the military in the last 5 years. The results are robust to expanding the time frame from 5 to 10 years. These data come from the DPI.

As a strategy for operationalizing the degree of party cohesion/factionalism, I rely on the coding scheme developed by Carey and Shugart (1995) as adapted and extended by Wallack et al. (2003). This scheme is designed to capture differences in the incentives to cultivate a personal vote (versus a party vote) across different electoral systems. A large number of scholars have argued that strong incentives to cultivate a personal vote undermine party cohesion and promote party factionalism (e.g., Katz 1986; Shugart and Carey 1992; Reed 1994; Lijphart 1994; Hicken 2002, 2007). The personal vote undermines party cohesion and promotes factionalism in at least three ways (Reed 1994). First, because in personal vote systems candidates typically do not owe their election to the party, they have less reason to be loyal to it once elected. Second, the independent campaign organization needed to win in candidate-centered elections gives politicians the means to stray from the party line without fear of major repercussions or leave the party all together. Third, in building an independent campaign base, candidates incur debts, make compromises, and develop loyalties to constituencies that may be different from other candidates from within the same party (ibid.).

Carey and Shugart suggest three variables that they argue shape the extent to which candidates running for office have an incentive to cultivate a personal vote. Each of the three variables, *Ballot, Pool, and Vote*, are coded as 0, 1, or 2, where higher values denote greater incentives to cultivate a personal vote.[12] Using the Carey and Shugart coding scheme as a template Wallack et al. (2003) collect data on incentives to cultivate a personal vote for 158 countries for the years 1978–2001.[13] They average across *Ballot, Pool,* and *Vote* to create a variable called *parindex*, which I use here as a proxy for party cohesion. *Parindex* ranges from 0 to 2 with higher values being associated with stronger incentives to cultivate a

---

[12] *Ballot* measures "the degree of control party leaders exercise over access to their party's label, and control over ballot rank in electoral list systems." *Pool* captures whether votes for one candidate affect the number of seats won in that district by the party as a whole. *Vote* codes the nature of voters' choice (for a party, candidate, or multiple candidates). (Carey and Shugart 1995, 418–21).

[13] Wallack et al. and Carey and Shugart differ in their treatment of single member district systems. See Wallack et al. (2002, 7) for more details.

personal vote (and greater tendencies toward party factionalism). *Parindex* is admittedly a very crude and indirect proxy for party factionalism/cohesion. However, it has the major advantage of being free of the endogeneity concerns that would accompany a more direct measure of party cohesion. Still, as I discuss later, *parindex* may ultimately be too crude a proxy to be useful.

Control Variables

I include a number of control variables to account for competing hypotheses. Most important is a control for social heterogeneity. We know that social heterogeneity interacts with electoral rules to shape coordination within electoral districts (Cox 1997), and it is reasonable to expect that the same will be true across districts. The independent effect of social heterogeneity on aggregation should be straightforwardly negative – higher levels of social heterogeneity (especially where groups are geographically concentrated) should hinder attempts to aggregate across districts. In terms of *inflation*, social heterogeneity should be associated with higher inflation scores. However, heterogeneity should also modify the effect of the institutional variables on inflation. Specifically, high levels of social heterogeneity should reduce the positive effect of centralization on aggregation. Likewise, for any given level of social heterogeneity, a greater centralization of authority should yield better aggregation.

As my proxy for social heterogeneity I use *ef* – a measure of ethnic fractionalization within a country. Clearly ethnic differences are only a single dimension of overall social heterogeneity, and ethnic fractionalization is not a perfect measure of ethnic heterogeneity. Ideally we might also want information about the polarization of ethnic groups, their geographic concentration or dispersion, and the extent to which cleavages are crosscutting or reinforcing.[14] Despite these weaknesses, ethnic fractionalization is a common proxy for social heterogeneity in the existing literature, and for this reason I choose to use it here. My measure of ethnic fractionalization comes from Fearon (2003) and is calculated as $1 - \Sigma g_i^2$ where g_i is the percentage of the population of the *i*th ethnic group. The *ef* data are available for 160 countries and

---

[14] See Selway (n.d.) for a review of different ways of thinking about social heterogeneity.

represent an improvement on the more common but frequently criticized index of ethno-linguistic fractionalization (EFL) (Posner 2004).

In addition to social heterogeneity, I also control for the age of the largest government party. One alternative explanation for the degree of aggregation is that it is simply a function of the age or institutionalization of the party system. In early elections, newly formed parties have not yet established the reputation or organizational capacity necessary to effectively run a national campaign. As time passes, some parties begin to build a reputation and capacity, whereas other, weaker contenders drop out of electoral politics or merge with other parties. Thus we might expect aggregation to improve along with the age and institutionalization of the party system. The older and more institutionalized the political parties, the better the aggregation.[15] *Log_govage* is designed to account for this alternative explanation. *Log_govage* is the logged age of the largest party in the government coalition. The variable is logged since I expect the marginal effect of a unit increase in a party's age on aggregation to decrease as the party grows older. In other words, a move from 5 to 10 years might be expected to have a bigger marginal effect than an increase from 50 to 55 years. The information for this variable comes from the DPI (Beck et al. 2001). (As a robustness check, I also control for whether a country was an advanced, industrial democracy, or a developing democracy, using a dummy variable for whether or not a country was a member of the OECD in 1990. The substantive findings are robust to the inclusion of this control.)

As a final control variable, I include information on the number of electoral districts across which candidates and parties must coordinate. The intuition behind this variable is that coordination/aggregation is more difficult as the number of districts increases. *Log_districts* is the log of the number of electoral districts in the lowest electoral tier for the lower house of the legislature. The variable is logged to reflect the expectation of a decreasing marginal effect of a unit increase in district as the number of districts increases.

As discussed earlier, the dataset I use to test these hypotheses includes information on 280 democratic legislative elections in 46 countries covering the period 1970 to 2002. These are countries for which both

---

[15] On party system institutionalization, see Mainwaring and Scully (1995) and Mainwaring (1999).

TABLE 3.2. *Summary Statistics*

Summary Statistics (Cross-Sectional Dataset)

Variable	Obs	Mean	Std. Dev.	Min	Max
inflation	46	.16	.14	0	.55
senate	46	.60	.49	0	1
subrevgdp	36	6.28	6.11	.21	21.22
military5	46	.15	.29	0	1
parindex	44	.87	.61	0	2
ef	44	.35	.25	0	.85
horizontal	46	.85	.63	0	2
decentralization	36	1.47	.77	0	3
log_govage	44	3.68	.88	1.47	5.13
log_districts	46	3.99	1.23	1.79	6.44
probability	21	.15	.20	0	.75
ENPres	36	1.98	1.77	0	5.5
proximity	44	.28	.40	0	1
log_avemag	44	1.31	1.16	0	5.01
ENPnat	46	3.92	1.81	1.95	9.40

Summary Statistics (Pooled Dataset)

Variable	Obs	Mean	Std. Dev.	Min	Max
inflation	273	.15	.15	−.04	.70
senate	273	.69	.46	0	1
subrevgdp	205	8.25	6.42	.13	23.44
military5	271	.12	.32	0	1
parindex	208	.83	.61	0	2
ef	263	.30	.23	0	.85
horizontal	271	.81	.51	0	2
decentralization	203	1.36	.62	0	2
log_govage	213	3.73	1.04	.69	5.16
log_districts	271	4.0	1.27	1.79	6.46
probability	141	.16	.23	0	1
ENPres	195	1.67	1.7	0	6.57
proximity	265	.20	.40	0	1
log_avemag	264	1.45	1.21	0	5.01
ENPnat	273	3.97	1.91	1.63	13.79

district level and national level election data were available.[16] Each country case contains nearly six elections on average, ranging from a low

---

[16] A project, funded by the National Science Foundation, to extend the district return dataset to more elections in more countries is currently underway.

of one election in five countries to 15 in the United States. See Table 3.1 for a complete list of the countries and their inflation scores. Table 3.2 contains the summary statistics for the dataset.

I test my hypotheses using both cross-sectional and pooled analyses. In the pooled analyses, I use OLS with robust standard errors clustered by country. This is a better modeling option than employing a fixed effects model with panel-corrected standard errors (PCSE) (Beck and Katz 1995) given the nature of the data (Franzese 2006; Golder 2006). First, fixed effects minimize the explanatory power of my time invariant independent variables. Clustering the standard errors by country allows me to produce consistent estimates of the standard errors while accounting for unit-heterogeneity in a way that does not require fixed effects (Franzese 2006; Golder 2006). Second, the accuracy of PCSEs increases as the number of observations per unit increase. Because many countries have only a few elections represented in the dataset, we might question the advisability of using PCSEs. Note, however, that while I report only results using clustered standard errors, using PCSEs instead does not change the interpretation of the results.[17]

To correct for serial correlation in longitudinal data, it is also common to include a lag of the dependent variable on the right-hand side. However, as Golder argues in a recent study on elections in presidential democracies, using a lagged dependent variable with comparative electoral data is problematic (2006). "First, observations in the dataset do not always come in regular intervals either within countries or across countries." (Golder 2006, 9) For example, the period between Thai elections ranges from 1 year to as many as 5 years. Given this irregularity, it is difficult to know how one would interpret the estimated coefficient on a lagged dependent variable. Second, the panel nature of the dataset (small T, large N) means that including a lagged dependent variable would significantly reduce the sample size and drop all countries for which I have data on only a single election (Golder 2006, 9). For these reasons, the models I present here do not include a lagged dependent variable.[18]

---

[17] In fact, in almost every case, the use of PCSEs yields stronger results.
[18] Including the lagged dependent variable does not generally change the nature of my inferences. With the lagged dependent variable included, the signs of other explanatory variables generally remain the same, though in some cases the variables are no longer statistically significant.

TABLE 3.3. *Horizontal Centralization (Dependent Variable: Inflation)*

Explanatory Variable	Cross-Sectional Analyses			Pooled Analyses		
	1	2	3	4	5	6
senate	0.06	0.03		0.08**	0.08**	
	(0.04)	(0.05)		(0.03)	(0.04)	
military5	0.24**	0.28**		0.19***	0.16**	
	(0.07)	(0.10)		(0.05)	(0.07)	
parindex	0.07**	0.02		0.06*	0.05	
	(0.03)	(0.03)		(0.03)	(0.03)	
subrevgdp		0.007*	0.007*		0.003	0.004
		(0.004)	(0.004)		(0.003)	(0.003)
horizontal			0.07*			0.10***
			(0.04)			(0.03)
ef		0.33***	0.34***		0.31***	0.33***
		(0.10)	(0.11)		(0.11)	(0.11)
log_govage		−0.04	−0.08***		−0.04**	
		(0.03)	(0.03)		(0.02)	
					−0.04***	
					(0.02)	
log_districts		0.005	0.01		−0.01	0.002
		(0.018)	(0.02)		(0.03)	(0.02)
Constant	0.03	0.09	0.21*	0.03	0.11	0.10
	(0.04)	(0.13)	(0.12)	(0.04)	(0.10)	(0.09)
R-squared	0.29	0.59	0.49	0.26	0.49	0.46
Observations	44	34	34	208	146	161

* $p < .10$, ** $p < .05$, *** $p < .01$; standard errors in parentheses

3.3.1 Results

Table 3.3 displays the results from six different simple additive models. Columns 1–3 display the results using the cross-sectional analyses. Columns 4–7 display the results from the same models run on the pooled dataset. The dependent variable in all of the models is the inflation score. Starting with models 1 and 2 and the corresponding models 4 and 5, the results in Table 3.3 provide strong support for the reserve domains hypotheses and some support for the bicameralism hypothesis as well. The presence of reserve domains, as measured by *military5*, significantly increases party system inflation in all four models. In two of the four models, bicameralism is significantly associated with poorer aggregation (as manifest by an increase in the inflation score). In the two remaining models, bicameralism has the correct sign but is not statistically significant. There is also strong statistical support for two of the three control variables. As expected, greater ethnic fragmentation is associated with poorer aggregation (higher inflation), whereas party systems with older parties appear to do a better job aggregating across districts than those with younger parties. The number of districts, however, appears to have no significant affect on the degree of cross-district coordination.

Fairing less well is my measure of party factionalism – *parindex*. *Parindex* is significant in two of the four models (and it does have the correct sign in the rest). However, even though my proxies for reserve domains and bicameralism are robust to alternative specifications, *parindex* is not. Across all the various models *parindex* is rarely significantly related to *inflation*, and in some models switches signs. *Parindex* does not perform any better if I recode it as dummy variable. In short, *parindex* does not appear to be a good proxy for party factionalism – not completely surprising given that it was at best a rather indirect measure of party cohesion.[19] In addition, including *parindex* in the models comes at a cost since it is available for fewer years than the rest of the sample.[20] Specifically, including *parindex* reduces the sample size by more than 23%. Both because of the variable's poor performance and in a desire to economize on observations, I opt to drop *parindex* from the remainder of the analyses in this chapter. However, I will revisit the party factionalism hypothesis in Chapter 5 in connection with the Thai case.

Recall that bicameralism and reserve domains are hypothesized to work together to affect the degree of horizontal centralization. In an attempt to capture this synthesis, I create an index labeled *horizontal*, which additively combines *senate* and *military5* to create a variable that ranges from 0 to 2. *Lower* scores on *horizontal* are associated with a *greater* concentration of power. In other words, we can think of *horizontal* as representing the degree of horizontal decentralization. In models 3 and 6 in Table 3.3, we see that *horizontal* is positively related to inflation as expected – greater horizontal decentralization is associated with higher party system inflation (poorer

---

[19] John Carey has developed a possible measure of party cohesion based on legislative voting records (Carey 2007). Unfortunately the dataset it is not available for enough of my sample to allow me to use it here.
[20] *Parindex* begins in 1978 while the rest of the sample begins in 1970.

aggregation).²¹ Specifically, the results from Table 3.3 model 6 suggest that a one-unit increase in *horizontal* (from 0 to 1 or from 1 to 2) is associated with an increase in the predicted inflation score of .10 (recall that the inflation score ranges from 0 to 1).²² When the power is highly centralized horizontally (*horizontal* = 0) the predicted inflation score is .09. As power becomes more decentralized, *inflation* rises to .19 (when *horizontal* is 1) and then to .29 (*horizontal* is 2). By contrast, a one standard deviation increase of *subrevgdp* (my proxy for vertical decentralization) causes only a .02 point increase in the inflation score (from .17 to .19). Table 3.9 displays these predicted inflation scores as well as predicted values for select other models from this chapter. Given that *horizontal* includes only two variables, it may appear more sensible to continue to include these variables in the model separately or to interact them. However, it is useful to have a single summary measure of horizontal centralization, especially when I turn to a set of interactions in subsequent models.

The Size of the Prize: Vertical and Horizontal Interaction

Table 3.3 by itself provides only weak support for the vertical centralization hypotheses – my measure of vertical (de)centralization is significant only half of the time. However, remember that one of the central arguments in Chapter 2 was that the payoff to being the largest party is a joint product of both vertical and horizontal centralization. A sufficiently high level of vertical centralization may be necessary to induce cross-district coordination, but absent an adequate degree of horizontal centralization, it is not sufficient. This suggests the following conditional hypothesis:

> **Joint Centralization Hypothesis:** The negative effect of vertical centralization on inflation is conditional on the degree of horizontal centralization. Inflation should be highest where there is both a high degree of vertical and horizontal decentralization and lowest where there a high degree of vertical and horizontal centralization.

---

[21] In the cross-sectional analysis, *military5* does the bulk of the work when the model is fully specified.
[22] Holding all other variables at their means.

In Table 3.4 I attempt to test this hypothesis by interacting *subrevgdp* with *horizontal*. Columns 1 and 3 summarize the results for the cross section and pooled analysis. As hypothesized when there is a high degree of horizontal centralization (*horizontal* is 0) an increase in the percentage of revenues controlled by subnational actors (*subrevgdp*) reduces aggregation (increases inflation). Specifically, a one standard deviation in *subrevgdp* when *horizontal* is 0 boosts the predicted inflation score from .06 to .11 (see Table 3.9).[23] Likewise when there is perfect vertical centralization (*subrevgdp* equals 0) greater horizontal decentralization is associated with poorer aggregation. The substantive effect is quite large – an increase of *horizontal* from 0 to 1 causes a .14 increase in the inflation score (from .01 to .15). As either variable increases, the marginal effect of the other declines as the negative coefficient on the interaction term shows. In short, the data demonstrate that even where there is perfect vertical centralization, horizontal decentralization will still undermine cross-district coordination. Likewise, when power is concentrated within the national government, party system inflation will still occur if subnational actors control substantial shares of power and resources. Aggregation is at its highest level when there is both horizontal and vertical centralization.

Note that when using interaction terms, the standard errors on the interaction term and the constituent variables are uninterpretable (Brambor, Clark, and Golder 2005; Kam and Franzese 2007). Instead, the question is the marginal effect of one of the interacted variables over the range of the other variable, and whether that effect is significant. Figure 3.1 graphically illustrates the marginal effect of vertical (de)centralization on inflation as the degree of horizontal (de)centralization changes.[24] The solid sloping line shows how the marginal effect changes as horizontal decentralization increases. We can judge whether this effect is significant by drawing 95% confidence intervals around the line. Wherever the confidence interval lies completely above or below the zero line, the marginal effect is significant. Where it straddles the line the marginal effect cannot be statistically distinguished from zero.

---

[23] Again, holding all other variables at their means.
[24] See Kam and Franzese (2007) and Brambor et al. (2005) on the advisability of presenting the results in this manner. I thank Brambor et al. for granting me access to their STATA .do file, which I use to create all the marginal effect graphs in this chapter.

TABLE 3.4. *Horizontal and Vertical Centralization (Dependent Variable: Inflation)*

Explanatory Variable	Cross-Sectional Analyses		Pooled Analyses	
	1	2	3	4
subrevgdp	0.01**		0.007**	
	(0.004)		(0.003)	
horizontal	0.09*		0.14***	
	(0.05)		(0.05)	
subrevgdp * horizontal	−0.01		−0.006	
	(0.01)		(0.004)	
decentralization		0.06**		0.07***
		(0.03)		(0.02)
ef	0.34***	0.32***	0.34***	0.37***
	(0.11)	(0.10)	(0.11)	(0.12)
log_govage	−0.07**	−0.06***	−0.04**	−0.05***
	(0.03)	(0.02)	(0.02)	(0.01)
log_districts	0.01	0.004	0.01	0.003
	(0.02)	(0.019)	(0.02)	(0.02)
Constant	0.17	0.21**	0.04	0.13
	(0.13)	(0.09)	(0.09)	(0.10)
R-squared	0.50	0.44	0.48	0.45
Observations	34	34	161	161

* $p < .1$, ** $p < .05$, *** $p < .01$; standard errors in parentheses

Figures 3.1a and 3.1b display the marginal effect of subnational governments' share of revenues (or the degree of vertical decentralization) on inflation. Figure 3.1a illustrates the cross-sectional model, while Figure 3.1b shows the pooled model. We can see in both figures that the marginal effect of vertical decentralization on inflation is positive and significant, but only at low levels of horizontal decentralization. As horizontal power becomes more dispersed, the marginal effect of vertical centralization is no longer significant. In short, these two graphs show that aggregation is highest (and *inflation* is lowest) where we have both vertical *and* horizontal centralization, as hypothesized. In other words, vertical and horizontal centralization jointly determine the size of the payoff for cross-district coordination. Figures 3.1c and 3.1d display the marginal effect of horizontal decentralization as vertical decentralization changes. The marginal effect of horizontal decentralization is positive and significant and decreases in vertical centralization. In other

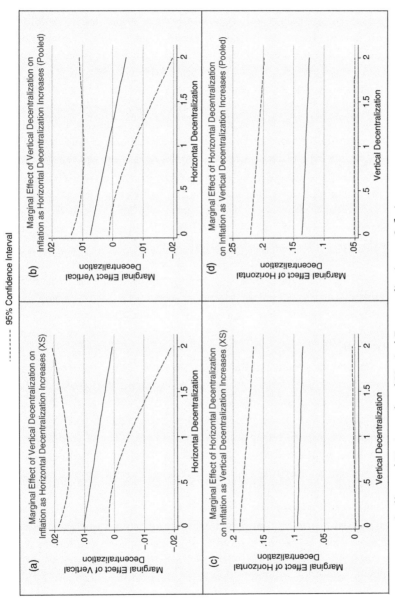

FIGURE 3.1. Marginal Effects of Horizontal and Vertical Decentralization on Inflation

words, as vertical decentralization increases, the marginal effect of horizontal decentralization moves toward zero (albeit gradually).

In order to interact the size of the payoff with other variables of interest as the theory calls for, it is useful to generate a single summary measure of the size of the payoff. To do this, I convert *subrevgdp* into a dichotomous variable, recoding all observations below the median as 0 and the remainder as 1. I then add it to *horizontal*. The resulting variable, *decentralization*, ranges from 0 to 3 and represents the combination of both the vertical and horizontal dimensions of centralization. Note that higher values on the variable correspond to higher levels of decentralization. Higher values of *decentralization* should be associated with a lower payoff, poorer aggregation, and ultimately, a higher inflation score. Columns 2 and 4 in Table 3.4 demonstrate that *decentralization* is indeed positively related to *inflation*, as expected.[25] For the remainder of the analysis I will use *decentralization* as my proxy for the size of the aggregation payoff.

To summarize the results from this section, the bicameralism and reserve domain hypotheses were both supported by the data. Second chambers and the presence of reserve domains are each associated with poorer aggregation. The data do not support the party factionalism hypothesis. This might suggest that the hypothesis is incorrect, or that my proxy for factionalism, incentives to cultivate a personal vote, does a poor job of capturing the theoretical concept. The index of horizontal decentralization (the combination of *senate* and *military5*) also produced the hypothesized effect on aggregation. Higher levels of horizontal centralization are associated with better the aggregation (and lower inflation scores). There was no support in any of the models for the alternative hypothesis that high levels of horizontal decentralization induce greater efforts at cross-district coordination (and hence lower inflation scores).

The results were also supportive of the joint centralization hypothesis. Horizontal and vertical centralization together determine the size of the aggregation payoff. Aggregation is best where power is concentrated both horizontally and vertically. The interaction models suggested that the marginal effect of vertical centralization on inflation

---

[25] In model 4, a rise in *decentralization* from 0 to 1 yields a change in the predicted inflation of .07 (from .06 to .20). (All other variables are held at their mean – see Table 3.9.)

is conditional on the level of horizontal centralization. Vertical centralization is indeed associated with a lower inflation score, but only where there is also substantial horizontal centralization. In short, diffusion of power within the national government is sufficient to undermine the effect of vertical centralization on inflation, as hypothesized. Finally, the proxy for the size of the aggregation payoff, the *decentralization* index, is positively related to party system inflation, as expected.

3.4 THE PROBABILITY OF CAPTURING THE PRIZE – PARLIAMENTARY SYSTEMS

The size of the payoff to being the largest party in government is not the only thing that shapes aggregation incentives. The probability that the largest party will capture that prize is also important. If the largest legislative party has little chance of capturing the reins of government, particularly executive office, then even a potentially large payoff will not be enough to induce national coordination. In parliamentary systems, the probability of capturing the prize depends on whether the leader of the largest party becomes the prime minister. If someone other than the leader of the largest party gets the chance to form and head the government, then this can undermine the incentives to coordinate across districts to forge a large national party.

Prime Minister Hypothesis: In parliamentary systems, inflation will be negatively related to the probability that the leader of the largest party becomes prime minister.

I operationalize the probability variable as a moving average of the number of elections since 1970 where the prime minister has not been a member of the largest party in the legislature (*probability*). The variable is continuous and ranges from 0 (the leader of the largest party has always been the prime minister) to 1 (the leader of the largest party has never been the prime minister). In short, *probability* captures the probability that the prime minister will NOT come from the largest legislative party. Higher values on probability should be associated with a higher inflation score. I believe *probability* is a reasonable proxy for the expectation candidates and party leaders might have when devising a coordination strategy. However, as a robustness check I also calculated two dichotomous variables. *Probability2* is coded 1 once someone other than the leader of the largest party serves as prime minister and *probability3* is 1 if someone other than the leader of the largest party served as prime minister in the last election. These two cruder proxies produce results consistent with *probability*, though they are occasionally insignificant. All three variables are calculated from data in the Database of Political Institutions (Beck et al. 2001).

Probability-Payoff Interaction

Recall that it is the interaction of the size of the payoff and the probability of capturing that prize that together jointly shape the expected utility of becoming the largest legislative party. In short, probability modifies the effect of *decentralization* on aggregation incentives.

> **Expected Utility Hypothesis:** The effect of the size of the payoff on inflation is conditional on the probability of capturing that payoff. Specifically, the marginal effect of *decentralization* on inflation is increasing in *probability*.

I test these hypotheses using a dataset of 156 elections in 21 parliamentary democracies from 1970 to 2002. I use both cross-sectional and pooled models. Given the structure of the data I again use OLS with robust standard errors clustered by country for the pooled analysis.

3.4.1. Results

Table 3.5 displays the results of the hypothesis testing – again divided into cross-sectional and pooled analyses. Given the small number of observations in the cross-sectional models, the results should be interpreted with some caution. It is heartening, therefore, to see the cross-sectional results replicated in the pooled analysis. Columns 1 and 4 contain the results of a simple additive model. We can see that *probability* is statistically significant with the right sign when added to the model in this way. The higher is the probability that the leader of the largest party will NOT capture the payoff, the higher is the associated inflation score. This is true, even controlling for the size of the

TABLE 3.5. *Aggregation in Parliamentary Democracies (Dependent Variable: Inflation)*

	Cross-Sectional Analyses			Pooled Analyses		
Explanatory Variables	1	2	3 (No Thailand)	4	5	6 (No Thailand)
decentralization	0.07**	0.04	0.05	0.08**	0.05	0.05*
	(0.03)	(0.05)	(0.05)	(0.03)	(0.03)	(0.03)
probability	0.23**	-0.14	-0.08	0.16*	-0.12	-0.03
	(0.10)	(0.32)	(0.30)	(0.09)	(0.18)	(0.17)
decent*prob		0.21	0.10		0.18	0.07
		(0.17)	(0.17)		(0.13)	(0.12)
ef	0.36***	0.32**	0.30**	0.53***	0.51***	0.48**
	(0.11)	(0.11)	(0.12)	(0.16)	(0.16)	(0.17)
log_govage	-0.07**	-0.07***	-0.07***	-0.03**	-0.02**	-0.02**
	(0.02)	(0.02)	(0.02)	(0.01)	(0.01)	(0.01)
log_districts	0.01	0.02	0.02	0.01	0.01	0.01
	(0.02)	(0.02)	(0.02)	(0.02)	(0.03)	(0.03)
Constant	0.11	0.18	0.18	-0.05	-0.01	-0.01
	(0.13)	(0.14)	(0.14)	(0.10)	(0.10)	(0.10)
R-squared	0.74	.74	.65	.66	.67	.64
Observations	19	19	18	101	101	98

* $p < .1$, ** $p < .05$, *** $p < .01$; standard errors in parentheses

payoff (*decentralization*). Note too that the effect of *decentralization* on inflation remains significant in these models.

Columns 2 and 5 summarize the results of the interactive models. To get a better sense of the interactive dynamics at work in these models, I once again include marginal effects graphs. In this case, the graphs display the marginal effect of *decentralization* as *probability* changes. Figures 3.2a and 3.2b show that the marginal effect of *decentralization* on inflation is always positive, though when *probability* is at or near 0 this positive effect is not statistically significant at the 95% level (though it is at the 90% level).[26] This suggests that the marginal effect of the size of the payoff is weakest where actors are virtually certain that the largest party will capture the premiership. However, as the probability that someone other than the leader of the largest party will become prime minister increases, the marginal impact of decentralization inflation increases as well. As hypothesized, the marginal effect of *decentralization* increases in *probability*. As I argued in Chapter 2, aggregation appears to be the poorest where *both* the size of payoff is small (*decentralization* is high) *and* the chance of capturing that payoff is low (*probability* is high). More concretely, the model in column 5 suggests that where power is highly decentralized (*decentralization* = 2) *and* there is little chance of capturing the payoff (*probability* = 1), the inflation score is a very high .42.[27] By contrast, where there is certainly that the largest legislative party will capture a valuable prize (*probability* and *decentralization* are both 0), the predicted inflation score is .08 (see Table 3.9).

Plots of the observations suggest that Thailand is an outlier with both an unusually high *probability* score and an equally high *inflation* score. Even though this result is consistent with the theory (as I will demonstrate in Chapter 5), I want to be certain the results are not being driven entirely by the Thai case. As a remedy, I reran the interactive models with Thailand excluded and display the results in columns 2 and 4. We can see that dropping the Thai case does indeed reduce the size of the coefficients on both *probability* and the interaction term. The marginal effects graphs

---

[26] In the pooled analyses, substituting expenditures for revenues in the *decentralization* index produces consistent but weaker results. Substituting expenditures makes no difference in the cross-sectional analyses.

[27] Holding all other variables at their means.

Testing the Theory

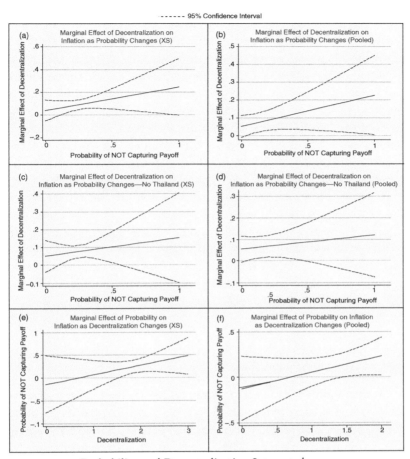

FIGURE 3.2. Probability and Decentralization Interacted

do not change much, however, when I exclude Thailand (see Figures 3.2c and 3.2d). The marginal effect of *decentralization* is still positive and increasing in *probability*, though with Thailand excluded, this marginal effect is no longer significant at high levels of *probability*.

Finally, the final two graphs in Figures 3.2e and 3.2f show the marginal effect of *probability* as *decentralization* increases. Note that where there is a high aggregation payoff (*decentralization* = 0), the marginal effect of probability on inflation is indistinguishable from zero. In other words, a high aggregation payoff can be enough to induce aggregation even if the probability of capturing that prize is low.

However, as the aggregation payoff declines, an increase in *probability* is associated with a rise in party system inflation. This positive marginal effect continues to increase as *decentralization* increases.

To summarize, the results of these models are consistent with both the Prime Minister and Expected Utility hypotheses. In the additive models, an increase in the probability that someone other than the leader of the largest party will capture the premiership is associated with greater inflation. (In those same models, the proxy for the aggregation payoff – *decentralization* – is significantly positive, as expected). The interactive models are consistent with my argument that aggregation incentives are a reflection of both the size of the aggregation payoff and the probability of capturing that payoff. *Decentralization*, my measure of the aggregation payoff, has its strongest marginal effect on inflation when combined with a high likelihood of not capturing the premiership. In other words, aggregation is the worst when there is both a low aggregation payoff and a low probability of capturing that prize, as hypothesized.

3.5 THE PROBABILITY OF CAPTURING THE PRIZE – PRESIDENTIAL SYSTEMS

In presidential democracies, the probability that the largest legislative party will also capture the presidency is a function of whether presidential and legislative elections are concurrent and the effective number of presidential candidates. The arguments about the probability of capturing the prize of government in presidential systems can be summarized with the following hypotheses.

> **Concurrency Hypothesis:** Inflation is lower when presidential and legislative elections are concurrent.
> **ENPresxConcurrency Hypothesis 1:** The effect of concurrent elections on inflation is conditional on the effective number of presidential candidates. As the effective number of candidates increases, the negative relationship between concurrency and inflation weakens.
> **ENPresxConcurrency Hypothesis 2:** The effective number of presidential candidates is positively related to inflation in concurrent elections.

In Chapter 2, I also argued that a ban on reelection for the president should increase the number of presidential candidates, ceteris paribus, which suggests the following hypothesis.

Reelection Hypothesis: The effective number of presidential candidates is positively correlated with restrictions on presidential reelection.

Data on the effective number of presidential candidates (*ENPres*) and the concurrency of elections come from Golder (2005).[28] To capture the proximity of legislative and presidential elections, I use a dummy variable that equals 1 if presidential and legislative elections are held in the same year, 0 if they are not.[29] For restrictions on presidential reelection, I use a variable coded as 1 if the sitting president is not eligible for reelection (*no_reelection*). This operationalization is preferable to a simple dummy variable for whether or not a country places term limits on a president. Coding the variable for term limits lumps together countries where presidents face a single term limit (e.g., Mexico or the Philippines) with countries that allow presidents to serve multiple but limited terms (e.g., the United States). Since what I ultimately care about is whether in any given presidential election there is an incumbent running, *no_reelection* seems like the logical choice.[30] *No_reelection* is calculated from data in the DPI (Beck et al. 2001).

I test these hypotheses using both cross-sectional and pooled models. I again use OLS with robust standard errors clustered by country for the pooled analyses for the reasons described previously. To test the hypotheses, I use three different datasets. The first is a subset of the dataset described in the previous sections and consists of 81 elections in 18 presidential democracies. I use this dataset to directly test the hypotheses relating aggregation to concurrency, the effective number of presidential candidates, and the interaction of these two variables.

Given that this first dataset is small I also indirectly test the same three hypotheses using Golder's legislative elections dataset (2005).

---

[28] The effective number of presidential candidates is calculated by dividing 1 by the sum of each candidate's squared vote share: $1/\Sigma v_i^2$.

[29] The results are robust to the substitution of a continuous variable measuring the distance between presidential and midterm elections on a 0 to 1 scale.

[30] Even better would be data on whether the incumbent actually runs. Unfortunately such data have not been gathered in a single dataset to my knowledge.

This dataset covers all democratic legislative elections in the world from 1946 to 2000 for a total of 784 elections.[31] The dependent variable from this dataset is the effective number of electoral parties at the national level (*ENPnat*). Ceteris paribus the effective number of legislative parties is positively correlated with the *inflation* score.[32] However, unlike *inflation*, *ENPnat* does not distinguish between the degree of aggregation across districts and the amount of coordination within those districts. To control for the district-level effects, I include the log of average district magnitude (*log_avemag*) and ethnic fractionalization (*ef*). We know that these two variables interact to determine the effective number of parties at the district level (Cox 1997). The district magnitude data come from Golder (2005) and the ethnic fractionalization data are from Fearon (2003) as described previously.

To test the reelection hypothesis I use a third data set – Golder's presidential elections dataset. This dataset includes 294 democratic presidential elections from 1946 to 2000. I focus only on direct election in presidential democracies and so exclude from my models elections in hybrid presidential-parliamentary regimes as well as any cases of indirect presidential elections (e.g., the United States).[33] This brings the number of observations in the dataset to 170. The dependent variable from this dataset is the effective number of presidential candidates (*ENPres*). The main explanatory variable is the presence (or absence) of a ban on reelection of the sitting president (*no_reelection*).

As discussed in Chapter 2, the effective number of presidential candidates (like the effective number of parties) is a product of an interaction between electoral rules and social structure (Golder 2006). Ethnic heterogeneity increases the effective number of presidential candidates only when accompanied by a permissive electoral formula (namely, majority runoff). I replicate this finding and then add the

---

[31] The total dataset includes 867 elections. This excludes Columbian elections from 1958 to 1970 when there was an agreement between Columbia's two major parties to alternate control of government and the share of legislative seats regardless of electoral results. Another 76 elections are dropped from the sample due to a lack of party vote share data, which are needed to calculate the effective number of electoral parties.

[32] Specifically, holding the average number of parties at the district level constant.

[33] Leaving indirect presidential elections in the dataset does not substantively alter the results.

Testing the Theory

no_reelection variable to see whether it has a significant independent effect on the effective number of presidential candidates. Ethnic heterogeneity is measured, as it has been previously, as the ethnic fractionalization (*ef*). *Runoff* is a dummy variable coded 1 if the presidential election formula is a runoff, 0 otherwise.

3.5.1 Results

Table 3.6 displays the results using my inflation dataset and Golder's legislative elections dataset. In columns 1, 4, and 5, the dependent variable is *inflation*. The effective number of electoral parties (*ENPnat*) is the dependent variable in columns 2, 3, 6, and 7. Looking first at the results from the *inflation* models, we can see that, as expected, party system inflation is lower where presidential and legislative elections are concurrent – *proximity* has a significant negative effect when *ENPres* is 0. Also in line with the first interaction hypothesis, the deflationary effect of concurrent elections diminishes as the effective number of presidential candidates rises. The coefficient on the interaction term *proximity* ENPres* is positive and significant in all of the model specifications. This relationship holds even when controlling for the size of the aggregation payoff as in model 5. (Note that *decentralization* is still positive and significant in model 5, even when controlling for the number of presidential candidates and proximity).

The story is similar if we substitute the effective number of electoral parties (*ENPnat*) for *inflation* as the dependent variable in models 2, 3, 6, and 7. Models 2 and 6 use my dataset. For a robustness check, I also run the same specifications using Golder's larger legislative elections dataset (models 3 and 7). The substantive results are the same regardless of which dataset I use. With *ENPnat* as the dependent variable, my analyses are similar to recent studies on the effect of presidential election on legislative fragmentation (Cox 1997; Mozaffar et al. 2003; Golder 2006). The findings are consistent with these existing studies.[34] Proximity reduces the effective number of electoral parties (proximity is negative and significant in all four specifications), but this effect is conditional on the effective number of presidential candidates. An increase in the number of candidates undermines the marginal negative

---

[34] See especially Golder (2006, 11–13).

TABLE 3.6. *Aggregation in Presidential Democracies*

	Cross-Sectional Analyses – Dependent Variable			Pooled Analyses – Dependent Variable			
Explanatory Variables	1 (inflation)	2 (ENPnat)	3 (ENPnat) (Golder)	4 (inflation)	5 (inflation)	6 (ENPnat)	7 (ENPnat) (Golder)
proximity	−0.68***	−6.95***	−5.02***	−0.43***	−0.19**	−4.30**	−3.43***
	(0.04)	(1.66)	(1.66)	(0.10)	(0.06)	(1.57)	(1.26)
ENPres	−0.04**	−0.14	1.32**	−0.04	−0.04*	−0.04	0.61*
	(0.01)	(0.61)	(0.60)	(0.03)	(0.02)	(0.39)	(0.36)
proximity*ENPres	0.18***	1.81**	0.28	0.13***	0.08***	1.31**	0.65*
	(0.02)	(0.72)	(0.86)	(0.03)	(0.02)	(0.51)	(0.37)
ef	0.11	0.74	1.84	0.19	0.49**	−0.67	2.43**
	(0.07)	(2.73)	(1.57)	(0.11)	(0.16)	(1.52)	(1.16)
log_govage	−0.02*			−0.05***	−0.09***		
	(0.01)			(0.01)	(0.02)		
log_districts	−0.01			−0.001	−0.03*		
	(0.01)			(0.01)	(0.02)		
log_avemag		0.69	0.75			−0.09	0.81*
		(1.09)	(0.60)			(0.70)	(0.41)
ef*avemag		0.73	−0.46			2.56	−0.34
		(2.12)	(0.89)			(1.98)	(0.83)
decentralization					0.13**		
					(0.04)		
Constant	0.44***	3.65*	2.04	0.42***	0.31***	3.19**	1.39
	(0.06)	(1.82)	(1.40)	(0.10)	(0.09)	(1.42)	(1.31)
R-squared	0.95	0.80	.56	.63	.77	.64	.39
Observations	15	16	26	61	45	74	182

* $p < .1$; ** $p < .05$; *** $p < .01$; standard errors in parentheses

effect of proximity on the number of parties (the interaction term, *proximity*ENPres*, is positive in all four specifications, significantly so in three).

In Figure 3.3, I display the marginal effect graphs for four of the seven models in Table 3.6, specifically models 1, 2, 4, and 6.[35] The graphs tell a remarkably consistent story. Concurrent presidential elections are associated with better aggregation (fewer parties and less inflation), but only where there is a small effective number of presidential candidates. Once the number of candidates rises to somewhere between 2.5 and 3.5, the marginal effect of concurrency disappears altogether. Focusing for a moment on just *inflation* (Figures 3.3a and 3.3c), we see that once the effective number of candidates is sufficiently large, concurrent elections are actually associated with a significant *increase* in inflation.

Table 3.7 presents the remainder of the presidential election models. In the first cross-sectional specification and models 4 and 5 in the pooled specifications, I isolate the impact of the effective number of presidential candidates on inflation and the number of parties when elections are concurrent (*proximity* = 1).[36] We can see that when presidential and legislative elections are concurrent, the effective number of presidential candidates is positively related to both party system inflation and the effective number of electoral parties, as hypothesized. If the effective number of candidates is in fact so important for shaping aggregation incentives, as it appears to be, then what determines the effective number of candidates?

In models 2 and 6, the effective number of candidates (*ENPres*) is the dependent variable, and I test whether reelection restrictions lead to more presidential candidates, controlling for the strength of the electoral system and social heterogeneity. The results provide some support for the hypothesis that restrictions on reelection are associated with more presidential candidates. In model 2, *no_reelection* is positive but just short of significant, while in the pooled analysis (model 6) the coefficient for *no_reelection* is both positive and significant. The lack of an incumbent does appear to have an inflationary effect on the effective

---

[35] The graphs for the other three models tell the same story.
[36] I do not report the results from the cross-sectional inflation model here due to the small number of observations in that specification. However, the results from that model are nearly identical to the pooled inflation model (#4).

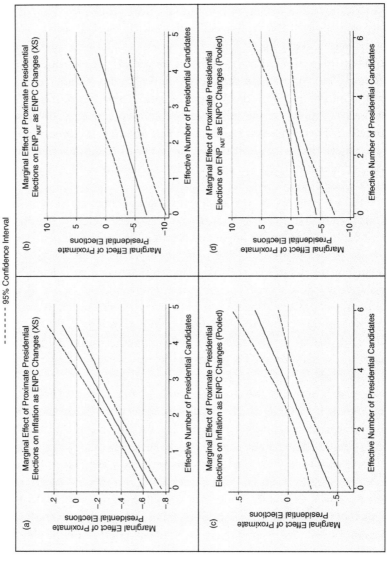

FIGURE 3.3. Marginal Effect of Proximate Presidential Elections as the Effective Number of Presidential Candidates Changes

TABLE 3.7. *Reelection Restrictions and the Effective Number of Presidential Candidates*

	Cross-Sectional Analyses – Dependent Variable				Pooled Analyses – Dependent Variable		
Explanatory Variables	1 (*ENPnat*) (Golder-leg)	2 (*ENPres*) (Golder-pres)	3 (*ENPres*) (Golder-pres)	4 (*inflation*)	5 (*ENPnat*) (Golder-leg)	6 (*ENPres*) (Golder-pres)	7 (*ENPres*) (Golder-pres)
ENPres	0.87** (0.30)			0.10*** (0.02)	1.29*** (0.20)		
log_govage				−0.03** (0.01)			
log_districts				0.01 (0.01)			
log_avemag	0.23 (1.06)				1.69*** (0.24)		
ef*log_avemag	−0.37 (1.52)				−0.83* (0.46)		
ef	0.27 (2.83)	0.47 (0.36)	0.89* (0.46)	0.15* (0.07)	1.67** (0.72)	0.12 (0.47)	0.98 (0.63)
no_reelection		0.43 (0.26)	0.42* (0.22)			0.55** (0.27)	0.53* (0.27)
runoff		0.11 (0.39)	0.53 (0.37)	−0.12 (0.09)		−0.42 (0.55)	0.53* (0.28)
ef*runoff		0.84 (0.89)				2.03* (1.16)	
no_reelection* runoff			0.04 (0.47)				0.11 (0.45)
Constant	0.57 (1.89)	2.04*** (0.31)	1.84*** (0.32)	0.77	−1.32* (0.71)	2.28*** (0.30)	1.88*** (0.39)
R-squared	.30	.32	.21	38	.51	.24	.19
Observations	13	31	31		104	104	104

* $p < .1$, ** $p < .05$, *** $p < .01$; standard errors in parentheses

number of presidential candidates, especially in the pooled analysis. But how do we account for the nature of the presidential electoral system? Do we observe more presidential candidates in the face of reelection restrictions when the presidential electoral system is permissive, and fewer when it is restrictive? To test whether this is the case, I interact *no_reelection* with *runoff* and display the results of these analyses in columns 3 and 7. (Recall that *runoff* is coded 1 if majority runoff, a permissive electoral rule, is used to elect the president, 0 otherwise.) *No_reelection* has a positive and significant effect on the number of presidential candidates, even when the electoral rule is restrictive (*runoff* equals 0). By contrast, Figure 3.4 suggests that under majority runoff, the marginal effect of *no-reelection* is no longer distinguishable from zero. It appears then, that reelection restrictions only have a discernable inflationary effect on the number of parties where the electoral system is restrictive. Where a permissive electoral system (i.e., majority runoff) already allows for a large number of candidates the effect of reelection restrictions is superfluous.

In summary, the data support the hypotheses laid out in this section. Proximate presidential elections are associated with better aggregation (and fewer parties), but this effect is conditional on the number of presidential candidates. In addition, when presidential and legislative elections are concurrent, the effective number of presidential candidates is positively related to both party system inflation and the effective number of electoral parties, as hypothesized. There is also some support for the hypothesized link between bans on presidential reelection and the effective number of candidates, even when controlling for the effect of the presidential electoral system and ethnic heterogeneity. Finally, the marginal effect of the reelection does appear to be conditional on the permissiveness of the electoral system.

3.6 SOCIAL HETEROGENEITY AND AGGREGATION

Even though social heterogeneity is not the focus of this study, it is worth taking a moment to think more carefully about the role it plays in shaping the incentives and capability of candidates to coordinate across districts. Throughout the preceding analyses, I controlled for the social heterogeneity (operationalized as ethnic fractionalization [*ef*]) but now

Testing the Theory

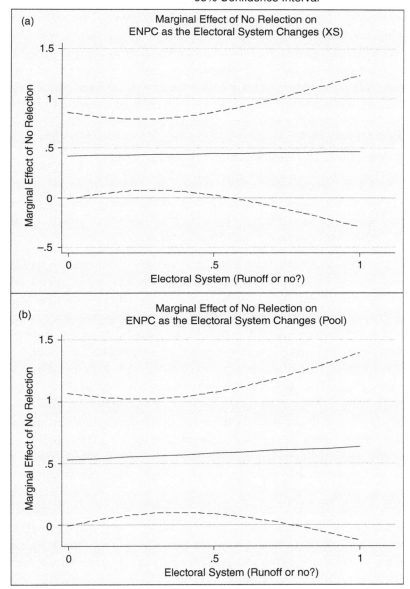

FIGURE 3.4. Marginal Effect of No Reelection as the Electoral System Changes

investigate how social heterogeneity might interact with the size of the aggregation payoff to affect aggregation. In Chapter 2, I argued that by itself social heterogeneity is neither necessary nor sufficient to produce poor aggregation. Instead, the effect of heterogeneity on aggregation is conditional on the size of the aggregation payoff. A large payoff may mitigate the negative effect of social heterogeneity on aggregation, and likewise, a small payoff may undermine aggregation incentives, even in the face of social homogeneity. Aggregation should be poorest when there is both a high degree of social heterogeneity and a small aggregation payoff. This suggests the following hypothesis.

Social Heterogeneity*Payoff Hypothesis: The marginal effect of social heterogeneity on inflation is conditional on the size of the aggregation payoff. Social heterogeneity increases inflation only where the aggregation payoff is not large.

I test this hypothesis with both cross-sectional and pooled analyses once again using OLS with robust standard errors clustered by country for the pooled analyses. I continue to operationalize social heterogeneity as ethnic fractionalization (*ef*) and use the *decentralization* index as a proxy for the size of the aggregation payoff. Table 3.8 displays the results. For comparative purposes, I've reproduced the additive models found in Table 3.4 as columns 1 and 3 in this table. Entered separately, both *decentralization* and *ef* have significant positive effects on inflation. When interacted, however, we see that the effects of ethnic fractionalization are conditional on the degree of decentralization. When power is centralized (*decentralized* = 0), the coefficient on ethnic fractionalization, while still positive, is no longer significant. This suggests that a high degree of centralization can still induce aggregation, even in the face of social heterogeneity. Alternatively, the positive and significant coefficient on *decentralization* implies that even when a polity is ethnically homogenous (*ef* = 0) a small aggregation payoff can still be sufficient to undermine aggregation. The marginal effect of each variable on inflation increases in the other (as the coefficient on the interaction variable signifies). The marginal effects graphs in Figure 3.5 show that, as hypothesized, the marginal effect of ethnic fractionalization is significant only for values of *decentralization* greater than 0.

TABLE 3.8. *Social Heterogeneity and Aggregation (Dependent Variable: Inflation)*

	Cross-Sectional Analyses		Pooled Analyses	
Explanatory Variable	1	2	3	4
decentralization	0.06**	0.06*	0.07***	0.06*
	(0.03)	(0.03)	(0.02)	(0.03)
ef	0.32***	0.32	0.37***	0.33
	(0.10)	(0.21)	(0.12)	(0.24)
log_govage	−0.06***	−0.06***	−0.05***	−0.05***
	(0.02)	(0.02)	(0.01)	(0.01)
log_districts	0.004	0.004	0.003	0.002
	(0.02)	(0.02)	(0.02)	(0.02)
decentralization* ef		0.002		0.04
		(0.09)		(0.13)
Constant	0.21**	0.21**	0.13	0.14*
	(0.09)	(0.08)	(0.10)	(0.08)
R-squared	.44	.44	.45	.44
Observations	34	34	161	161

* $p < .1$, ** $p < .05$, *** $p < .01$; standard errors in parentheses

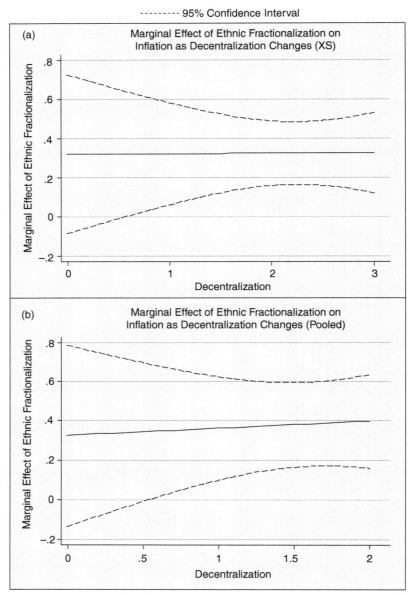

FIGURE 3.5. Marginal Effect of Ethnic Fractionalization on Inflation as Decentralization Increases

Testing the Theory

TABLE 3.9. *Predicted Values Table*

Value of Key Independent Variables (holding all other variables at their means)	Predicted Inflation Score
Table 3.3 Model 6	
horizontal is 0	.09
horizontal is 1	.19
horizontal is 2	.29
subrevgdp is at its means (8.25)	.17
subrevgdp is one standard deviation above the mean	.19
Table 3.4 Model 3 (Interaction Model)	
horizontal is 0 and *subrevgdp* is at its mean (8.25)	.06
horizontal is 1 and *subrevgdp* is at its mean (8.25)	.15
horizontal is 2 and *subrevgdp* is at its mean (8.25)	.24
horizontal is 0 and *subrevgdp* is 0	.01
horizontal is 0 and *subrevgdp* is one standard deviation above the mean	.11
Table 3.4 Model 4	
decentralization is 0	.06
decentralization is 1	.13
decentralization is 2	.20
Table 3.5 Model 5 (Interaction Model)	
decentralization is 0 and *probability* is 0	.08
decentralization is 1 and *probability* is 0	.13
decentralization is 2 and *probability* is 0	.18
decentralization is 1 and *probability* is 1	.19
decentralization is 2 and *probability* is 1	.42
Table 3.6 Model 5 (Interaction Model)	
ENPres is 2 and *proximity* is 1	.15
ENPres is 3 and *proximity* is 1	.19
decentralization is at its mean (1.36) and *proximity* is 1	.14
decentralization is one standard deviation (1.98) above the mean and *proximity* is 1	.22
Table 3.8 Model 4 (Interaction Model)	
decentralization is 0 and *ef* is at its mean (.3)	.06
decentralization is 1 and *ef* is at its mean (.3)	.13
decentralization is 2 and *ef* is at its mean (.3)	.20
decentralization and *ef* are at their means	.15
decentralization it at its mean and *ef* is one standard deviation above the mean (.53)	.24
decentralization is 2 and *ef* is one standard deviation above the mean (.53)	.29
	Predicted ENPres
Table 3.7 Model 7 (Interaction Model)	
no_reelection is 0 and *runoff* is 0	2.4
no_reelection is 1 and *runoff* is 0	2.9
no_reelection is 1 and *runoff* is 1	3.5

3.7 CONCLUSION

The analysis in this chapter provides substantial support for the theory I advanced in Chapter 2. I find that aggregation is indeed the product of two factors: (a) the size of the aggregation payoff and (b) the probability that the largest legislative party will capture that payoff. In addition, the focus solely on the distribution of power and resources between national and subnational actors (vertical centralization) misses a key part of the institutional story. Horizontal centralization, or the distribution of power within the national government, combines with vertical centralization to affect the size of the aggregation payoff and shape aggregation incentives. The results show that even where there is a high degree of vertical centralization, horizontal decentralization is enough to undermine cross-district coordination. The reverse is also true. When power is concentrated within the national government party system, inflation can still occur if subnational actors control substantial shares of power and resources.

In terms of the components of horizontal centralization, bicameralism and reserve domains are both important, but there was little support for the argument that party factionalism shapes aggregation through its effect on horizontal centralization. At this stage, it is difficult to judge whether the poor showing of the factionalism hypothesis should be ascribed to a shortcoming in the theory or whether it is the result of the choice of a poor proxy for party factionalism. In Chapters 4 and 5, I will revisit the factionalism hypothesis as part of the effort to explain aggregation in Thailand.

In addition to the size of the payoff, the evidence suggests that the probability of capturing that prize also plays an important role in shaping aggregation incentives. In parliamentary systems, a low probability that the largest legislative party will also capture the premiership undermines aggregation. As the chance that someone other than the leader of the largest party will become prime minister grows, the marginal effect of a decrease in the aggregation payoff is amplified. Party system inflation is at its highest where a low probability combines with a small aggregation payoff.

In presidential systems, the probability of capturing executive office is a function of the number of presidential candidates and the proximity of presidential and legislative elections. Similar to other studies, I find that proximate elections lower the number of electoral parties but only where the effective number of presidential candidates is low. A unique contribution of this study is to demonstrate that proximity and the number of presidential candidates also have an effect on aggregation. Proximity lowers party system inflation where there are relatively few presidential candidates, and the number of presidential candidates itself has a substantial negative impact on cross-district coordination. The more presidential candidates there are, the more difficult it is for legislative candidates, voters, parties, and donors to identify and coordinate around the frontrunners. The cost is poorer aggregation. There is also evidence that the effective number of presidential candidates tends to be higher where incumbents do not run for reelection.

The results of the large-N analyses then generally support the theory of aggregation incentives laid out in Chapter 2. The models behave in the ways we would expect given the theory and the hypotheses derived from it. In subsequent chapters, I shift my focus from a large-N cross-national comparison to an in-depth examination of aggregation and nationalization in two developing democracies – Thailand and the Philippines. These two countries have both undergone institutional reforms that the theory predicts should alter aggregation incentives. As such, Thailand and the Philippines are useful natural experiments that I can use to further test the theory. In addition, an in-depth analysis of coordination in these two countries also allows me to move beyond the correlations and associations established in this chapter toward identifying some of the causal mechanisms that link the theory's explanatory variables to this study's dependent variables: aggregation, and, ultimately, the number of parties and party system nationalization.

4

Aggregation, Nationalization, and the Number of Parties in Thailand

4.1 INTRODUCTION

In the previous two chapters, I developed and tested a theory of aggregation incentives. In the next three chapters, I use the theory to help explain the nature of party system development in Thailand and the Philippines. As discussed in the introduction, Thailand and the Philippines provide interesting variations on both the dependent and independent variables, which allow me to further investigate the causal mechanisms lying between the explanatory variables of interest (the size of the aggregation payoff and probability of capturing that prize) and the outcome of interest – the degree of aggregation. Even though elections in each country have often produced a comparatively large number of parties at the national level, aggregation has generally been much better in the Philippines vis-à-vis Thailand. In the following three chapters, I first describe the nature of intra-district and cross-district coordination in Thailand and the Philippines, utilizing unique datasets of district-level electoral returns in each country. Then, using the theory described in Chapter 2, I explain why the party system in each country looks as it does. In so doing, I answer the question of why, given similar majoritarian electoral institutions, there has until recently been more parties in Thailand than in the Philippines. Finally, I utilize episodes of institutional reform in each country to conduct comparative statics tests of the theory. The theory helps account for (a) the dramatic fall in the number of national parties after the 1997

Thailand: Aggregation, Nationalization, Number of Parties

constitutional reforms in Thailand and (b) the demise of the two-party system since the return of democracy in the Philippines in 1986.

In this chapter and the next, the focus is on coordination, the number of parties, and nationalization in Thailand. In Chapter 5, I marry the theory of aggregation incentives with the Thai case in an effort to both deepen the theory and illuminate the nature of the Thai party system. In this chapter, I lay the necessary groundwork for that analysis by taking an in-depth look at the Thai party system. This is useful both because Thailand is a country that is unfamiliar to most readers and because the electoral system used during most of Thailand's electoral history (the block vote) is one that is comparatively rare (and hence unstudied).[1]

The remainder of the chapter proceeds as follows. I first briefly review the history of the Thai party system and provide a basic description of its characteristics.[2] I then describe the features of the Thai electoral system in use from 1978 to 1996 and derive a set of hypotheses regarding coordination and the number of parties at the district level.[3] Thailand's unusual electoral system allows for an ideal comparative statics test of electoral theories such as Duverger's law and Cox's $M + 1$ rule. Using district-level election data, I assess the validity of these hypotheses and explore deviations from the mean across time and across regions in Thailand. This focus on intra-district coordination will show that the average number of political parties in each district is about what one would expect given Thailand's electoral environment. I also examine regional differences in the extent of district coordination and provide empirical support for the oft-made claim by Thai scholars that the South of Thailand behaves differently from the rest of the country. Finally, I compare the average district-level party system with the national party system in an effort to document the extent to which aggregation and aggregation failures contribute to an inflated party system. I find that the number of political parties in Thailand cannot be explained by coordination or coordination failures within districts. I then look at cross-district coordination/aggregation and show that poor aggregation is chiefly to blame for the size of the Thai party system and the lack of party nationalization.

---

[1] By contrast, I spend less time detailing the Philippines electoral system since the Philippines uses the well-known and oft-studied single-member district plurality system for its House of Representatives elections.
[2] For a more thorough description, see Hicken (2002).
[3] Chapter 5 considers the post-1996 electoral system.

4.2 DICTATORSHIP, DEMOCRACY, AND THE DEVELOPMENT OF THE THAI PARTY SYSTEM

Thailand is the only country in Southeast Asia that was never colonized.[4] Through skilled leadership, clever diplomacy, and an impressive modernization campaign, Thailand's monarchs (chiefly King Mongkut and his son King Chulalongkorn) were able to maintain their country's independence. Thailand also stands out as the first independent state in the region to formally adopt democratic institutions. In 1932, the absolute monarchy was overthrown and replaced with a constitutional monarchy.

Over the next 40 years, Thailand alternated between short-lived (semi-)democratic governments and longer periods of rule by military and bureaucratic elite (Riggs 1966). The first quarter of century following the end of the absolute monarchy saw Thai politics dominated by leaders of the 1932 coup, especially by two military leaders, Pahonyothin (leader of the 1932 coup group) and Phibun Songkhram, who together served for about 24 years as prime ministers. During this period, coups became a regular feature of political life as different factions within the bureaucratic and military elite jostled for advantage. Although there was a House of Representatives (whose major role was to elect a prime minister) and competitive elections regularly took place, political parties played no real role and were in fact banned for much of the period. In short, elected actors did not represent a significant check on the powers of the ruling elite. Governments during this period rarely found it necessary to resort to brute force to maintain power. Instead, the political dominance of the military-bureaucratic elite was founded more upon the weakness of extra-bureaucratic societal forces (e.g., political parties, interest groups, labor unions) than upon repression and exclusion.

This changed in 1957 when Field Marshal Sarit Thanarat seized power. Sarit, the first army chief who did not belong to the 1932 coup generation, simply dispensed with democratic trappings. Political and civil liberties were put on hold, elections were eliminated, and political parties were banned as Sarit replaced the partially elected parliament

[4] This section draws on several excellent histories/reviews of Thai politics/parties/elections, including Wilson (1962), Riggs (1966), Darling (1971), Neher (1976), Preecha (1981), Likhit (1985), Murashima (1991), Parichart, Chaowana, and Ratha (1997), and Nelson (2001).

Thailand: Aggregation, Nationalization, Number of Parties

with one completely appointed by the prime minister (himself). This state of affairs lasted until 1968 when Sarit's successor, Thanom Kittikachorn, promulgated a new constitution in a bid to shore up his legitimacy. The new constitution included provisions for a fully elected House of Representatives. Thanom lifted the restrictions on political parties and held an election in 1969, with Thanom staying on as prime minister. This brief democratic opening was brought to an end in 1971 when Thanom staged a coup against his own government, abrogating the constitution, banning political parties, and reinstalling military rule.

A student uprising finally brought down Thanom's military government in 1973, and a vibrant, but short-lived, democratic period followed, complete with two democratic elections (1975 and 1976) and the formation of dozens of political parties. This democratic period ended with the 1976 military coup and the imposition of martial law. After two years of military rule a new constitution was adopted; it aimed to put the country on the path back to democratic government while avoiding what some had viewed as the anarchy and excess of the 1973–6 democratic period. The 1978 Constitution established a bicameral legislature with an elected House of Representative and an appointed Senate.[5] After an initial transitional period, the rules and institutions established under the 1978 Constitution were largely constant until the constitutional reforms of 1997.[6]

The development and evolution of the Thai party system roughly parallels Thailand's democratic history. Parties were organized and flourished under liberal governments or constitutions, but were marginalized or banned under more authoritarian regimes. From the end of the absolute monarchy in 1932 to the end of World War II, Thailand had no political parties.[7] A group calling itself the People's Party (*Khana Ratsadorn*) ruled for much of the period, but it was less a political party than a label adopted by the small group of military and bureaucratic elite responsible for the 1932 coup (Neher 1976). In fact, attempts to form

---

[5] The Senate could not formally block legislation, though it could force a delay. Chapter 5 discusses the role of the Senate in more detail.
[6] A 1991 military coup brought an end to the 1978 constitution, but its replacement, adopted in 1992, largely replicated the 1978 rules and institutions.
[7] I focus here on government parties or parties that competed for office electorally. This excludes the Communist Party of Thailand, which was organized in 1942 and waged a war against the Thai state from the mid-1960s through the mid-1980s.

genuine political parties, such as the National Party (*Khana Chart*), were blocked by the country's leadership (Anusorn 1998). It was not until the liberal 1946 Constitution that politicians were able to freely organize political parties (Kramol 1982).

A variety of factors combined to prevent the emergence of strong, institutionalized national parties between 1946 and 1978. The lack of a nationalist, independence struggle in Thailand meant the country was slow to develop mass political movements that served as the basis for political parties elsewhere in the developing world (e.g., the PNI and PKI in Indonesia). In addition, an unstable and unpredictable political environment hindered the development of stronger Thai parties. Between 1932 and 1978, coups occurred about every 3 years. Constitutions have also traditionally been short-lived. Between 1932 and 2005, there have been a total of 16 constitutions – on average a new constitution about every 4.5 years. Some of these constitutions allowed for parties and an elected legislature – many did not. In addition, as discussed previously, prior to 1978 whenever democratic institutions or political parties came in conflict with entrenched military/bureaucratic authorities they were quickly eliminated. Not until the 1980s were parties allowed to legally exist for more than two consecutive elections. Table 4A in the appendix to this chapter summarizes the constitutional and electoral history of Thailand since 1932.

The repeated dissolution of the legislature and the recurring bans on political parties, together with frequent coups made it very difficult for party development to occur. Faced with an uncertain future, party leaders during liberal periods lacked strong incentives to invest in party-building activities like the creation of party branches or the cultivation of a party label. Government instability also encouraged parties and politicians to adopt short-term, particularistic perspectives during the brief periods of time when they were in power.

Thus, for much of Thailand's post-1932 history, political parties (when they weren't banned outright) were bit players in Thai politics. Indeed, many considered them as largely epiphenomenal to politics and policymaking in Thailand.[8] This began to change during the 1970s and

---

[8] Perhaps the clearest expression of this view can be seen in Riggs's classification of Thailand as the epitome of the bureaucratic polity (1966). Drawing on his knowledge of the Thai case, Riggs described the bureaucratic polity as a polity with a concentration of power in the hands of a narrow bureaucratic and military elite, and where

Thailand: Aggregation, Nationalization, Number of Parties

1980s. The democratic, party-led governments of the mid-1970s together with the return of regular democratic elections in the 1980s worked to gradually increase the importance of elected office, along with the primary vehicle for obtaining that office, political parties. One indication of this change was the efforts of urban business elite to organize political factions and gain control of political parties in the 1970s (Anek 1989; Sidel 1996; Pasuk and Baker 1997). In the 1980s, the provincial business elite also entered politics in a major way by organizing their own political factions and then moving to organize new parties or take over existing ones (Ockey 1991, 2000; Robertson 1996; McVey 2000). The assassinations of politicians and political candidates that emerged in the 1980s are ironically another reflection of the growing value of political office. For the first time in Thai history, parliamentary membership was worth killing for (Anderson 1990).

Despite the growing value of political office, and by extension, the importance of parties as a means of capturing that office, the basic characteristics of the party system remained virtually unchanged.[9] The Thai party system throughout the 1980s and 1990s exhibited a lack of party cohesion. Virtually every Thai party was composed of multiple factions (*phak phuak*), each of which vied for preeminence within the party.[10] Parties and party factions were organized around powerful leaders who worked to attract the strongest candidates or factions to their group. Unlike democracies like Japan where factions are institutionalized within a given party, factions in Thailand frequently switched parties. Party switching by both factions and by individual candidates was rampant. As a result, party label was of relatively little value to either voters or candidates.

---

representative organizations such as parliaments, parties, and interest groups have a minimal role. With a few notable exceptions (e.g., Anderson 1977) Riggs's view of Thai politics was the dominant view until the mid-1980s and 1990s when a host of scholars began to question whether the bureaucratic polity label still applied to Thailand (Prizzia 1985; Pisan and Guyot 1986; Mackie 1988; Anek 1989, 1992; Pasuk and Baker 1995).

[9] What did change was the relevance of the party system for policymaking. As parliament became a more powerful institution and politicians wrested more control over policymaking, the party system became an important determinant of policymaking patterns (Hicken 2001, 2002).

[10] See Chambers's recent dissertation on the role of political factions in Thai politics (2003).

Thai political parties and politicians also tended to have subnational, rather than national constituencies. With the partial exception of the Democrat Party, no Thai party could be considered a national party. Very few parties had nationwide support, and candidates and parties tended to focus on local, narrow constituencies. In sum, parties and their members generally lacked a national focus.

The Thai party system was also "under-institutionalized." According to Mainwaring and Scully (1995), institutionalized party systems (a) manifest regular patterns of party competition, (b) contain parties with stable roots in society, and (c) have party organizations that matter.[11] None of these features held for the Thai party system. Parties did not exhibit regular patterns of competition. In fact, party fortunes fluctuated greatly from election to election. Between 1983 and 1996 the electoral fortunes of Thailand's political parties taken together varied dramatically from election to election as measured by Pedersen's electoral volatility index (Pedersen 1983).[12] Thailand's electoral volatility score was a 34.[13] Viewed in comparative terms this number is quite high (Table 4.1).

Parties also lacked stable roots in society. Most Thai parties were short-lived.[14] Of the 43 parties that competed in at least one election between 1979 and 1996, only 10 survived to compete in the 2001 elections alongside more than 20 new parties. On average, these 43 parties competed in fewer than three elections before disbanding. Almost half (20 parties) competed in only one election. The average age of parties with at least 10% of the House vote in the 1996 election was 20 years. Again, some comparative figures for other countries helps put this number in context (Table 4.2).

Finally, Thai parties have not developed strong party organizations.[15] Although parties were legally required to organize party branches, few

---

[11] They also list a fourth criterion: Major political actors accord legitimacy to the electoral process and to parties.
[12] Pedersen's electoral volatility index measures the net change in the vote (or seat) shares of all parties from election to election. The index is the sum of the net change in the percentage of votes (seats) gained or lost by each party from one election to the next, divided by two: $(\sum |v_{it} - v_{it+1}|)/2$.
[13] On average the results of the last election predict the results of the subsequent election with an accuracy rate of only 66%.
[14] The Democrat Party is an exception.
[15] See King (1996) for a detailed examination of the organization and orientation of two Thai parties: Palang Dharma Party and New Aspiration Party.

TABLE 4.1. *Lower Chamber Electoral Volatility*

Country	Time Span	No. of Elections	Mean Volatility
United States	1944–94	25	4.0
United Kingdom	1974–97	6	8.3
Uruguay	1974–94	3	10.4
Italy	1946–96	13	12.0
France	1945–93	14	18.3
Argentina	1973–95	7	18.8
Venezuela	1973–96	6	22.5
Costa Rica	1974–98	7	25.0
Poland	1991–74	3	28.4
Brazil	1982–94	4	33.0
Thailand	1983–96	7	34.0
Russia	1993–99	3	60.0

Sources: Author's calculations; Mainwaring 1999; Parliamentary Elections around the World (http://www.universal.nl/users/dreksen/election); Elections around the World (http://www.agora.stm.it/elections/); Centre for the Study of Public Policy (http://www.cspp.strath.ac.uk//intro.html); Election Resources on the Internet presented by Manuel Álvarez-Rivera (http://electionresources.org/).

branches were ever opened (Kanok 1993; Chaowana 1997; Anusorn 1998).[16] In addition, those party branches that did exist were often less party offices than campaign headquarters or constituency offices for members of parliament (King 1996; Party Interviews 2000).

In short, Thai parties in the 1980s and 1990s were less cohesive unitary actors with well-defined national policy platforms than ephemeral electoral alliances of locally oriented politicians. This is despite the fact that (a) demand for democratic institutions by the Thai public appears to have broadened and deepened during the period,[17] and (b) the balance of power between political parties/elected politicians and conservative forces (the military and bureaucracy) was clearly shifting in favor of the parties and politicians (the 1991 coup

---

[16] The Democrat Party did organize a large number of branches, but according to at least one study they were largely ineffective at generating grassroots support for the party (Chaiwat 1992).

[17] The large-scale protests in favor of democratic government that occurred both in 1973 and again in 1992 are evidence of the domestic demand for democratic government, at least among some segments of society. More evidence of a growing acceptance of democratic institutions can found in LoGerfo (1996). His survey of urban and rural Thais found that both groups held "democratic attitudes" regarding parliament.

TABLE 4.2. *Years Since Founding of Parties with 10% of the Lower Chamber Vote, 1996*

Country, Election Year	Average Age
United States, 1996	154
Uruguay, 1994	115
Argentina, 1995	54
Costa Rica, 1994	47
France, 1993	43
Chile, 1993	40
Italy, 1996	39
Venezuela, 1993	29
Thailand, 1996	20
Brazil, 1994	13

Sources: Mainwaring 1999; author's calculations.

notwithstanding). Part of the explanation lies in the nature of Thailand's electoral system. Thailand's block vote system (described in more detail later) pitted candidates from the same party against each other in the same district and gave voters multiple votes with a right to split those votes among candidates from different parties.[18] The incentives of this system were such that candidates placed a premium on cultivating a personal vote thereby undermining party cohesion and the value of the party label (Hicken 2002, 2007b).

One of the strongest indications of the dominance of personal reputation over party label is the large discrepancy in the vote shares of copartisans. If candidates used party strategies, and voters voted on the basis of party label, then the difference between the totals of copartisans in the same district (the vote differential) should be small. Large vote differentials, on the other hand, signal the importance of the

---

[18] Thailand's system did not generate the degree of intra-party competition that occurs in systems where there are fewer seats than copartisan candidates in a given district, such as in single non-transferable vote systems, but it did pit candidates from the same party against one another. As a result, neither candidates nor voters could rely on party label to help differentiate between candidates from the same party. Instead, most candidates tended to rely on personal vote-getting strategies and personal support networks rather than campaigning on the reputation or policy position of the party. The fact that voters had multiple votes – an invitation to split their vote – and that votes were not pooled among copartisans further strengthened the incentive to pursue a personal strategy.

Thailand: Aggregation, Nationalization, Number of Parties

TABLE 4.3. *Vote Differentials*

	Average Ratio between 1 and 2	Average Ratio between 1 and 3	Average Ratio between 2 and 3
Democrat Party	1992: 4.1:1	1992: 6.1:1	1992: 1.8:1
	1995: 7.9:1	1995: 8.6:1	1995: 1.5:1
	1996: 6.0:1	1996: 8.9:1	1996: 2.5:1
Chart Thai	1992: 14.2:1	1992: 25.1:1	1992: 4.8:1
Chart Thai	1995: 15.6:1	1995: 18.9:1	1995: 4.7:1
NAP	1996: 8.6:1	1996: 11.1:1	1996: 4.0:1

Sources: Ministry of Interior, election reports (1986, 1988, 1992a, 1992b, 1995, 1997).

personal vote and a personal strategy.[19] In addition, parties that have a stronger party label should have smaller vote differentials than parties with weak party labels. Table 4.3 presents the average vote differential for two parties, the Democrat Party and the largest party other than the Democrats in the last three elections before the 1997 constitutional reforms. These parties are the Chart Thai Party in September 1992 and 1995 and the New Aspiration Party (NAP) in 1996. In the 1995 and September 1992 elections the Democrats and Chart Thai were the two largest parties in terms of seat share, and in the 1996 election the Democrats and NAP were the largest. The Democrat Party was viewed as having strongest label of any Thai party during this period while both Chart Thai and the NAP were the epitomes of a factionalized, candidate-centered party (King 1996; Murray 1996; King and LoGerfo 1996). One would thus expect the vote differential to be smaller between Democrat co-partisans than between co-partisans from Chart Thai or NAP. Table 4.3 presents the differentials between the first- and second-, first- and third-, and second- and third-place copartisans. A ratio of 4.1:1 means that the first candidate received 4.1 times as many votes as the second candidate.

---

[19] Another indicator of personal strategy is the extent to which copartisans rely on a shared network of vote canvassers (*hua khanaen*). In-depth research on the subject is still needed, but interviews with party officials and anecdotal evidence suggests that sharing was not the norm. Each copartisan invested the resources to develop a network designed to get the vote out for just that candidate. The large vote differentials among copartisans support this view – such differentials would likely be much smaller if candidates relied on the same *hua khanaen* network.

As expected, the vote differentials of copartisans are large, with first place candidates getting as much as 25 times more votes than their copartisans. The results displayed in Table 4.3 also support the hypothesis that Democrat Party copartisans, on average, are separated by smaller margins than candidates from either Chart Thai or the NAP. Still, even though the differentials for Democrat copartisans are smaller, they are still quite large – at best the top Democrat in a district received more than four times the number of votes as his or her copartisan.[20]

Another indirect measure of the extent to which candidates relied on and voters responded to personal rather than party strategies is the prevalence of split district returns. How often did voters in multiseat districts elect candidates from more than one party? Where candidates and voters place great value on party label, split returns should be less frequent than where party labels are weak and personal strategies are the norm. Indeed, given Thailand's electoral system, the only way a multiseat district can return candidates from more than one party is if voters disregard party labels and either split their votes between candidates from different parties or fail to cast their full allotments of votes.

As can be seen in Table 4.4 split returns occurred in over 50% of the districts nationwide in each of the six pre-reform elections. This supports the claim of weak party labels and the importance of personal strategies. No clear trend, either increasing or decreasing, is evident over time. Split returns did drop nationally in the 1996 election, but the constitutional changes in 1997 make it impossible to tell whether this represented a trend or an anomaly.[21] Comparing across regions, we see

[20] There is also evidence of parties running a single strong candidate in a district along with two also-rans added just to meet the electoral requirement. (Parties were required to field a full slate of candidates for any district they wished to contest and the total number of candidates run by any political party had to be equal to at least 1/4 to 1/2 (depending on the year) of the total membership of the House of Representatives.) The vote totals between the second- and third-place copartisans are significantly closer than between the first-place copartisan and either 2 or 3. Indeed, parties were very open about the fact that they hired and ran "ghost candidates" in order to fill electoral requirements. Muon Chon party leader Chalerm Yubamrung admitted that in the 1986 election most of his party's candidates were not "real" but were used to make up the required number of candidates. The party was able to run a majority of "real" candidates in 1988 but still ran 65 "real" candidates to 35 "unreal" (BP 1988).

[21] It is possible to explain the big drops in split ticket voting for Bangkok without arguing that party labels are becoming more important. Briefly, the rise in split ticket

Thailand: Aggregation, Nationalization, Number of Parties

TABLE 4.4. *Percentage of District Returns Split between Parties*

	1986	1988	1992a	1992b	1995	1996
Overall	57	77	62	65	65	52
Bangkok	25	69	16	33	69	39
Central Region	70	71	53	53	62	53
Northeastern Region	86	91	82	87	79	54
Northern Region	69	74	68	90	84	77
Southern Region	36	81	47	5	9	17

Sources: Ministry of Interior, election reports (1986, 1988, 1992a, 1992b, 1995, 1997).

that even with the 1996 drop in split returns, six of the nine regions still had split returns in over 50% of their districts. The most striking result of the regional comparison is the relatively low incidence of split returns in the South, the traditional stronghold of the Democrat Party. The exception is the 1988 election when a faction within the Democrat Party broke away and formed a new party. Section 4.3 takes a closer look at candidate and voter behavior by region.[22]

To summarize, after nearly two decades of democratic elections and party competition, Thai political parties remained weak, factionalized, and under-institutionalized. In fact, as discussion turned to the topic of constitutional reform in the mid-1990s a major focus of reformers was the party system. Specifically, reformers criticized the lack of cohesion and discipline within parties (evidenced by factionalism and frequent party switching), the parochial interests of parties and their members (as opposed to a national focus), and the large number of parties winning seats in parliament. I turn my attention in the remainder of this chapter to the last of these issues – the large number of parties in Thailand.

voting in Bangkok in 1995 is an anomaly driven by the entrance of a new political party, Palang Dharma, which was able to win a seat in several of Bangkok's districts that were formally held by the Democrat Party. In 1996, the Democrats recaptured many of these seats so the percentage drops. For an excellent analysis of the Palang Dharma Party, see King (1996).

[22] A study of the 1986 election that used both split return and candidate differential data also found that voters nationwide preferred to elect individuals rather than parties. According to the study, only 27% of the votes cast could be considered party votes. The same study found that party voting was more common in Bangkok (Manut 1987).

4.3 INTRA-DISTRICT COORDINATION AND THE NUMBER OF PARTIES

Since parties were formally legalized in 1955, the norm in Thailand has been multiple parties in parliament and short-lived multiparty coalition governments.[23] In fact, in the 50 years since 1955, only twice has a single party been able to capture a majority of the seats in the legislature.[24] The effective number of parties at the national level has been in double digits during some elections. On average each election during the last three decades (1975–96) produced 7.7 parties (6.2 if measured by seat shares) (see Table 4.5).[25] This large number of parties translated into large, multiparty coalition governments with between five and six parties in government on average (Table 4.5).

The large number of parties in Thailand was a source of concern for policy makers and observers who felt that the large number of parties has contributed to Thailand's governance problems (see, for example, Kanok 1993; Pasuk and Baker 1998; Vatikiotis 1998; MacIntyre 1999; Haggard 2000). They were certainly not alone in this concern. Indeed, as discussed in Chapter 1, the problems associated with a hyper-inflated party system represent a common theme in the comparative politics literature.

The purpose of the remainder of this chapter is to begin to uncover the sources of Thailand's multiparty system. Why were there so many parties in Thailand? How much of the size of the party system (measured by the number of parties) was a function of Thailand's unusual

---

[23] One of my favorite quotes describing this state of affairs comes from a 1976 monograph by a Thai academic. "Unstable stability of stable instability is the way of life for Thai government, exhibited clearly in the parliamentary democracy system" (Somporn 1976).

[24] This occurred in the February 1957 election where the party of the military strongman Phibun Songkhram (the *Seri Manangkasila* Party) won 53.8% of the seats and in the 2005 election when the Thai Rak Thai (TRT) Party won nearly 75% of the seats. The Thai Rak Thai nearly duplicated this feat for a third time in 2001 but fell just short of a majority with 49.6% of the seats. After the election, two parties chose to merge with the TRT giving the TRT a majority.

[25] The effective number of parties is defined as 1 divided by the sum of the weighted values for each party. The weighted values are calculated by squaring each party's vote (or seat) share (v_j): ENP $= 1/(\sum v_j^2)$ (Laakso and Taagepera 1979). Using votes shares yields the effective number of electoral parties while the seat share gives the effective number of legislative parties. For the remainder of this chapter I use vote shares.

TABLE 4.5. *Effective Number of Parties in Thai Elections: 1976–1996*

Election Year	Effective Number of Parties (by vote shares)	Effective Number of Parties (by seat shares)	Number of Parties in Governing Coalition
1975	10.3	7.6	7
1976	7.0	4.1	4
1979[a]	11.6	8.2	7
1983[a]	5.9	5.6	4
1986	8.0	6.1	4
1988	9.8	7.7	6
1992a	6.7	6.0	5
1992b	6.6	6.1	5
1995	6.8	6.4	7
1996	4.6	4.3	6
Average	7.7	6.2	5.5

[a] The first election under the 1978 constitutions was held in 1979 but political parties were not formally legalized until the 1981 Political Party Act. However, they did exist informally and were allowed to organize and campaign. In the 1979 and 1983 elections, candidates were allowed to run as independents. In 1979, 619 independents ran and captured 31.5% of the vote and 20.9% of the seats. Their numbers were much smaller in 1983 with 417 independents capturing 7.5% of the votes and 7.4% of the seats. The question then arises how to count independents. The alternatives are to count all independents together as a single "independent" party or to count each independent separately as a party of one. The former may understate the number of parties, while the latter may overstate. Since I believe the reality of the Thai situation was closer to many parties of one rather than a single independent party I have reported ENP where each independent is counted separately. In calculating ENP by vote share, there was an additional challenge – the lack of readily accessible data on individual independent candidate vote shares. Where those data were lacking I calculated the average vote share for independent candidates (total independent vote share/total number of independent candidates) recognizing that this will inflate ENP. If, rather than counting each independent separately, I group all independents together in one "party" ENP by vote share would be 5.4 in 1979, 5.7 in 1983 for an average of 7.1 over the period. ENP by seat share would be 6.1 in 1979, 5.4 in 1983 for an average of 6.0.
Sources: Ministry of Interior, election reports (1986, 1988, 1992a, 1992b, 1995, 1997); Manut (1986).

block vote electoral system and the coordination of voters, candidates, and parties within districts? To answer these questions I analyze how coordination, as well as failures to coordinate, contributed to the number of political parties in Thailand.

As discussed in Chapters 1 and 2, the inflation of the party system can arise as the product of either of two separate types of coordination: intra-district or cross-district coordination (aggregation). Intra-district, or district-level coordination produces a large party system where either (a) permissive electoral rules do not generate incentives for coordination around a small number of parties or candidates within a given district or (b) impediments exist that prevent coordination on a small number of competitors, even where there are apparent electoral incentives for coordination (Duverger 1954; Taagepera and Shugart 1989; Cox 1997). I demonstrate that intra-constituency coordination has not been the primary source of multiple parties – the average number of parties in each constituency is much lower than the number of parties nationally, and about what one would expect given Thailand's electoral system. This is an important contribution. Because of the unusual nature of the block vote system, the application of tools such as Duverger's law (Duverger 1954) or Cox's $M + 1$ rule (Cox 1997) to the Thai case is not immediately obvious. Nevertheless, I show that it is possible to predict the number of parties at the district level from the electoral system.

Cross-district coordination has been much more problematic in Thailand. Cross-district coordination or aggregation failures occur when different parties run in various districts across the country. I argue that even though intra-district coordination in Thailand is fairly good, aggregation has been very poor resulting in a large number of parties and poor nationalization. I will begin with a discussion of the different features of the Thai electoral system and their impact on the effective number of parties at the district level.

4.3.1 The District-Level Party System in Thailand (1978–1996)

One of the major determinants of the number of parties locally is the type of electoral system within which parties, candidates, and voters must work.[26] The electoral system Thailand used for most of its history – the block vote – is unusual and warrants some description.[27]

---

[26] The second major determinant is whether or not societal cleavages are present (e.g., ethnic, religious, or linguistic cleavages). With the possible exception of an urban-rural cleavage, Thailand largely lacks the deep social cleavages found in many of its neighbors (e.g., Malaysia, Indonesia, Burma). At the district level, the urban-rural cleavage has not played a role in determining the number of parties as districts tend to be either urban or rural. The extent to which the urban-rural cleavage has affected aggregation is discussed in Chapter 5.

[27] Other uses of the block vote include elections in Mauritius and nineteenth-century Great Britain and elections for the Philippines Senate.

Thailand: Aggregation, Nationalization, Number of Parties

TABLE 4.6. *Basic Electoral System Data*

	1983	1986	1988	1992a	1992b	1995	1996
Total Districts	134	138	142	142	142	155	156
Total Seats	324	347	357	360	360	391	393
Three-Seat Districts	65	80	82	85	85	88	88
Two-Seat Districts	60	49	51	48	48	60	61
One-Seat Districts	9	9	9	9	9	7	7

Sources: Ministry of Interior, election reports (1986, 1988, 1992a, 1992b, 1995, 1997), Manut (1986), Law (1987).

Under the 1978 and 1992 constitutions, Thailand was broken down into between 142 and 156 electoral districts (depending on the election year), which together were responsible for filling between 360 and 393 seats in the House of Representatives.[28] Electoral districts were broken down into one-, two-, and three-seat districts. Most Thai districts had a district magnitude of three ($M = 3$) or two ($M = 2$), while a few were single seat districts ($M = 1$).[29] Seats were allocated by province (*changwat*), with each province receiving the number of seats commensurate with its population (one seat for every 150,000 people). See Table 4.6 for a summary of these data for the last six elections prior to the new 1997 Constitution. If a province had a large enough population for more than three seats, the province was divided into more than one district, and the seats were distributed so as to avoid single-seat districts. For example, if the population of a province warranted four seats, the province would be divided into two districts, each with two seats. Seven seats would be divided into three districts of three, two, and two seats. Single-seat districts occurred only in provinces with a population less than 225,000.[30]

Under the block vote, voters were allowed to vote for as many candidates as there were seats in a district, and seats were awarded to the top vote-getters on the basis of the plurality rule. Voters could not group their votes on one candidate (cumulation was forbidden) but

---

[28] Thailand has a bicameral legislature consisting of an elected House and (until the 1997 constitutional reforms) an appointed Senate.
[29] In Thailand, electoral units are the termed "constituencies" rather than "districts."
[30] Each additional 75,000 people above 150,000 was counted as an additional 150,000. A province with 200,000 people would receive one seat while a 225,000-person province would receive two seats.

panachage was allowed (i.e., voters could split their votes between candidates from different parties). Finally, voters were not required to cast all of their votes – they could partially abstain (plumping).[31] Parties were required to field a full team of candidates for any district they wished to contest (e.g., three candidates in a three-seat district).

Given Thailand's electoral system, how many parties would we expect? The answer is not immediately obvious. The block vote electoral system has not been studied much by students of electoral systems. However, it is possible to make some predictions. The expectations for the effective number of parties in each Thai constituency should vary according to the district magnitude and according to one's expectations about the importance of Thai party labels.

To begin with, the $M + 1$ rule (Cox 1997), a generalization of Duverger's law, is a useful predictor of the effect of an electoral system on the number of parties at the district level.[32] The $M + 1$ rule states that no more than $M + 1$ candidates/parties are viable in any single seat districts ($M = 1$) and no more than $M + 1$ parties are viable in multiseat districts ($M > 1$). In other words, in single-seat districts, the expected number of parties would be two; in two-seat districts, three parties, etc.

The expectations of the $M + 1$ rule rest on an assumption of strategic coordination by candidates, parties, and voters. Candidates and parties decide whether to enter a race partly on the basis of their chance of winning a seat or seats (*strategic entry*) (Cox 1997). Using the example of a single-seat district, third-place candidates or parties have an incentive to withdraw from the race or not to enter at all, or in the case of political parties, to join with one of the two front-running parties. If coordination among candidates or parties over strategic entry fails, then *strategic voting* can reduce the number of viable contenders in a given constituency. Voters, realizing that their votes are wasted if they cast them for third-place contenders, have an incentive to transfer their votes to their most preferred of the two strongest contenders. In a single-seat constituency, voters who under normal circumstances would prefer the third-place contenders will instead vote for their most preferred of the top two contenders so as not to waste their votes.

---

[31] See Cox (1997, 42–3) for a general discussion of *cumulation, panachage,* and *plumping.*

[32] Duverger's law states that electoral systems with single-member districts and plurality voting rules will produce a two-party system (Duverger 1954).

Thailand: Aggregation, Nationalization, Number of Parties

Strategic Entry Assumptions:	Strategic Voting Assumptions:
1. The identity of the frontrunners must be common knowledge.	1. Voters must be short term instrumentally rational.
2. The primary goal of candidates or parties must be victory in the current election	2. Voters must have access to "reasonably accurate and publicly available information" on candidate or party standings.
	3. There must be myopic (price-taking) adjustment on the part of voters.

Source: Cox, Gary. 1997. *Making Votes Count*. Cambridge: Cambridge University Press.

FIGURE 4.1. $M + 1$ Rule Assumptions

However, certain assumptions must be met in order for the $M + 1$ rule to completely hold (Cox 1997).[33] These are listed in Figure 4.1.

For the most part, these assumptions are met in Thai elections with two caveats. First, it is important to note that vote buying is common in Thai elections (Hicken 2007b). To the extent that vote buying and selling dictates how voters cast their votes, strategic voting assumptions one and three may not hold. If voters base their vote on which candidates give them the most money rather than which candidates have the best chance at winning seats, then they are not "short term instrumentally rational" in the manner described in Figure 4.1. This is not to say such voters are not rational; rather, they have different goals than those of the instrumentally rational voter. Likewise, vote-selling voters may not adjust their votes even after receiving information that their vote buyer is a trailing candidate.

Vote buying, in the form of votes for cash or goods, certainly occurs in Thailand (Sombat 1993; Arghiros 1995; Anek 1996; Surin and McCargo 1997; Nelson 1998; Callahan 2000; Hicken 2007b) but there is some question about how this affects election results. If one candidate engages in vote buying within a district, other candidates will have an incentive to do the same. Some scholars report that the result is that Thai voters often accept money from many candidates and parties and then vote for their preferred candidate(s) anyway (Sombat 1999). If this is the case, then vote buying might not have a large effect on strategic voting. In addition, campaign managers and vote canvassers/vote buyers buy votes in a strategic manner.

---

[33] These are the necessary assumptions to generate a *tendency* to bipartism in a single-member district. For the assumptions necessary to produce *pure* bipartism, see Cox (1997, 76–9).

During the final days prior to voting, many campaign managers opted to abandon weaker members of their team who seemed to have little prospect of being elected. Financial resources could then be directed towards buying votes on behalf of the one or two candidates with the best electoral prospects. (Callahan 2000, 35)

A second caveat is that the informational assumptions behind strategic voting and strategic entry may sometimes be problematic. First, accurate polling data can be hard to come by in Thailand, especially in rural districts. Thus some candidates and voters may lack the information necessary to distinguish the frontrunners from the rest of the candidates. Second, party labels often help communicate information on the viable candidates and parties in any given district and thus help candidates and voters coordinate their behavior. However, when party labels mean little to voters or candidates, and party support in a given district varies widely from election to election, then it will be more difficult for voters to obtain "reasonable and accurate" information on party and candidate standings. Even if party labels are weak, though, there are other cues to which voters and candidates can look to assess candidate/party viability. These would include a candidate's personal reputation and electoral history; the family, group, or faction to which a candidate belongs; or the amount of money the candidate spends campaigning (or buying votes) (Napisa 2005).

In summary, for the most part, the assumptions that underlie the $M+1$ rule are met in the context of Thai elections, although with the possible exceptions noted previously. Given this, for single-seat districts, a straightforward application of Duverger's law and the Cox's $M+1$ rule is possible (Duverger 1954; Cox 1999). In Thailand's single-seat districts, one would expect the average effective number of parties to be around two – slightly more where the assumptions behind the $M+1$ rule are not met.

What about Thailand's two- and three-seat districts? There the application of the $M+1$ rule is less obvious. The $M+1$ rule has not often been applied to cases where voters have multiple votes, as Thai voters do in two- and three-seat districts. When voters have multiple votes, does the $M+1$ rule still apply? Will the effective number of parties still vary by district magnitude? The answer depends on what we assume about the value of party labels to Thai voters. If voters truly cast their votes according to party labels, the $M+1$ rule will not apply – the effective

Thailand: Aggregation, Nationalization, Number of Parties

number of parties should be around two across all districts, regardless of district magnitude.

To see why, consider a single-seat district ($M = 1$) where the NAP candidate wins the most votes and so wins the seat. Now add two seats to that district and give the voters in that district two additional votes. If voters truly cast their votes according to party label, then they will cast their additional votes for the two additional NAP candidates, and the NAP will win all three seats. If on the other hand party labels are *not* the primary cue for voters when casting their votes, then they may well cast their additional votes for candidates from other parties. If this is the case then the $M + 1$ rule should apply, with larger seat districts having more parties.

How important were party labels in Thailand? As the preceding section demonstrated, labels were generally weak – party label meant little to either candidates or voters. This suggests that, given Thailand's pre-1997 block vote electoral system, we should expect the average effective number of parties in each district (ENP_{avg}) to be near $M + 1$ for all districts. However, if it is the case that party labels are in fact meaningful to voters, then the number of parties should be near two in all districts, regardless of district magnitude. These expectations are summarized in Figure 4.2.

The Southern Exception

Before presenting the data, one additional observation is useful. Recall that in addition to polling data, voters might rely on party label or candidate/party electoral history as signals of which parties and candidates are viable in a given district. In most Thai districts, there is no party with a significant electoral history, nor do party labels carry with them a habitual allegiance on the part of voters or candidates. The exception to this general statement can be found in Thailand's Southern region. The South has long been the stronghold of the Democrat Party – Thailand's oldest party. Of all the parties, the Democrats have traditionally had the strongest party label.[34] This party label, combined with the history of Democrat strength in the South, means that voters, parties, and candidates should have an easier time identifying viable candidates in Southern

---

[34] This is relative to other Thai party labels. In fact, the Democrat Party label is not as strong as one might expect given the party's long history due in part to numerous intra-party factional conflicts throughout much of the party's history (Somporn 1976; Surin 1992).

>
> $M = 1$
> ENP_{avg} near 2
>
> $M = 2$
> ENP_{avg} near 3
>
> $M = 3$
> ENP_{avg} near 4
>
> If party labels are valuable, ENP_{avg} should be near 2 across all district magnitudes.

FIGURE 4.2. Expectations for ENP_{avg}

districts compared to other regions of the country. As a result, one would expect the effective number of parties in the South to consistently be among the lowest in Thailand. One would also expect there to be very little difference between one-, two-, and three-seat constituencies in terms of the effective number of parties – all should be near two, with one caveat. During the mid- to late 1980s, the Democrat Party was riddled with factional problems, culminating in a split in the party and the formation of a breakaway party in 1988, the Prachachon Party. Thus one would expect ENP_{avg} in the South to be near or less than two and lower than ENP_{avg} in other regions of the country with the exception of the 1986 and especially the 1988 elections.

4.3.2 Testing the Expectations

In order to test these expectations, I collected district-level electoral data for five general elections: 1986, 1988, September 1992, 1995, and 1996. Elections prior to 1986 were excluded from the dataset because of some differences in the electoral laws prior to 1986.[35] The March 1992 elections were also excluded due to incomplete district level electoral data. For each district I calculated the effective number of parties in that district. In multiseat districts, vote totals for candidates of the same party were

---

[35] One of the biggest differences was that prior to the 1986 election candidates were not required to belong to a political party.

Thailand: Aggregation, Nationalization, Number of Parties

TABLE 4.7. *Regression Results: Effect of District Magnitude on the Effective Number of Parties at the District Level*

Dependent Variable: Effective Number of Parties at the District Level (ENP$_{avg}$)	1986–1996	1986–2005
District Magnitude (M)	.26**	.50***
	(.03)	(.03)
Constant	2.56	1.91
	(.21)	(.06)
R-squared	.02	.15
Number of Observations	725	1525

**Significant at the .001 level; ***Significant at the .000 level; Standard errors in parentheses

added together and used to calculate a party vote share.[36] The data from the five elections were then combined in a single dataset. Standard OLS regressions were run to determine whether there was a relationship between district magnitude and the effective number of parties. The statistical analysis reveals a significant positive relationship between district magnitude and the effective number of parties at the district level (Table 4.7).

As expected, the ENP$_{avg}$ varies by district magnitude. Higher district magnitudes are associated with more parties. This is additional evidence that party label is not the primary guide for Thai voters when they cast their votes. (The results are even stronger when one includes constituency results from the 2001 and 2005 elections, which used only single-seat districts.) Figure 4.3 graphs the effective number of parties averaged across one-, two-, and three-seat districts over the period. Again, the difference between one-, two-, and three-seat districts is evident. The effective number of parties is also near where we would expect given the $M + 1$ rule. In three-seat districts ENP is 4 or less in every election. In two- and single-seat districts, ENP is slightly higher than the $M + 1$ limit in the first couple of elections, and then falls to within the $M + 1$ range in later elections.[37]

---

[36] In two cases the election results failed to list a vote total for a candidate. In both cases I calculated an estimated vote total by splitting the difference in the vote totals for the next highest and next lowest candidates. In both 1986 and September 1992 four districts had to be thrown out because of missing data.

[37] Note that it is harder to draw inferences about single-seat districts due to the relatively small number of single-seat districts in each election.

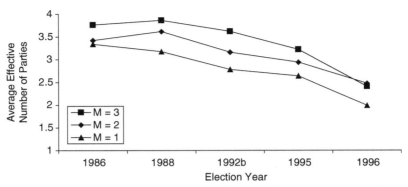

FIGURE 4.3. Average Effective Number of Parties by District Magnitude

Note in Figure 4.3 that ENP_{avg} falls from 1988 onward for all three district magnitudes. What's behind this steady fall in the number of parties? One might argue that the decline in the number of parties over time is evidence that party labels have become more important signals to voters and candidates as parties have built up an electoral history at the district level. As a result, it has become easier over time for voters, candidates, and parties to distinguish frontrunners from the also-rans. Indeed, this may be the case in certain constituencies, especially in the South as is discussed in more detail later. However, the fortunes of most political parties still vary greatly from election to election. This suggests that the decline in the number of parties over the period is a result of other factors quite apart from an increase in the value of party labels. For example, the electoral history of certain candidates, incumbents, or factions may be built up over time even if they switch parties from election to election (Napisa 2005). Thus, although a given candidate's party label may communicate little information about the candidate's chances, the candidate's (or his/her faction's) previous showing in the district might be all the information voters, parties, and other actors need to coordinate as the $M + 1$ rule predicts. Another possible explanation for the decline in ENP_{avg} is new electoral system shock. When a new electoral system is adopted, it may take candidates and voters time to understand the incentives of the new system and adjust their behavior accordingly. Thus one would expect ENP_{avg} to decline over time.[38]

---

[38] Although the block vote electoral system had been used in Thai elections before 1979, 1979 marks the beginning of regular elections. Also, 1986 marked the first

Thailand: Aggregation, Nationalization, Number of Parties

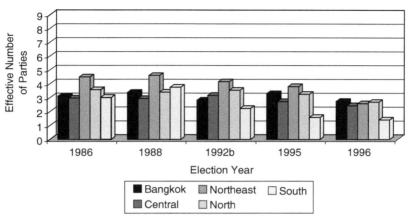

FIGURE 4.4. Average Effective Number of Parties per District by Region

To summarize, the evidence is fairly consistent with the $M + 1$ rule. ENP_{avg} varies by district magnitude and is at or near the $M + 1$ level. In other words, the intra-district dynamics seem to be working as expected.

Regional Variation

Figure 4.4 displays the average effective number of parties by region. As expected, in the last three elections Southern districts had, on average, a much lower effective number of parties than districts elsewhere in Thailand – 2.4 over the period compared with 3.3 for the rest of the country. For most elections the Southern ENP_{avg} reflected the strength of the Democrat label in the region – around two or less. However, one can also see the factional conflict in the Democrat party reflected in the 1986 and 1988 elections. While the Southern ENP_{avg} for 1986 is still one of the lowest in the country, it is still much higher than it is throughout the 1990s. In 1988, the year in which Democrats and former Democrats ran against each other in several constituencies, the effective number of parties in the Democrat's Southern stronghold is the second highest in the country. Excluding the 1988 election yields an ENP_{avg} of 2.1 for the South.

In summary, the large number of parties in Thailand at the national level does not appear to be a function of the electoral system or

election under the new constitution where candidates were required to be members of political parties.

district-level coordination failures. The average effective number of parties at the constituency level is quite small (3.2 on average), much smaller than the effective number of parties nationally. How, then, do we account for the large number of parties at the national level?

4.4 THE NATIONAL PARTY SYSTEM: CROSS-DISTRICT COORDINATION (AGGREGATION)

I argued in previous chapters that Duverger's law and Cox's $M + 1$ rule operate at the district level. The result is numerous district-level party systems each with its own effective number of parties. How do the local party systems map onto the national party system? How well do parties coordinate or aggregate across districts? Recall that if the same parties are the frontrunners in all districts nationwide, then the effective number of parties nationally should be equivalent to the average number of parties in each district. The difference, then, between the effective number of parties nationally and the average effective number of parties at the district level is a measure of the extent of aggregation between the local and national party systems ($D = \text{ENP}_{nat} - \text{ENP}_{avg}$). The larger the difference is, the poorer the aggregation will be (Cox 1999; Chhibber and Kollman 1998, 2004). ENP_{avg} and ENP_{nat} for Thai elections are displayed in Figure 4.5. Note that even though ENP_{avg} averages 3.2, the effective number of parties nationally (ENP_{nat}) averages 7.2. We can convert this difference into Cox's inflation measure using the formula $I = 100 * [(\text{ENP}_{nat} - \text{ENP}_{avg})/ \text{ENP}_{nat}]$.[39] As discussed in Chapter 1, the inflation score communicates the percentage of the effective number of parties nationally that is due to poor aggregation – higher numbers reflect worse aggregation. Figure 4.6 displays the inflation scores for each of Thailand's elections.

As Figures 4.5 and 4.6 indicate, aggregation was poor between the local and national party systems during the pre-1997 period. The average effective number of parties at the district level ranges from 2.4 to 3.7, but the effective number of parties nationally goes from 4.6 to 9.8 (Figure 4.5). In other words, between 48 and 62% of the national party system's size can be attributed to poor aggregation (Figure 4.6).

---

[39] In Chapter 3, I used a version of the inflation score that ranged from 0 to 1. Here I multiply it by 100 to convert it to a 0 to 100 scale.

Thailand: Aggregation, Nationalization, Number of Parties

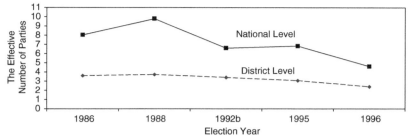

FIGURE 4.5. Effective Number of Parties: District Versus National

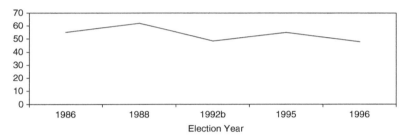

FIGURE 4.6. Inflation of the National Party System

Thailand's average inflation score over the period is 54, meaning 54% of the size of the national party system is the result of poor aggregation while 46% is due to the average number of parties at the district level. This inflation score is quite high by comparative standards (see Table 3.1).

Where specifically are aggregation failures occurring? Does the degree of cross-district coordination vary across different government administrative levels? For example, is it the case that coordination is good within provinces or regions, but not across them? To answer these questions, I calculate the extent to which candidates in provinces with multiple electoral districts link across those districts. Next, I examine aggregation between candidates across provinces within a given region. Finally, I determine how much aggregation occurred across different regions. Figure 4.7 displays the results.

Figure 4.7 traces the inflation of the party across each administrative level. I take the average effective number of parties and inflation scores for

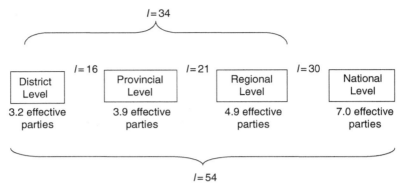

FIGURE 4.7. Where the Thai Party System Gets Inflated (Multidistrict Provinces Only)

all elections and all levels of government and show step by step where inflation occurs as one moves from the district to national level. Clearly, Thai parties failed to coordinate across the various administrative regions in Thailand. Specifically, 30% of the size of the national party system is due to poor aggregation across Thailand's 76 regions ($I = 30$). Measured in terms of percentage change, the party system grows by 45% between the regional and national levels. However, poor aggregation is even more pronounced at the subregional level. Between the district and regional levels, the party system expands by 52% for an inflation score of 34. Broken down even further, it becomes clear that there are aggregation failures both between the provinces ($I = 21$) and between districts within the same province ($I = 16$).[40]

4.5 CONCLUSION

Returning to the question posed at the beginning of the chapter: Why were there so many parties in pre-1997 Thailand? The large number of parties was not a function of a permissive electoral system or social cleavages that produced coordination failures at the district level. Thailand's block vote plurality electoral system is not an extremely

---

[40] The aggregation data from Figure 4.7 allow me to examine the extent to which Thailand has evolved into a party system made up of several major parties that dominate different regions of the country as some have suggested (see Surin and McCargo 1997). For an analysis, see Chapter 5.

permissive electoral system (though it is more permissive than a single-seat plurality system). As a result, candidates, voters, and parties *were* able to coordinate on a modest effective number of parties in each district. The level of intra-district coordination was such that Thailand would have had between three and four parties in the House of Representatives if parties had been able to perfectly aggregate across districts. I found also that the average effective number of parties at the district level varied by district magnitude in a manner consistent with what one would expect given the electoral system. (This is also further evidence of the weakness of Thai party labels.)

Rather than intra-district coordination failures, the source of Thailand's inflated party system was poor aggregation – the failure of candidates to better coordinate across districts. The data show that aggregation was poor between the districts, provinces, and regions. This finding begs some obvious questions. Namely, why has aggregation been so poor in Thailand relative to other countries? This is the subject to which I turn in Chapter 5.

4.6 APPENDIX

TABLE 4A. *Thailand's Constitutional and Electoral History*

Constitution	Duration	Nature of Assembly	Elections Held[a]	Total number of MPs[b]	Number of MPs Elected[b]	District Magnitude	Election Method
1932 (I)	5 months 13 days	Unicameral	None	70	0	—	—
1932 (II)	13 years 4 months 29 days	Unicameral	1933	156	78	1 to 3	Plurality (indirect)
			1937	182	91	1	Plurality
			1938	182	91	1	Plurality
			1946	192	96[c]	1	Plurality
1946	1 year 5 months 30 days	Bicameral[a]	1946	178	178[c]	1	Plurality
1947	1 year 4 months 14 days	Bicameral	1948	99	99	1 to 4	Plurality
1949	2 years 8 months 6 days	Bicameral	1949[d]	120[d]	120	1 to 4	Plurality
1952	6 years 7 months 12 days	Unicameral	1952[e]	246	123	1 to 6	Plurality
			1957 (Feb.)	283	160	1 to 6	Plurality
			1957 (Dec.)	281[f]	160[f]	1 to 6	Plurality
1959	9 years 4 months 23 days	Unicameral	None	240	0	—	—
1968	3 years 4 months 28 days	Bicameral	1969	219	219	1 to 15	Plurality
1972	1 year 9 months 28 days	Unicameral	None	299	0	—	—
1974	2 years	Bicameral	1975	269	269	1 to 3	Plurality
			1976	279	279	1 to 3	Plurality

114

Year	Duration	Chambers	Election	Total seats	Elected seats	District magnitude	Formula
1976	11 months 28 days	Unicameral	None	340	0	–	–
1977	1 year 1 month 13 days	Unicameral	None	360	0	–	–
1978	12 years 2 months 1 day	Bicameral	1979	301	301	1 to 3	Plurality
			1983	324	324	1 to 3	Plurality
			1986	347	347	1 to 3	Plurality
			1988	357	357	1 to 3	Plurality
1991 (I)	9 months 8 days	Unicameral	None	292	0	–	–
1991 (II)	5 years 10 months 2 days	Bicameral	1992 (March)	360	360	1 to 3	Plurality
			1992 (Sept.)	360	360	1 to 3	Plurality
			1995	391	391	1 to 3	Plurality
			1996	393	393	1 to 3	Plurality
1997	8 years 11 months 8 days	Bicameral	2001	500	500	1	Plurality
			2005			100 (national party list)	PR
2007	Current Constitution	Bicameral	2007	480	480	1 to 3	Plurality
						10 (8 regional party lists)	PR

[a] Elections listed are for the lower chamber (House of Representatives). The Thai Senate was an appointed body until the 1997 Constitution. The 2007 Constitution made the Senate into a partially appointed body, with half of the seats appointed.
[b] Members of the lower chamber (House of Representatives) of parliament when there are two chambers.
[c] Two rounds of elections were held in 1946. The first, held under the rules of the 1932 Constitution, was for the 96 elected seats in the assembly. After a new constitution was adopted in 1946, a second, supplementary round of elections was held to bring the number of MPs up to 178.
[d] A bi-election was held in 1949 to fill the 21 new seats created by the 1949 Constitution.
[e] The 1952 elections were held in February, one month prior to the formal adoption of the new constitution.
[f] In February 1958 the number of appointed members was reduced to 95. In March 1958 a by-election was held to fill an additional 26 elected seats, bringing the total number of elected seats to 186.

5

Explaining Aggregation in Thailand

5.1 INTRODUCTION

What does the theory of aggregation incentives as described in Chapter 2 tell us about the roots of cross-district coordination failures in pre-1997 Thailand? Why was aggregation so poor? Drawing on the theory presented in Chapter 2, I argue that poor aggregation incentives in Thailand reflected a diffusion of power within the national government (due to party factionalism and an appointed Senate) and uncertainty over the procedure for selecting the prime minister. In short, the expected utility associated with being the largest party in parliament was relatively low in pre-1997 Thailand. This discouraged greater attempts at cross-district coordination. I also discuss and evaluate possible alternative explanations (i.e., social heterogeneity and regionalism). I then devote the rest of the chapter to analyzing the effects of constitutional reform in light of the theory. Since the new Thai constitution and electoral system adopted in 1997 altered some of the variables I claim help shape aggregation incentives, this episode of institutional reform is an ideal opportunity for the use of comparative statics. In short, the constitutional reforms present me with a natural experiment that I can use to test the predictive power of the theory. The theory helps explain how and why the Thai party system has changed since the constitutional reforms. Specifically, I show that improvements in the aggregation payoff resulting primarily from new tools to combat party factionalism contributed to a dramatic improvement in cross-district coordination and an accompanying fall in the effective number of electoral parties. The final section concludes with a few words about aggregation in light of the 2006 coup and the subsequent constitutional reforms. The new 2007 Constitution was an attempt by Thailand's conservative forces to return Thai politics to the pre-Thaksin era, and it thus reduced many of the new aggregation incentives introduced in 1997. An analysis of the preliminary results from the December 2007 elections demonstrates that, as expected, aggregation declined in the wake of these reforms.

5.2 EXPLAINING POOR LINKAGE IN PRE-1997 THAILAND

5.2.1 The Size of the Aggregation Payoff – Vertical and Horizontal Centralization

The case of Thailand supports the argument that a concentration of power at the national rather than the subnational level (*vertical centralization*) is not enough to produce strong aggregation incentives. Thailand is a unitary state. Governors appointed by the Ministry of Interior (MoI) headed the country's 76 provinces. The few locally elected offices during the pre-1997 period "remained in the MoI's sphere of power" (Nelson 1998, 34). Nearly without exception Thailand is characterized by academics, bureaucrats, and politicians as an extremely centralized state – political and economic power remain heavily concentrated at the center (Bangkok) (Nelson 1998).[1] For example, over the 1980s and 1990s, the central government controlled 92% of all government expenditures and 95% of all government revenues (World Bank n.d.). As a percentage of GDP, subnational government's share of total revenues and expenditures was just a bit more than 1% (World Bank n.d.). Much of the revenue subnational governments would collect went directly to Bangkok – for example, 90% of the sales and excise taxes and 60% of the local surcharges collected by local governments were transferred to Bangkok (Hunsaker 1997, 144).[2]

If we focus solely on vertical centralization, we would expect Thailand to have excellent aggregation. However, as Chapter 4 demonstrated, this is not the case. In short, the concentration of power and

---

[1] For more information regarding the dominance of the central government over local administrative units in Thailand, see Nelson (1998) and Missingham (1997).
[2] To say that power is extremely centralized is not to say that local government units have no power. Hunsaker (1997) demonstrates that municipalities can and do bargain with the central government over revenue grants.

resources at the national level in Thailand does not translate into sufficiently strong incentives for cross-district coordination. Instead, one must look to the second component of the aggregation payoff – the concentration of power within the national government, or horizontal centralization.

Leaders of the largest party in pre-1997 Thailand faced significant checks on their power, which reduced the perceived payoff to aggregation. In Chapter 2, I argued that the presence of bicameralism, reserve domains, and party factionalism all reduce the size of the aggregation payoff. Each of these was present in pre-1997 Thailand. First, Thailand has a bicameral legislature consisting of a House Representatives (*saphaphuthaenratsadorn*) and Senate (*wuthisapha*). The House of Representatives was the primary legislative body – its approval is required for all legislation. The Senate could delay a bill but the House can eventually pass legislation over the objection of the Senate. Strictly speaking then, the Senate was not a formal veto gate and theoretically could have served as only a mild check on the authority of the largest party in the House. However, while the Senate did not have the formal power to block legislation, it was none-the-less difficult for elected governments to ignore the interests of the Senate. Until 1997, the Senate was an appointed body. During the 1980s, these appointees were generally former military officials and bureaucrats. Representing as it did the interests of Thailand's conservative forces – who, recall, had a long history of intervening to shut down democratic institutions – the Senate's position on a matter carried a good deal of weight. This was especially true when the Senators were relatively united on an issue. In effect, the Senate functioned as a reserve domain. The existence of an unelected Senate stocked with representatives of the military and bureaucracy meant that the parties that controlled the House and cabinet still did not hold all the reins of power.

Throughout much of the 1980s, another portion of the potential aggregation payoff was off limits to party leaders – macroeconomic and budgetary policy. This reserve domain emerged as the result of a compromise between elected politicians, Thailand's conservative forces, and Prime Minister (and former general) Prem Tinsulanonda.[3]

---

[3] For more on this compromise, see Hicken (2001, 2005), Christensen et al. (1993), and Doner and Ramsey (1997).

As part of this "pork-policy compromise," macroeconomic and budgetary policy was shielded from elected politicians and run by Prem-backed technocrats. In exchange, the political parties were given control of the sectoral ministries (Commerce, Industry, Education, Agriculture, etc.) and were allowed to run them as they saw fit provided they avoided major scandal and respected the budgetary ceilings set by the technocrats (Hicken 2001, 2005).

By the early 1990s, both of these reserve domains were withering away. In 1988, an elected politician became Thailand's prime minister for the first time since 1976 and immediately did away with the pork-policy compromise by seizing control of macroeconomic and budgetary policy (Hicken 2001, 2005). In addition, the composition of the Senate gradually changed so that over time business interests came to make up a larger and larger portion of Senate appointees. Yet, while these reserve domains were in place, they represented a significant diffusion of political authority and a disincentive for aggregation.

A third reserve domain exists in Thailand, one that did not wane during the 1990s – the institution of the monarchy. While the Thai king typically plays a largely ceremonial role in politics, Thai constitutions have reserved signification powers for the king in the area of legislation. Namely, by refusing to sign a bill into law, the king can effectively veto that legislation, and it then requires a two-thirds vote of both houses to pass the bill over the king's objections. Although the king has rarely, if ever, invoked this power, the fact remains that even a leader of the large, majority party faced a potential check on his authority.[4]

Another factor contributing to the horizontal diffusion of power – one that did not change over the course of the 1980s and 1990s – was the factionalized nature of Thai parties. As discussed in Chapter 4, Thai political parties were extremely factionalized, due in large part to the nature of Thailand's pre-1997 electoral system. Because of the rampant party factionalism, the leader of a political party was more like a first among equals than the head of a political hierarchy. The fact that the leader of the largest party might still find his power checked by rival

---

[4] In addition, the revered status of Thailand's current long-serving king means that on the occasion when the king weighs in on a political or policy matter, politicians disregard that advice at some cost. The clash between elected Prime Minister Thaksin Shinawatra and the monarchy was a major factor behind Thaksin's ouster from office in a September 2006 coup.

factions within his own party discouraged greater attempts at aggregation. Party factionalism was a major cause of the frequent cabinet reshuffles and short-lived governments that so characterized Thailand's pre-reform system as disgruntled faction leaders actively sought to bring down their rivals, including sometimes the nominal head of the party – the prime minister (see Chambers 2003).

Consider the history of the New Aspiration Party. The NAP vaulted to power as the largest party in 1996 after luring several factions to the party with promises of cabinet portfolios. The party, with its eight factions, was still far short of a majority in parliament with only 32% of the seats.[5] It was therefore forced to invite five other parties to join with it in coalition – most of which were also composed of multiple factions.

During its term in office, the various factions within the NAP were perpetually in conflict. Indeed, factional conflicts were among the factors behind the government's slow and inconsistent response to the economic crisis of 1997 (MacIntyre 1999; Chambers 2003). NAP faction leaders clashed with each other over how to respond to the growing crisis, what strategy to adopt regarding proposed constitutional reforms, and most of all over the allocation of portfolios. Chavalit Yongchaiyudh, the party's leader, was often reduced to the role of mediator and referee in a bid to keep all the factions on board and the party together. Unhappy with their share of the payoff after yet another cabinet reshuffle in October of 1997, some NAP factions began looking for greener pastures in other parties. Faced with this threat and unable to govern effectively while sitting astride the NAP hydra and five other coalition partners, Chavalit finally stepped down in November 1997. Over the next few years, the party steadily disintegrated as faction after faction abandoned the party. What remained of the party was finally folded into the Thai Rak Thai Party in 2002.

What is instructive about the NAP case is not how unusual it is but rather how typical. Factional conflict within the ruling party and/or within its coalition partners was a major cause of the collapse of nearly every democratic government prior to NAP (Chambers 2003). Recall that these were not large national parties. Each governing party controlled only a relatively modest plurality of parliamentary seats and drew support from only one or two regions. Yet even these moderately sized,

---

[5] See Chambers (2003) for details on these eight factions.

Explaining Aggregation in Thailand

nonnational parties were unable to manage internal conflict between factions. Historically, Thai parties that try to grow beyond a modest number of MPs implode in relatively short order (Chambers 2003).[6] The lesson internalized by nearly all party leaders and politicians during the 1980s and 1990s was that attempts to better coordinate across districts in an effort to build a larger, national party would not be worth the cost to party cohesion. Indeed, in numerous interviews with party officials, the dangers and drawbacks associated with factionalism was frequently cited as a major reason why coordination in a bid to form large, national parties was rarely attempted (Party Interviews 1999, 2000).

In short, Thai party leaders and would-be-prime ministers understood the challenges associated with the factionalized nature of Thai parties. Even when a prospective prime minister had the opportunity to create a nationwide majority party through aggregation, the specter of factional conflict undermined the appeal of such an option.

To summarize, power was vertically centralized in pre-reform Thailand, but within the national government itself power was dispersed. The existence of party factionalism, an upper chamber, and significant reserve domains, especially during the 1980s, reduced the payoff to being the largest party in government. This small aggregation payoff in turn contributed to weak aggregation incentives and the poor cross-district coordination that characterized pre-reform Thailand.

5.2.2 Prime Ministerial Selection Method

In parliamentary systems like Thailand's, the method of selecting the prime minister determines the probability that becoming the largest party will translate into control of government. If the rules or norms of parliament are such that the leader of the largest party always has the first opportunity to form a government and usually succeeds, then aggregation may be worthwhile. If, on the other hand, actors other than the leader of the largest party often form or get a chance to form the government, then aggregation incentives are weaker.

In Thailand, the leader of the largest party did successfully head a new government after the September 1992, 1995, and 1996 elections, but this

---

[6] The threshold of sustainability seems to be between 80 and 90 members of parliament (Chambers 2003).

was not always the norm. After the 1979, 1983, 1986, 1988, and March 1992 elections, non-elected individuals (military figures) were invited to form a government either immediately after the election, or after political party leaders failed in their attempts. In 1988, the man invited to be prime minister, General Prem Tinsulanonda, turned down the invitation; and the head of Chart Thai, the largest party, became prime minister. After a non-elected individual was again invited to form the government after the March 1992 elections (resulting in mass protests), a constitutional amendment was passed requiring that the prime minister be a member of the House of Representatives. Prior to the amendment, however, the high probability that the leader of the largest party would not get the opportunity to form a government undermined the incentives to try to create a large national party.

To summarize, the pre-1997 institutional environment generated weak aggregation incentives. Even though power was vertically centralized, within the national government power was less concentrated. The existence of party factionalism together with a Senate and the presence of reserve domains placed checks on the power of the largest party and kept the potential payoff to aggregation low throughout the period. In addition, for much of the pre-1997 period the selection procedure for the prime minister was uncertain. This uncertainty together with the small aggregation payoff undermined incentives to coordinate across districts. Note, however, that as reserve domains diminished and a constitutional amendment was adopted prohibiting non-elected prime ministers, aggregation did somewhat improve. The average inflation score for the 1980s, when reserve domains were strongest and the government was regularly headed by a non-elected premier, is 58. After the 1992 constitutional amendment, the average inflation score falls to 50 – still high as expected given the enduring factionalism, but noticeably lower than the previous decade.

5.3 ALTERNATIVE EXPLANATION: SOCIAL HETEROGENEITY AND REGIONALISM

It is worth taking a moment here to review some alternative explanations for Thailand's high inflation rate. In Chapter 3, I noted that when there is social heterogeneity and cleavage groups are concentrated in separate regions, cross-district alliances may be difficult to build (though I also argued that heterogeneity interacts with the size of the aggregation payoff). In general, Thailand lacks the pronounced and politicized social cleavages found in many of its neighbors. While its ethnic fractionalization score is a notable .43 (Fearon 2003), ethnicity has not been a major basis of political or party competition. In fact, "ideology, religion, ethnicity, and policy issues have generally played a minor role in the [Thai] electorate's voting behavior" (Surin and McCargo 1997, 135).

To the extent a significant cleavage exists in Thailand, it would be an urban–rural cleavage, and some scholars do claim that the urban–rural divide hinders the development of national parties. Due to their very different constituencies, this argument goes, Bangkok-based candidates and provincially based candidates have a hard time forming alliances. In short, Thailand is a country with "two separate political cultures and two competing agendas" (Pasuk and Baker 1998, 245). The gap between these urban and rural interests, it is argued, is too great for any single party to bridge (Anek 1996).

I do not dispute the existence of a division between Bangkok and the provinces; however, I do question whether this gap is insurmountable. There are parties that have been able to simultaneously draw support from both Bangkok and the provinces, most notably the Democrat Party which has, at times, done well in Bangkok and the more rural Southern region. More recently, in 2001 the Thai Rak Thai Party was able to win the support of both provincial and urban voters. Its share of the Bangkok vote (42%) is nearly identical to what it received in the rest of the country, outside of the South (44%). In addition, urban- and rural-based parties have been able to form alliances with each other once in power. An example is the 1995 grand coalition of the provincially based Chart Thai and New Aspiration Party with the Bangkok-based Palang Dharma and Nam Thai Parties. There is no a priori reason that similar cross-constituency alliances could not be formed prior to elections under the umbrella of a single party, as indeed they have been in recent elections. In addition, Chapter 4 demonstrated that coordination failures are pronounced even within regions where there is *no* significant urban–rural divide.

This brings me to a second, but related, alternative explanation. Some scholars suggest that Thailand has evolved into a party system made up of several major parties that dominate different regions of the country (see Surin and McCargo 1997). If this is true, then this could suggest that region is an important cleavage in Thailand and a hindrance to better aggregation. Indeed, there is a good deal of evidence in support of the regionalization argument. Most parties do draw the bulk of their support from a particular region and, as I argued in Chapter 4, the Democrat Party has traditionally dominated Southern elections. If different parties dominated other regions of the country in the same way, aggregation across regions could certainly be difficult. Indeed, the parties do have difficulty linking across regions as the cross-regional inflation score of 30 in Figure 5.1 suggests. Nonetheless, two points of caution are worth noting regarding claims that Thailand is developing or has developed a regionalized party system. First, the fact remains that aggregation is poorer between the district and regional levels ($I = 34$) than it is between the regional and national levels ($I = 30$) (see Figure 5.1). In other words, the evidence suggests that even candidates from within the same region have difficulty joining together under a common party label.

A second concern with the regionalization claim is whether regions outside of the South are really dominated by one or two political parties. To examine this question I calculate the effective number of parties for each region of Thailand (ENP_{reg}) by aggregating party vote shares by region. I then compare the number of regional parties (ENP_{reg}) with the average effective number of parties (ENP_{avg}) at the district level in each region. ENP_{avg} tells us how many parties there are on average in each district in a given region. ENP_{reg} tells us how many parties there are region wide – aggregating across the various districts in a region. ENP_{reg}, then, is similar to ENP_{nat} but on a regional scale. By comparing these

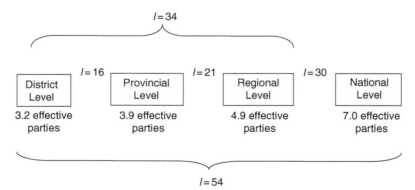

FIGURE 5.1. Where the Thai Party System Gets Inflated (Multidistrict Provinces Only)

Explaining Aggregation in Thailand

two numbers I can determine whether there is a difference between the average number of parties found in a region's districts and the total effective number of parties for that region. In a region with one or two dominant parties, one would expect the effective number of parties at the district level (ENP$_{avg}$) to be low – the dominant party (or parties) should be the clear frontrunner in any given constituency. In addition, aggregation between districts should be good – truly dominant parties should be the frontrunners in most of the districts region-wide, and thus ENP$_{reg}$ should be near ENP$_{avg}$. Finally, if one or two political parties truly dominate regions to a degree similar to which the Democrats dominate the South, then ENP$_{avg}$ and ENP$_{reg}$ for non-South regions should compare favorably to ENP$_{avg}$ and ENP$_{reg}$ for the South.

Figure 5.2 compares the effective number of regional parties (ENP$_{reg}$) for each Thai region with the average effective number of parties in each region's districts (ENP$_{avg}$) (Figure 5.2a). It is clear from this figure that even at the regional level aggregation is poor. In nearly every region there is a large gap between the effective number of parties at the district and regional levels. Even when this gap narrows in 1996, 33% of the regional party system can still be explained by poor aggregation ($I = 33$). Figure 5.2 also shows that, as expected, aggregation in the Southern region is very good. There is very little difference between the number of parties at the regional level (ENP$_{reg}$; Figure 5.2b) and the number of parties at the constituency level (ENP$_{avg}$; Figure 5.2a) – except for the year of the split in the Democrat Party (1988). In addition, both ENP$_{avg}$ and ENP$_{reg}$ are generally lower in the South than in other regions, again with the exception of 1988. These results suggest that outside the South, no party has been able to dominate an entire region. Regionally *based* parties do draw the majority of their support from one particular region, and they may indeed have difficulty forming alliances with candidates or parties in other regions, but as Figure 5.2 demonstrates, these parties have plenty of difficulty forging alliances across districts within their own region.[7]

---

[7] Bangkok is an exception. While Bangkok's ENP$_{avg}$ is comparable in most elections to ENP$_{avg}$ for the Central and Northern regions, ENP$_{reg}$ is much lower in Bangkok. In short, there is better aggregation in Bangkok than in any other region outside of the South. Even though Bangkok has more parties running in a given constituency than the South, those parties tend to be the same from constituency to constituency. Thus, the difference between ENP$_{avg}$ and ENP$_{reg}$ is very small.

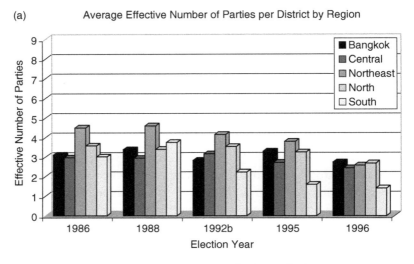
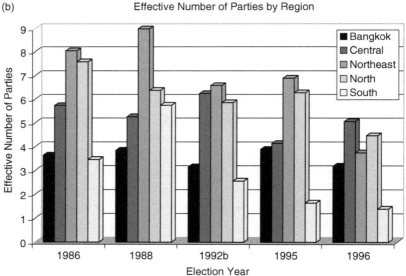

FIGURE 5.2 Average Effective Number of Parties per District by Region (a) and (b) Effective Number of Parties by Region

If social or regional cleavages cannot adequately account for the lack of cross-district coordination in Thailand, then other factors must be coming into play to prevent aggregation. Why hasn't there been greater coordination between urban and rural areas, or across regions by candidates and parties? A major reason is certainly the lack of incentives to do so. Given stronger aggregation incentives it seems likely that candidates/parties would find a way to bridge these divides. As we will see in the next section, this is indeed the case.

5.4 AGGREGATION AND THE 1997 CONSTITUTIONAL REFORMS

In 1997 Thailand adopted a new constitution. The first House of Representatives election under this constitution was held in 2001.[8] For the first time since democratic elections were restored in 1979, a single party, the newly formed Thai Rak Thai Party, nearly captured a majority of the seats in the House. (Shortly after the election, two smaller parties decided to merge with Thai Rak Thai, giving the party a legislative majority.) As a result, the effective number of parliamentary parties fell quite dramatically to 3.1 from an average of 6.1 during the previous six elections (Table 5.1). A similar decline is evident in the effective number of electoral parties (as measured by vote shares) – from 7.1 to 3.8. This trend continued in 2005 with the effective number of electoral parties falling further to 2.4. I argue that this change in the effective number of parties nationally is a direct result of the constitutional changes Thailand adopted in 1997. Specifically, I argue that reducing district magnitude (M) led to improved strategic coordination within districts. However, it is the stronger incentives for coordination by parties and candidates *across* districts that are primarily responsible for reducing the number of parties. In short, the constitutional changes increased aggregation incentives, resulting in a decline in the number of parties nationally.

Whenever one is interested in the effects of institutional changes endogeneity and direction of causation issues are a concern. Specifically one must consider whether the constitutional changes *and* subsequent changes to the party system are both simply reflections of the interests and capabilities of major political actors. In the Thai case, however, treating the constitutional changes as relatively exogenous seems reasonable. First, the constitutional drafting process was generally free

---

[8] In 2000, Thailand's first ever Senate elections were held. The new Senate had only delaying power, and Senators could not belong to a political party. See more on this later in this chapter.

TABLE 5.1. *Effective Number of Parties in Thailand*

Election Year	Effective Number of Parties (by seat shares)	Effective Number of Parties (by vote shares)
1986	6.1	8.0
1988	7.7	9.8
1992a	6.0	6.7
1992b	6.1	6.6
1995	6.4	6.8
1996	4.3	4.6
Average: 1986–96	6.1	7.1
2001[a]	3.1	3.8
2005[a]	1.6	2.4

[a] The 2001 and 2005 election used a mixed-member system with 400 seats elected from single-seat districts and 100 seats elected using national party lists with proportional representation. The effective number of parties for these elections is calculated using all House votes and all House seats.

Sources: Ministry of Interior, election reports (1986, 1988, 1992a, 1992b, 1995, 1997); Nelson (2002). Electoral Commission of Thailand (2005).

from partisan political influence (Prudhisan 1998). The drafting process was carried out by a body entirely separate from the legislature and specially created for the purpose of writing a new constitution (the Constitutional Drafting Assembly – CDA). The CDA consisted of indirectly elected representatives from each of the country's provinces alongside appointed experts in the fields of public law, political science, and public administration. By statute, the CDA draft was subject only to an up or down vote in the legislature and could not be amended.[9] Within the CDA itself, the majority of the work of constitutional design and drafting was delegated to a select committee of academics and technocrats with no clear partisan affiliations.

Second, consistent with the fact that the drafting was outside of the control of Thailand's existing political elite, the constitutional reforms threatened the interests of many of Thailand's traditional power centers.[10] It is not surprising then that support for the CDA draft constitution was greeted in some quarters with wariness and even outright

[9] In the event of a no vote, the draft would then go before the people in the form of a referendum.
[10] The nature of the reforms was very much the reflection of middle class (Bangkok) preferences (Connors 2002). See also McCargo 2002.

opposition. The political elite of many of the major political parties and factions, including the ruling NAP, expressed strong reservations about the draft. The fact that most ultimately voted to adopt the draft constitution, despite their very serious misgivings, is a function of two factors. First, the Constitutional Amendment Bill required an up or down vote of the draft by parliament without amendment. This made it impossible for legislators to pick apart the draft or delay it via the amendment process. Second, the coincident occurrence of the Asian economic crisis, a chain reaction that began in Thailand in late June/early July 1997, effectively raised the stakes connected with passage or rejection of the draft. The crisis struck just as the drafting process was wrapping up. It shone a spotlight on some of the shortcomings in the Thai political system (MacIntyre 2002). In the minds of many voters and investors, the constitutional draft became a symbol of the government's commitment to difficult but needed political and economic reforms. Constitutional reform and the broader reform agenda became so linked, in fact, that the stock market and currency markets reacted quickly and noticeably to expressions of opposition or support by leading government officials. In the end, the potential economic and political costs of a no vote outweighed the risks of reform, and the draft was adopted by a vote of 518 to 16 (with 17 abstentions).

Finally, it is difficult to draw a clear link between existing political interests and reform processes and outcomes. As mentioned previously, the leaders of the largest party during the drafting period were not enthusiastic supporters of the proposed constitution and only came around once the crisis-related implications were apparent. The party that many believed stood to gain the most from the new rules, the Democrat Party, was in the political opposition throughout the drafting and passage process. Finally, the party that ultimately benefited the most from the reforms, the Thai Rak Thai Party, did not exist when the constitution was being drafted and adopted, nor were its future leaders, most notably Thaksin Shinawatra, involved in the drafting process. In short, in this case it does not seem unreasonable to treat the constitutional reforms as exogenous to the subsequent changes in the party system.

In the rest of the chapter, I first review the 1997 constitutional reforms and use the aggregation incentives theory to generate hypotheses on the effect of these reforms on the number of parties. I then test these hypotheses using data from the 2001 and 2005 elections.

TABLE 5.2. *Constitutional Reforms*

	1978/1991 Constitutions	1997 Constitution
House of Representatives	• 1–3 seat constituencies • Block vote	• Mixed-member system • 400 single-seat constit. • 100 national party list seats
Senate	• Appointed	• Elected using SNTV, non-partisan
Party Switching	• Allowed	• 90-day membership requirement
Decentralization	• Limited	• Mandated

5.4.1 The Effect of Political Reform on Aggregation Incentives and the Number of Parties

The 1997 constitution and subsequent party and electoral laws drastically revamped Thailand's electoral and political landscape. Reforms included changes in the way elections are administered, the establishment of several semiautonomous oversight agencies, and the creation of an elected Senate – the first ever in Thailand. Here, however, I will focus on the reforms that might be expected to bear on aggregation and the number of political parties. These reforms are summarized in Table 5.2.[11]

Decreased District Magnitude
One of the most striking changes in the 1997 Constitution was the move to 400 single-seat districts in place of the multiseat districts that were previously the norm. As discussed in the last chapter, electoral theory suggests that lowering district magnitude should also lower the effective number of parties at the district level.

Whether the move to single-seat districts actually leads to an average effective number of parties of two, corresponding to the $M + 1$ rule, depends on how well the assumptions behind the $M + 1$ rule hold.[12] There are several reasons to expect ENP_{avg} to be slightly larger than 2 for the 2001 election. First, it may take time for candidates and voters to divine and respond to the incentives generated by a new electoral system. The new electoral system necessitated a redrawing of district

---

[11] For discussion of other important reforms and their effects, see Hicken (2006).
[12] See the last chapter for a discussion of these assumptions.

boundaries, in some cases pitting incumbent against incumbent and in others leaving districts without incumbents. Party allegiances also shifted as party leaders and potential candidates attempted to anticipate what reforms would mean for various parties' electoral prospects. In short, these changes meant that some of the cues that facilitate strategic coordination by voters and candidates (e.g., electoral histories, party labels) were lacking.

Second, to the extent that vote buying and selling (long features of Thai elections) continue to dictate how some voters cast their votes, some of the strategic coordination assumptions may not hold. Vote buying certainly occurred in the 2001 election, as it did in past elections, but as discussed in Chapter 4, there is some question about how this impacts election results.[13] If one candidate engages in vote buying within a district, most other candidates will have an incentive to do the same. The result is that Thai voters often accept money from many candidates and parties and then vote for their preferred candidate(s) anyway. If this is the case, then vote buying might not have a large effect on strategic voting.

To summarize, the uncertainty connected with a new electoral system combined with the occurrence of vote buying may keep the effective number of parties above 2. Over time, one would expect ENP_{avg} to fall as voters and candidates adjust to the new rules and as vote buying diminishes as a result of development and increased enforcement of anti-vote-buying laws.[14]

Decentralization

One of the most striking features of the 1997 Constitution was its call for greater decentralization. Political and economic power has traditionally been highly centralized in Thailand. To the extent decentralization actually lead to greater political and economic power at the subnational level, aggregation incentives should have decreased. However, the decentralization provisions of the constitution had not been implemented at the time of the 2001 elections. The process of decentralization

---

[13] See Callahan (2002) and Hicken (2007b) for discussions of the effect of the constitutional reforms on vote buying.
[14] During the 2001 election, the newly created Electoral Commission penalized and/or disqualified several candidates found guilty of vote buying and other illegal practices. Elections were re-run in many districts where electoral law violations were found. See Nelson (2002).

did commence under Thaksin (post-2001), but although local elections were held and some budgetary power was decentralized, progress towards meaningful decentralization remained slow (Painter 2005).[15] Eventually vertical decentralization should reduce the size of the aggregation payoff, but not enough time has passed to assess whether this is indeed the case.

Greater Power for the Prime Minister

The change in the 1997 Constitution with the biggest bearing on aggregation incentives was increased powers for the prime minister relative to factions within his own party. Two changes are particularly worth noting. First, cabinet members were now required to give up their seats in parliament if they chose to join the cabinet. Since parties or ministers that chose to leave the cabinet, or were expelled by the prime minister, could no longer return to parliament, the stakes associated with breaking with the prime minister were much higher. Second, the 1997 Constitution placed new restrictions on party switching. In order to compete in future elections, candidates had to be members of a political party for at least 90 days. The rule was designed to curb the 11th hour party switching by individuals and factions that traditionally occurred in the run-up to Thai elections. Once the House was dissolved, elections had to be held within 45 days (if the House's term expired) or 60 days (if parliament was dissolved) – not enough time for would-be party switchers to meet the membership requirement. The prime minister, with the power to dissolve the House and call new elections, gained the most from this change.[16] The prime minister could credibly threaten to call new elections if party factions tried to bolt, thus forcing the members of the faction to sit out one election.[17] According to the theory, enhanced power for the prime minister over intra-party factions increases the payoff to being the largest party in government. If the theory is correct, this should result in better aggregation and fewer parties.

---

[15] In fact, the reforms carried out under the banner of decentralization have actually recentralized authority under the prime minister's office (Painter 2005).
[16] Formally it was the king who dissolved the House and called for new elections upon the advice of the prime minister.
[17] For this reason, some prominent Thai factions were in favor of amending the constitution to allow for easier party switching.

Explaining Aggregation in Thailand

TABLE 5.3. *Summary of Constitutional Changes*

Constitutional Change	District Party System (Reduce or inflate ENP_{avg})	National Party System (Aggregation Incentives Stronger or Weaker)
Decrease district magnitude	Reduce	–
Greater power for PM	–	Stronger
Decentralization (not fully implemented)	–	(Weaker)

Table 5.3 summarizes the reforms just discussed along with the expected effects of these changes on the district level and national party systems.[18]

On balance then, Thailand's 1997 constitutional reforms pushed in the same direction – toward a reduction in the number of parties at the national level (ENP_{nat}). A portion of this reduction should reflect fewer parties at the district level (ENP_{avg}) due to the move to single-seat districts. However, since the average effective number of parties in pre-reform Thailand was already quite modest (3.2), any large decline in the number of parties nationally should be the result of better aggregation between districts. I summarize these expectations in hypothesis form here:

Hypothesis 1: The move from multiseat to single-seat districts will be associated with a fall in ENP_{avg}.

Hypothesis 2: Aggregation in the post-reform elections will improve relative to pre-reform elections as measured by the inflation score (I).

Hypothesis 3: The post-1997 elections should have a smaller ENP_{nat} post-reform than previous elections.

Hypothesis 4: Better aggregation should play a larger role in lowering ENP_{nat} than the decline in ENP_{avg}.

---

[18] In the appendix, I include a discussion of two other reforms – the addition of an elected Senate and a national party list tier for House elections – and explain why these reforms do not generate strong predictions about changes in aggregation incentives, though they do have important bearing on other dimensions of the party system.

5.4.2 Empirical Results

To test these hypotheses I compiled district- and national-level electoral returns for the 2001 and 2005 elections to the Thai House of Representatives. (2001 was the first election to be held under the 1997 Constitution.) The data from these two elections were then compared to data from five pre-reform elections to determine whether the local party and national party systems have changed in the hypothesized manner.[19] All of the hypotheses are supported by the data.

At the district level, a move to single-seat districts was accompanied by a decline in ENP_{avg} as hypothesized (H_1). ENP_{avg} for the elections prior to 1997 was 3.2. During the 2001 election, ENP_{avg} fell by nearly 16% to 2.7. It fell a further 35% to 2.0 in 2005 (see Table 5.5). An OLS regression with robust standard errors reveals that the average effective number of parties in each district is significantly lower in post-reform elections (see Table 5.4). Voters and candidates clearly responded strategically to the change in the district electoral system – specifically the reduction in district magnitude. Also as expected, the average effective number of parties did not immediately fall to 2 in 2001, but by the 2005 election the contest in each district was, on average, a two-party affair.

If voters and candidates at the district level were able to coordinate on a smaller number of parties than they had in past elections, were they able to do the same across districts? Did aggregation improve as hypothesized (H_2)? Figure 5.3 compares the effective number of parties at the district and national levels before and after constitutional reform.[20] Note the narrowing of the gap between the effective number of parties nationally and the average effective number of parties locally in 2001 and 2005. This is evidence of improved aggregation. Better

---

[19] These were the 1986, 1988, September 1992, 1995, and 1996 elections. The March 1992 election is once again excluded due to incomplete district-level electoral data.

[20] Since the post-1997 Thai system contains both constituency and party list votes one must decide whether to combine those votes to produce ENP_{nat} and the inflation scores or to use only the votes cast in the constituency elections. There are pros and cons to either approach. The numbers I report in the text, tables, and figures are calculated using total party vote shares – that is I combine the party list and constituency votes for each party. Excluding party list votes produces slightly higher ENP_{nat} and inflation scores for 2001 and 2005, but my inferences remain the same. I report the scores excluding party list votes in footnotes where applicable.

Explaining Aggregation in Thailand

TABLE 5.4. *Regression Results: The Effect on Reform on the Average Effective Number of Parties at the District Level*

Dependent Variable: Effective Number of Parties at the District Level (ENP$_{avg}$)	1986–2005
Post-reform Election	−0.86***
(Equals 1 if the election is 2001 or 2005, 0 otherwise)	(0.05)
Constant	3.22
	(0.04)
R-squared	.15
Number of Observations:	1525

***Significant at the .000 level; standard errors in parentheses

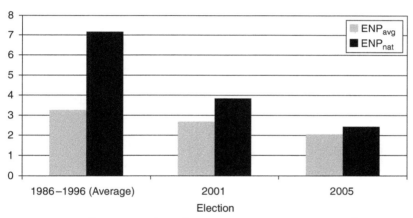

FIGURE 5.3. Effective Number of Parties: District Versus National

aggregation is also reflected in the decline of the inflation measure *I* from 54 to 30 in 2001 and 16 in 2005 – a total fall of 70% (see Table 5.5).[21] Whereas before the reforms poor aggregation accounted for the majority of the size of national party system (54%) in 2005, only 16% of the effective number of parties nationally is attributable to poor cross-district coordination.

The result of fewer parties at the local level (lower ENP$_{avg}$) and improved aggregation is a sharp reduction in the effective number of parties nationally (ENP$_{nat}$) consistent with Hypothesis 3. ENP$_{nat}$ fell to

---

[21] Excluding party list votes yields an inflation score of 37 in 2001 and 20 in 2005 for an overall decline of 63% from pre-reform inflation levels.

TABLE 5.5. *Pre- and Post-reform Elections Compared*

	ENP_{avg}	ENP_{nat}	Inflation
1986–1996 elections (average)	3.2	7.2	54
2001 election	2.7	3.8	30
2005 elections	2.0	2.4	16

3.8 in 2001 and 2.4 in 2005 from an average of 7.2 prior to 1997.[22] The data also support Hypothesis 4 – better aggregation was a bigger factor in reducing the effective number of parties nationally than the decline in the average effective number of parties at the district level. The shift to single-seat districts reduced the effective number of parties by 1.2 parties. By contrast, improved aggregation reduced the effective number of parties by 3.6 parties. The story is the same in percentage terms. The effective number of parties contracted by 67% nationally compared to only 38% at the district level. Table 5.5 summarizes the results of the 2001 and 2005 elections and compares them with pre-1997 electoral averages.

5.5 THE RISE AND FALL OF THAKSIN SHINAWATRA AND THE 2007 CONSTITUTION

Constitutional Reform and the Rise of the Thai Rak Thai Party

In the next chapter, I focus on aggregation incentives and aggregation in the Philippines. However, before turning to that task, it is worth taking some time to discuss one of the most striking features of Thai politics in the wake of the 1997 reforms – the rise and success, and subsequent fall of the Thai Rak Thai Party and its leader, Thaksin Shinawatra.[23] Thai Rak Thai was the largest party in the 2001 election. Prime Minister Thaksin subsequently became the first elected prime minister to serve out a full four-year term, and his party was reelected in a landslide in 2005. How, if at all, did the constitutional reforms discussed in this chapter contribute to the success of Thaksin and his party? Stated differently, what role did institutional changes

---

[22] Excluding party list votes the ENP_{nat} is 4.3 in 2001 and 2.6 in 2005.
[23] This section draws on Hicken (2006).

play vis-à-vis some of the other possible explanations for the success (i.e., Thaksin's enormous wealth)? The question is more than just academic – if the changes in the Thai party system since 1997 are due solely to Thaksin/Thai Rak Thai's particular assets, then that leaves institutional approaches with nothing to explain – in a word, they are superfluous.

Thaksin and his advisors do deserve credit for designing an electoral strategy that combined promises of protection and political power to domestic business interests (in dire straits after the crisis) with a populist campaign that promised the government would now take an active role in eliminating poverty and increasing social welfare (Hewison 2004). With respect to social welfare, the government promised and, once in office, implemented policies such as the million baht village fund, the 30 baht health care schemes, a debt moratorium for farmers, and the One Tamboon, One Product (OTOP) plan. These policies were not completely new. Similar proposals had floated around party and policy circles for years in Thailand, but they had never before found their way into election campaigns in a serious way, in part because politicians lacked incentives to campaign on such policies (Hicken 2002). The adoption of the 1997 Constitution altered these incentives in important ways, and Thai Rak Thai took advantage of the new institutional environment, with its increased incentives and rewards for party-centered campaigns and programmatic appeals. In short, electoral reforms meant that a national programmatic appeal was a much more viable/appealing strategy than it had been under previous constitutions.[24]

More germane to the focus of this chapter on aggregation incentives, Thaksin also benefited enormously from the increased power the new constitution gave the prime minister. Thaksin enjoyed a degree of leverage over his coalition and factional rivals that *none* of his elected predecessors ever possessed. As discussed previously, this leverage stemmed from his ability to completely exclude his factional rivals from political power via his power to call early elections. How, though, can we assess the importance of these new institutionally derived powers

---

[24] Other parties also recognized the opportunity to pursue new electoral strategies and attempted to do so. They were less successful in part because of their association with the crisis and/or the costly economic reforms adopted in its wake.

relative to Thaksin's personal and financial assets, which were also considerable. What about the counterfactual? Would Thaksin have been able to organize and hold together Thai Rak Thai without the new leverage the constitution granted him? Although it is impossible to definitively answer this question, there is evidence that supports the argument that the new powers and larger aggregation payoff were necessary and that his vast personal wealth was not sufficient to produce a stable Thai Rak Thai majority.

First, under the previous constitution, Thaksin served as head of the Palang Dharma Party. Thaksin by this time was already enormously wealthy, yet under his leadership the party was rife with factional conflict and failed miserably at the polls, despite a strong showing in a previous election. Even with his vast financial resources, he was unable to grow the party or even hold the party together. The party finally disintegrated under his watch.

Second, as discussed earlier, the few past attempts by politicians previous to Thaksin to forge larger parties all ended in failure, regardless of the assets and capabilities of the party's leadership. Historically, Thai parties that tried to grow beyond a modest number of MPs imploded in relatively short order, a victim to factional conflicts (Chambers 2003). Indeed, knowledge of this fact undermined the expected aggregation payoff for most politicians and discouraged greater attempts at aggregation before 1997. By contrast, before being banned by the coup-government in 2007, Thai Rak Thai accomplished back-to-back majority electoral victories – something no party in Thai history has ever done.

Finally, it is clear that there were factions within Thai Rak Thai that, given the chance, would have jumped ship before the 2005 elections. The most prominent example is Sanoh Thienthong and his Wang Nam Yen faction. Sanoh left the New Aspiration Party and joined Thai Rak Thai prior to the 2001 election bringing his large faction with him. His faction played an important role in Thai Rak Thai's electoral victory. New Aspiration was not, though, Sanoh's original home. He had been a prominent member of the Chart Thai Party but switched to the New Aspiration Party prior to the 1996 election, helping propel it to victory at the polls. As part of the Thai Rak Thai government, Sanoh grew increasingly restless. He campaigned for an amendment to the constitution that would eliminate the party-switching restrictions and became increasingly critical of the party's leadership, including Thaksin. In cabinet reshuffles and in negotiations over how (and whom) to run in the 2005 election, his faction was increasingly left out in the cold. Under earlier rules, there is little doubt Sanoh would have left Thai Rak Thai and joined another party, as he had in the past. Yet, despite his dissatisfaction with his position in the party (he famously likened being in the party to being in prison)[25] and the likelihood that his position would only worsen, Sanoh and his faction remained with Thai Rak Thai for the 2005 election. The 90-day rule made switching parties (and forfeiting the right to participate in the April election) an unpalatable proposition for even some of the unhappiest members of Thai Rak Thai.

In summary, even though Thaksin's personal assets no doubt played a role in the rise and success of Thai Rak Thai, it is difficult to believe he would have been as successful without the greater rewards for aggregation the new constitution provides. The new tools available to keep intra-party factions in check helped make greater coordination across-districts worth the substantial cost. Indeed, the utility of these tools was recognized by Thaksin's opponents – Thailand's conservative forces. After ousting him from power, these opponents immediately commenced to revise the constitution to deny future elected prime ministers similar tools.[26] I next turn to the details of the 2007 constitutional reforms and their implications for aggregation.

Aggregation Incentives and the 2007 Constitution

Once in power, Thaksin worked steadily to centralize power in the hands of Thai Rak Thai, and within the party, in the hands of Thaksin and his associates (Hicken 2006).[27] The centralization of power around the prime minister, together with his methods, eventually generated a backlash from certain segments of the public and, ultimately, from Thailand's conservative forces, culminating in the September 19, 2006, military coup. The proximate justification for the coup was Thailand's increasingly intractable political crisis – triggered by the sale of Shin Corp. (founded by Thaksin and still owned by his family) to a

---

[25] "Sanoh in Open Rebellion," *Bangkok Post* (June 9, 2005).
[26] For more details about events leading up to the 2006 coup, see Hicken (2007c).
[27] This section draws on Hicken (2007c).

Singaporean firm in January 2006. However, even though the ongoing political crisis was the immediate justification for the coup, the events of September 19 had deeper roots. Over the course of his tenure, Thaksin had become a threat to Thailand's conservative forces. He butted heads with segments of the military over his policies toward the South and his efforts to use the military reshuffle process to install Thaksin loyalists in positions of authority within the military (McCargo and Ukrist 2005). Likewise, Thaksin's efforts to turn the bureaucracy into an effective agent of the government met with resistance from career civil servants and those with loyalties to other parties or institutions. However, the most important conflict was that between Thaksin and the monarchy. As Thaksin's term in office progressed, Thaksin and the monarchy (the king and the members of the Privy Council) clashed over extra-judicial killings in the war on drugs, government policy toward the Thai South (McCargo 2006), and Thaksin's efforts to create a new network of power loyal to him, displacing the monarchy's own carefully cultivated network of power and influence (McCargo 2005; Ockey 2005; Handley 2006). In the end Thaksin's enormous popularity and his efforts to centralize power were a challenge to the power and popularity of the monarchy. When the military intervened, the monarchy supported the move and endorsed the subsequent military-appointed government.[28] Constitutional reform was immediately put forward as one of the central planks of the coup leaders' (and interim government's) reform agenda. Their stated goal was to use constitutional reform to correct some of the perceived shortcomings of the 1997 Constitution and the excesses of the Thaksin era.

The drafting of the new charter differed in key respects from the drafting of the 1997 Constitution. Recall that the drafting assembly for the 1997 Constitution was partially an elected body outside the direct control of any particular party or faction. By contrast, the body convened to draft the 2007 Constitution was not independent – all of its members were directly or indirectly appointed by the coup-installed government. The coup leaders consistently denied trying to manage the drafting process from behind the scenes. Nonetheless, they controlled the make-up of the drafting assembly and were not shy about sharing

---

[28] Whether the members of the royal inner circle played an active role in bringing the coup about is a subject of on-going debate.

Explaining Aggregation in Thailand

their preferences with the drafters (*The Nation* 2006).[29] The drafting assembly completed its work in July of 2007, and on August 19, 2007, the charter was adopted in a national referendum with 57.8% of the vote.

The 2007 Constitution represents an attempt to undermine the capacity of political parties and elected leaders to challenge Thailand's conservative forces in the future. In short, a major goal behind the charter was to prevent the rise of another Thaksin – a powerful prime minister at the head of a relatively cohesive, nationally oriented party. The new constitution contained a number of important reforms (including the introduction of a partially appointed Senate and redesigned party list tier), but my focus here is on the reforms that bear on intra-district coordination, aggregation, and ultimately nationalization.

The new constitution retains Thailand's mixed-member system but, in a nod to the pre-1997 electoral system, replaced the 400 single-seat districts with multiseat districts elected using the block vote. Most nominal tier districts once again contain two or three seats – only a handful have a single seat. Voters have as many votes as there are seats in a district and are allowed to vote for the candidates of their choosing. The top vote-getting candidates will receive the seats in each district. The return to multiseat districts should increase the average effective number of parties in each district. However, even with this increase, we would still expect the number of parties in each district to be relatively modest, given that the number of seats in each district is capped at three.

In addition to the abandonment of single-seat districts, a major impetus toward greater party system fragmentation and less nationalization will likely be the undermining of the incentives for cross-district aggregation and national party building. Specifically, the new constitution dramatically reduces the relative power of the prime minister. This means future prime ministers will find it more difficult to build and maintain anything close to a large, cohesive national party. To begin with, the constitution strips the prime minister of much of his leverage over factions within his own party. Politicians are no longer required to give up their House seats in order to join the cabinet, meaning the costs

---

[29] It is important to note that the junta leaders appear not to have gotten all that they wanted. Some controversial proposals for which coup leaders expressed support, such as eliminating the party list, instituting a "crisis council," or allowing for a non-elected prime minister, were defeated after much debate and public criticism.

of breaking with the prime minister are lower than under the 1997 constitution. The new constitution also effectively removes barriers to party switching. Candidates must still belong to a party at least 90 days prior to a general election. However, an exception is now made for any sudden or unexpected dissolution of the House. In the case of such an early dissolution, candidates must belong to a party for only 30 days in order to be election eligible. Since elections must be held within 45 to 60 days after a House dissolution, the effect of this change is to take away the prime minister's ability to threaten an early election as a way to keep potentially promiscuous party members from jumping ship.

The 2007 Constitution reduces the size of the prize associated with the premiership in two additional ways. First, new constitution includes provisions to ensure that future governments cannot guarantee their security in office by capturing a supermajority of the parliament. Thaksin was able to achieve effective immunity from no confidence challenges after winning more than 75% of the seats in the 2005 elections, leaving the opposition with less than the 40% of the seats required by law to launch a no confidence debate. The new constitution lowers the seat requirement for launching a debate to 20% (Section 158). More fundamentally, the constitution also allows half of the opposition MPs to join together to launch a censure debate against the government if the total number of opposition MPs is less than the 20% of the total House membership typically required (Section 160). In effect, what this means is that, short of winning every seat, no party can ever again secure immunity from censure debate.[30]

Second, the new constitution limits the potential power of the premiership by placing a two-term limit on the office. This measure was designed to make it impossible for Thaksin to return as prime minister and to prevent the rise of a future Thaksin. Term limits are a rare thing in a parliamentary context, and Thailand is one of only a few countries to have adopted term limits for its prime minister. At most, Thai prime ministers will be able to serve 8 years in office before being forced to step down. In reality, most governments will likely not survive the full 4-year term in the new institutional environment, and hence even very popular prime ministers will likely serve less than the possible 8 years.

---

[30] Section 160 cannot be invoked until the government has been in office at least 2 years.

Explaining Aggregation in Thailand

If the theory outlined in Chapter 2 is valid, we should expect an increase in the number of parties and a decrease the degree of nationalization as a result of the 2007 reforms. To begin with, the number of parties in each district should grow modestly due to the increase in district magnitude. However, the number of parties nationally should increase by a greater amount due to the decrease in aggregation incentives and resulting deterioration of cross-district coordination.

The first election under the new constitution was held on December 23, 2007. As of publication, the official district-level results from the election were not available. However, preliminary unofficial district-level results were available via various newspaper Web sites.[31] The inferences from these data should be treated as indicative rather than authoritative, both because the results are still unofficial, and because data from about 20% of the districts are incomplete. We should also be cautious about drawing conclusions from a single election – particularly one that follows such a major political shock as the 2006 coup was. However, to the extent the 2007 election was unusual, the bias should work against the hypotheses of declining aggregation and more parties. The 2007 elections took place in a highly polarized environment with the population divided into two camps. The first group consisted of the supporters of ousted Prime Minister Thaksin Shinawatra, who remains very popular in Thailand. Though the Thai Rak Thai Party was disbanded and Thaksin was barred from standing in the election, the Palang Prachachon Party (PPP) took up the banner of the pro-Thaksin forces and received active support (financial and otherwise) from Thaksin. The anti-Thaksin forces made up the second camp in the 2007 race, and their primary standard bearer was the Democrat Party, Thailand's oldest party and the party widely viewed as the most viable alternative to Thaksin and the PPP. Given this highly polarized environment, it would not be surprising to observe *no* measurable change in aggregation or the number of parties. The imperatives of polarization would potentially be more than enough to compensate for the weaker aggregation incentives generated by the 2007 Constitution.

---

[31] *Matichon* and *The Nation*, two daily newspapers, both reported district-level results. The analysis here uses data from *Matichon* (http://info.matichon.co.th/election/elec50/politarea.php?z=1).

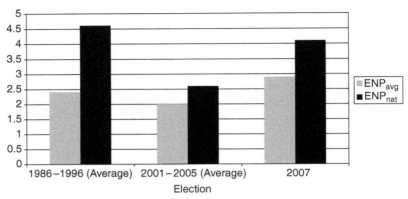

FIGURE 5.4. Effective Number of Parties: District Versus National

It is therefore interesting to see that despite the potentially mitigating effects of polarization, the results of the 2007 election support the hypotheses outlined earlier. As expected, we see a modest increase in the average effective number of parties at the district level, from 2 to 2.9 – an increase of 45% (see Figure 5.4). The number of parties nationally also increases from 2.6 to 4.1 – an increase of 58%. As expected, with weaker aggregation incentives, there was a deterioration of cross-district coordination.[32] This is reflected in a 24% increase in the inflation score, from an average 23 in 2001 and 2005 to 29 in 2007.

5.6 CONCLUSION

In any polity, the number of political parties is shaped by the extent to which voters and candidates are able to coordinate their behavior. Most analyses of strategic coordination have focused on the strategic entry decisions of parties/candidates and the strategic voting decisions of voters – all at the district level. As a result of this work, researchers are relatively well equipped to make sense of district level electoral outcomes. Indeed, analysis of the district-level party systems in Thailand revealed that the effective number of parties did vary by district magnitude prior to 1997, in line with theoretical expectations (Chapter 4), and that a shift to single-seat districts in 1997 caused the effective number of parties to fall (this chapter).

---

[32] The inflation score does not rise to pre-1997 levels, consistent with the higher polarization in 2007 compared to the pre-1997 elections.

However, theoretical tools such as Duverger's law and the $M + 1$ rule, restricted as they are to predictions at the district level, cannot sufficiently account for the effective number of parties nationally. Instead, we need to understand when candidates have incentives to coordinate across districts – to link together under a shared party label.

I have argued that these aggregation incentives are a function of (a) the payoff to being the largest party at the national level (the aggregation payoff) and (b) the odds that the largest party will capture that payoff. In this chapter, I used the theory developed in Chapter 2 to help explain the lack of aggregation and large number of parties in pre-reform Thailand and the effects of the 1997 constitutional reforms. In pre-1997 Thailand, an appointed Senate, factionalized party system, and reserve domains combined to limit the size of the potential aggregation payoff. The practice of selecting someone other than the leader of the largest party as premier for much of the period also reduced the expected utility of aggregation. Given the weak aggregation incentives, cross-district coordination in pre-reform Thailand was poor, and the result was a large number of parties at the national level. The 1997 constitutional reforms magnified candidates' aggregation incentives chiefly by increasing the premier's leverage over internal party factions. This increased the potential size of the aggregation payoff resulting in better aggregation and fewer national parties. The 2007 Constitution once again reduced the power of the prime minister, thereby undermining aggregation incentives and leading to a decline in aggregation and an increase in the number of parties nationally.

5.7 APPENDIX

The Effect of the Senate and Party List Tier on Aggregation

Two other 1997 constitutional reforms worth noting are the switch to a fully elected Senate and the addition of a national party list tier for House elections. As I discuss here, neither of these reforms (or the counterreforms in 2007) generates strong, consistent predictions about changes to aggregation incentives.

Changes to the Senate
The 1997 Constitution replaced the appointed Senate with a fully elected body. However, the effect of this change on aggregation incentives was

negligible. First, the Senate's formal powers did not change a great deal – the Senate still had only delaying power.[33] Second, the Senate was now directly elected but it remained outside the direct, formal control of Thailand's political parties, as was the case before the reforms.[34] Senators were constitutionally prohibited from belonging to a political party and were allowed only one term – drafters wanted to create a legislative body that would remain above the petty political squabbling that in their view characterized the House (Suchit 1999). Thus, even where a party controlled the House of Representatives, the Senate could potentially remain outside of the control of the prime minister.[35] Third, recall that much of the power of the appointed Senate stemmed from its role as a reserve domain for Thailand's conservative forces. In short, the authority of the old Senate was a function of whom it represented (military and bureaucracy) rather than its formal powers. By the time of the 1997 constitutional reforms, the Senate had already largely ceased to operate as a reserve domain through the appointment of nonmilitary/bureaucratic individuals to the Senate. In short, the change to an elected Senate in 1997 may have be an important step forward for Thai democracy, but we would not expect it to have a substantial impact on aggregation incentives.

The changes to the Senate under the 2007 Constitution may not have such an innocuous effect on aggregation incentives.[36] The 2007 charter replaced the fully elected Senate with a new, partially appointed body. Specifically, the new Senate consists of 150 seats: 76 of those seats are to be filled via elections in Thailand's provinces – one seat for each province. The remaining 74 seats will be selected by a special committee that will choose members from among experts and prominent figures in a

---

[33] The new Senate did have added responsibilities for appointing members of the new superintendent and oversight institutions the constitution established.

[34] The first Senate elections were held in 2000.

[35] There are, of course, many informal means for parties and the prime minister to exert influence on the Senate, and in practice there were significant ties between many Senators and political parties. For example, many Senators were relatives of prominent party politicians (Nelson 2000). Thaksin was also accused of trying to bring the Senate under his thumb through various means (though it is hard to say whether his leverage over the Senate was a result of it becoming an elected body or rather the advent of stable majority party government (and the end of short-lived coalition governments.)) To the extent an elected Senate did provide for more influence for political parties and the prime minister on the Senate, this should have improved aggregation incentives, which is consistent with the data.

[36] This discussion draws on Hicken (2007c).

variety of fields. The selection committee includes the president of the Constitutional Court, the president of the Election Commission, the president of the Office of Auditor General, the president of the National Counter Corruption Commission, the parliamentary ombudsman, a judge from the Supreme Court of Justice, and a judge from the Supreme Administrative Court.[37]

There is an important distinction between this new Senate and appointed Senates from Thailand's past. Under the 1978 and 1991 Constitutions, Senators were appointed by the king, and the appointment then had to be countersigned by the prime minister. In practice, the prime minister often played an important role in recommending potential Senators to the king for his endorsement. Under the 2007 charter, the prime minister no longer has a direct role to play in the appointment process.[38] He is not a member of the selection panel, and he no longer countersigns the selection list. This raises the possibility that the Senate could once again become a serious reserve domain for Thailand's conservative forces.

In the end, the reintroduction of appointed senators should reduce the leverage future prime ministers will have over the Senate. In fact, given that the prime minister is now completely cut out of the selection process, his influence over the Senate may be even less than it was during the late 1980s and 1990s. The fact that the Senate still possesses only delaying power in legislative mitigates somewhat the effect of these changes, but on balance the switch to a partially appointed Senate could potentially undermine aggregation incentives.

National Party List Tier

Following a growing trend (see Shugart and Wattenberg 2000) the 1997 Constitution drafters established a mixed-member or two-tiered system in Thailand. The 400 seats of the nominal tier were elected from single-member districts on a plurality basis as described previously. One hundred additional seats made up the list tier and were elected from a single nationwide district via proportional representation. (The

---

[37] Disturbingly, the Senate itself selects many of these appointees in the first place, at best muddying the lines of accountability, at worst raising the possibility of a quid pro quo.

[38] Note the monarch also appears to play no direct role in the selection process, which is different from the 1978 and 1991 Constitutions.

2007 Constitution reduced the list tier to 80 seats and divided up the national district into eight separate regional districts.) Each party was required to submit a list of candidates for voters to consider, and voters cast two votes: one vote for a district representative and one for a party list. Candidates had to choose between either running in a district or running on the party list. The two tiers were not linked in any way (i.e., votes from one tier did not transfer to the other tier).

How might the change to a mixed-member system lead to changes in aggregation incentives and the number of parties? There is no straightforward expectation since the addition of a national party list tier generates competing incentives. On the one hand, the mixed-member system as used in Thailand gives Thai voters multiple votes, and we know that multiple votes tend to put upward pressure on the effective number of parties (Lijphart 1994, 118–24). In addition, the national party list potentially makes it easier for small, subnational parties to win seats in parliament. Since seats are awarded on a proportional basis, small parties that in the past could not win, nor even field enough candidates to meet the electoral requirement, can now win seats as long as they obtain over 5% of the party list votes. If many more small parties won seats under the new system, this would increase the effective number of parties.

Pushing in the opposite direction are the stronger incentives to coordinate across districts generated by the presence of the national list tier. The presence of the national list tier is in part an electoral bonus for linking together to form a large, national party (and to that extent, the change to *regional* part lists in 2007 should undermine aggregation incentives). Parties large enough to be competitive across the nation should capture more list tier seats than provincial or regional parties with limited national appeal. Locally strong parties but nationally weak parties may be able to capture some seats in the nominal tier, but national parties should dominate the list tier seats both at the national level and in any given district.

In conclusion, even though the list tier may have important consequences for other aspects of Thailand's party system (Hicken 2006), its effect on aggregation is theoretically indeterminate.

6

Term Limits, Aggregation Incentives, and the Number of Parties in the Philippines

6.1 INTRODUCTION

In many respects, the party systems of Thailand and the Philippines look very similar. In both countries, party labels have historically been weak, party switching is rampant, and party cohesion is low. Where Thailand and the Philippines diverge is in the number of parties at the national level. Recall that in Thailand the average effective number of parties nationally prior to constitutional reform was 7.2. The corresponding figure for the Philippines over the course of its democratic history is a more modest 2.6. However, as in Thailand, there is substantial variation over time in the number of parties. Specifically, in the democratic period before martial law the effective number of parties at the national level averaged 2.3. After the fall of Marcos, the number of parties increased to 3.6 on average. Why this large increase? The inflation of the party system post-Marcos has long been a puzzle for scholars of Philippine politics, and this chapter provides an answer to that puzzle that is superior to existing explanations. How, too, do we explain the differences in the size of the Philippine and Thai party systems? Drawing on the theory from Chapter 2, I explain, first, why the post-Marcos party system has been much larger than the pre–martial law party system and, second, why cross-district coordination differs across the two countries. I demonstrate that differences in the number of parties between Thailand and the Philippines are primarily a product of aggregation and not variations in the two countries' electoral systems.

This chapter proceeds as follows. I first briefly review the history of the Philippine party system and provide a basic description of its characteristics. I next apply the aggregation incentives theory to the pre- and postauthoritarian Filipino party systems to explain the growth in the effective number of national parties since 1986. I argue that adopting a one-term limit on the presidency introduced greater uncertainty into presidential elections. The result is delayed aggregation and the reverse of the concurrency effect usually observed in presidential elections (Shugart 1995). Finally, I compare the local and national party systems in Thailand and the Philippines and demonstrate that the difference in the number of parties nationally is foremost a reflection of different levels of aggregation (and aggregation incentives) across the two countries. For most of its democratic history, aggregation incentives in the Philippines were stronger than those in Thailand, but recent institutional reforms in both countries have brought about a reversal.

6.2 THE HISTORY AND DEVELOPMENT OF THE PHILIPPINES PARTY SYSTEM

The Philippines has one of the oldest democratic traditions in Asia.[1] Under U.S. colonial auspices, elections for both national and local offices were the norm in the Philippines from the early 1900s. After a brief interruption during Japanese occupation, elections resumed in 1946 in a fully independent Philippines. Elections were a mainstay of Filipino life until 1972 when President Ferdinand Marcos declared martial law. After 14 years of dictatorship, democratic government was restored in 1986. The post-Marcos constitutional drafters chose to reinstate the pre-Marcos American-style presidential system, with an elected president, a House of Representatives and a Senate.

What has the Filipino party system looked like during the two democratic periods since independence? (See Box 6.1.) As I will discuss in more detail later the post–Marcos party system was different from

---

[1] Thanks in part to the country's relatively long electoral history, Filipino elections and parties have received more scholarly attention than their Thai counterparts. See for example, Hayden (1950), Grossholtz (1964), Corpuz (1965), Landé (1965, 1996), Liang (1970), Wurfel (1988), Tancango (1992), Carlos and Banlaoi (1996), Banlaoi and Carlos (1996), Carlos (1998a, 1998b, 1998c); Hartmann, Hassall, and Santos (2001), and Hutchcroft and Rocamora (2003).

Box 6.1: Four Periods of Filipino Party Development

U.S. Colonial Period: 1901–1946. As the U.S. colonial administration organized first local, then national elections, several parties formed to compete for elected office. By the 1907 election, the Nacionalista Party (NP) had become the largest party, and it remained the largest party in virtually every election from 1907 to 1941. However, the NP did not go unchallenged. Factional infighting caused regular defections from the NP, and strong second parties ran against the NP in many elections.

Two-party Period: 1946–1972. After independence, two parties emerged as the dominant electoral forces – the Nacionalista Party and the Liberal Party. These two parties were the largest parties in every national election from 1946 to 1972. The relatively stable two-party system masked significant factional splits within the two parties and frequent party switching or 'turncoatism' by politicians.

Marcos Dictatorship: 1972–1986. After President Marcos declared martial law in 1972, all existing parties were dissolved, including Marcos's own NP. In their place, Marcos organized Kilusang Bagong Lipunan (KBL or New Society Movement). The KBL was the de facto party of the government and dominated elections during the Marcos years. Several opposition parties were organized in the late 1970s and early 1980s. During the 1980s, several of these parties allied together to form the United Democratic Opposition (UNIDO).

Post-Marcos Period: 1986–. The defeat of Marcos in 1986 brought the return of elected government and most of the democratic institutions from the pre-Marcos period. The two-party system did not return, however. Instead, a multiparty system has emerged marked by frequent party turnover.

its predecessor in at least one important respect – the number of national parties. A relatively stable two-party system had been the norm pre-Marcos – with the Nacionalista and Liberal Parties vying for power in every election. However, it was a multiparty system that materialized after democracy returned. Although this change is interesting and significant, the change from a two-party to multiparty system masks an underlying constancy on other dimensions of the Philippine party system. Parties in both periods are characterized by factionalism, frequent party switching (called turncoatism in the Philippines), and party labels that generally mean little to voters or candidates. Like

Thai parties, Philippines parties are generally organized around a powerful leader, or a temporary alliance of leaders, and tend to be primarily concerned with distributing the spoils of government to themselves and their local supporters.

The lack of intra-party cohesion is one of the most notable features of Filipino parties (Landé 1965, 1996; Machado 1978; Banlaoi and Carlos 1996). Parties are generally not unified actors, but instead are atomized and/or composed of competing factions or "wings." Factionalism emerged early as a property of the party system and continues to be a feature of many parties. Another indication of the lack of cohesion is the tradition of party switching, or turncoatism. Party switching is a regular part of every election in the Philippines, including elections for the highest office in the land. Ramon Magsaysay and Ferdinand Marcos left leadership positions in the Liberal Party to run for president under the Nacionalista label. In 1992, Fidel Ramos formed LAKAS-NUCD to support his presidential bid after he failed to win the LDP nomination. At lower levels of government, party switching occurs both before and after elections and has important implications for the political economy of policymaking (Hicken 2002). Party switching in the Philippines is generally in one direction – toward the president's party. The Philippines president controls valuable resources – namely pork and political appointments. As a result, candidates make an effort to align themselves with the strongest presidential contenders prior to elections. Once the presidential elections are complete, many who find themselves in the parties of losing candidates rush to join the president's party. Indeed, within the House of Representatives enough party switching can occur to change the status of the president's party from the minority to the majority party, as happened after the election of Presidents Macapagal, Marcos, Aquino, and Ramos (Liang 1970; Banlaoi and Carlos 1996; Landé 1996).

Switching to the president's party in an effort to maximize governmental largess is a fact of life at all levels of government, from members of Congress to local officials. Table 6.1 presents party switching data from the 1995 election as an example. The pattern of switching is clearly evident in the behavior of incumbent House members and governors. Overall, more than 48% of incumbent representatives switched parties between the 1992 and 1995 elections, with most switching shortly after the 1992 election was complete. Of the turncoats, nearly 90% joined

TABLE 6.1. *Party Switching Prior to the 1995 Election*

Percentage of incumbent House members that switched	48.5
Percentage switched to LAKAS-NUCD	89.9
Percentage switched to other parties	10.1
Percentage of incumbent governors that switched	35.1
Percentage switched to LAKAS-NUCD	88.5
Percentage switched to other parties	11.5

Sources: Author's calculations from Commission on Elections (1992, 1995).

President Ramos's LAKAS-NUCD party. This is supportive of Kasuya's (2001a) finding that for all House elections (1946–71; 1992–8) an average of 49.3% of opposition incumbents switched to the president's party by the next election.[2] The pattern is similar among incumbent governors. Prior to the 1995 election, 35% of incumbent governors had switched parties, and of those, 88.5% had moved to the president's party.

The high rate of party switching is indicative of weak party labels in the Philippines. Another indication is the relatively high level of electoral volatility – particularly since the return of democracy in 1986. During the pre–martial law period, the dominance of the Liberal and Nacionalista Parties is reflected in a relatively low electoral volatility score of 18.5. In comparative terms, this tally places the Philippines on par with France and Argentina (Table 6.2). Since 1986 the electoral fortunes of Filipino parties have been much more unstable.[3] Electoral volatility for the 1992, 1995 and 1998 elections is more than double the pre–martial law figure at 37.3, more than the volatility in Brazil and Thailand.[4]

---

[2] Kasuya also found a similar pattern in the Senate where an average of 33.3% of opposition incumbents switched to the president's party between elections (2001a, 23).

[3] Calculating electoral volatility for the Philippines post-1986 is difficult due to shifting party alliances and the fact that candidates often run under more than one party label. As a rule of thumb I treated each party in a temporary electoral alliance as a separate party. For candidates that ran under more than one party label, I credited the votes to the largest party with which the candidate was affiliated (measured by vote share in that election). In the few cases where candidates declared themselves independent but also ran under a party label, those candidates were treated as independent.

[4] Vote share data are not available for the 1987 election. For the 1992 election, the vote shares data are available for only 174 of the 200 districts. For the 1998 election, vote share data are based on parties' performance in the nominal tier seats. An alternative way to measure electoral volatility is to calculate changes in seat rather than vote shares. Seat share data tells the same story – greater volatility post-Marcos. During the 1946–69 period, volatility was 28.0 versus 45.4 from 1987 to 1998.

TABLE 6.2. *Lower Chamber Electoral Volatility*

Country	Time Span	No. of Elections	Mean Volatility
United States	1944–94	25	4.0
United Kingdom	1974–97	6	8.3
Uruguay	1974–94	3	10.4
Italy	1946–96	13	12.0
France	1945–93	14	18.3
Philippines I	**1946–69**	7	18.5
Argentina	1973–95	7	18.8
Venezuela	1973–96	6	22.5
Costa Rica	1974–98	7	25.0
Poland	1991–94	3	28.4
Brazil	1982–94	4	33.0
Thailand	1983–96	7	34.0
Philippines II	**1992–98**	3	37.3
Russia	1993–99	3	60.0

Sources: Mainwaring (1999); author's calculations from Hartmann, Hassall, and Santos (2001); Parliamentary Elections around the World (http://ww.universal.nl/users/dreksen/election); Elections around the World (http://www.agora.stm.it/elections/); Centre for the Study of Public Policy (http://www.cspp.strath.ac.uk//intro.html); Election Resources on the Internet presented by Manuel Álvarez-Rivera (http://electionresources.org/).

There are other indications that party labels mean little to candidates. Guest candidatures – where a party invites a candidate from another party to run under its banner without formally switching parties – are not uncommon. It is also not unusual for candidates to eschew attachment to a single party, opting instead to run as an independent or as a joint candidate – a candidate running under more than one party banner. In the 1992 election, candidates with joint affiliation or with no party affiliation whatsoever captured 7% of the House seats.[5] In 1995, they captured 15%. Interestingly, nearly 7% of the 1995 seats went to candidates who carried the banners for the government party *and* one of the opposition parties.

Like candidates, voters do not place a high value on party label. Voters frequently split their votes between candidates from different parties (Mangahas 1998). Nowhere is this more evident than in the election of president and vice-president. Filipino voters cast two separate votes, one for a presidential candidate and one for a vice-presidential candidate.

[5] This excludes candidates that ran as part of the formal LAKAS-LDP electoral alliance.

These votes need not be for candidates from the same political party. Taking advantage of this rule, voters frequently split their votes between candidates from two different parties. As a result, both the 1992 and 1998 presidential elections returned a president and vice-president from different political parties. In 1998, the vote shares of presidential and vice-presidential running mates differed by an average of 18.7 percentage points.

Filipino parties also tend to have less than national constituencies, like their Thai counterparts. Few, if any post–Marcos parties could be described as national parties. Parties have been unable to cultivate lasting nationwide support (witness the high level of electoral volatility) and most lack a national policy focus. Even during the pre-1972, two-parties system, the Nacionalista and Liberal Parties are best seen as shallow alliances of locally based and locally focused politicians, rather than cohesive national political parties with distinct policy visions. Politicians' electoral fortunes depend primarily upon their ability to deliver targeted benefits to narrow constituencies rather than collective goods to more national constituencies. In short, candidates, and their respective parties, have a focus that is more local than national.

One indication of this subnational focus is the lack of a serious national policy or ideological orientation by Filipino parties.[6] Party platforms are notable for their lack of distinctive ideological or national policy content. An extreme example occurred in the run up to a recent election. Several different parties, including parties in both the government and opposition, ended up hiring the same group of consultants to write their party platforms. Because of the strong similarities across all of the platforms the consultants adopted a simple rule to keep each distinct – use a different font for each.[7] As this anecdote illustrates, the major differences between parties are not differences over national policy. Elections then are not battles between different ideologies or party programs but rather struggles between personalities for the control of government resources.

To summarize, far from being cohesive unitary actors, political parties in the Philippines are factionalized or atomized. Party switching occurs

---

[6] The only exception to this is parties on the Left – which have generally performed poorly at the polls – and some new party list parties each of which can capture a maximum of three seats in the House.

[7] Interview with political consultant, July 2000. Anonymity requested.

regularly, and party labels carry little weight for either voters or candidates. In addition, party constituencies are more local than national. In the words of one scholar: "Far from being stable, programmatic organizations, the country's main political parties are nebulous entities that can be set up, merged with others, split, resurrected, regurgitated, reconstituted, renamed, repackaged, recycled or flushed down the toilet anytime" (Quimpo 2005). This characterization of the Philippine party system is consistent with a lack of party system institutionalization, as defined by Mainwaring and Scully (1995). Recall that Mainwaring and Scully define institutionalized party systems as those in which (a) there is a regular pattern of electoral competition, (b) parties have stable roots in society, and (c) parties have organizations that "matter." While a stable two-party system was the norm prior to 1972, parties in the post–Marcos period have yet to exhibit regular patterns of competition. As the electoral volatility figures suggest, party fortunes vary greatly from election to election.

Political parties also lack stable roots in society. One indication of this is the high degree of electoral volatility. Another is the average age of the largest parties since the return of democracy. One might have expected that a return to democracy would bring a return to prominence of the Nacionalista and Liberal Parties – the two parties that dominated the pre–martial law period. In many Latin American countries, there was just such a continuity of political parties before and after periods of authoritarian rule. In the Philippines, however, a return to democracy brought with it a whole host of new parties. The average age of parties with at least 10% of the House vote in the 1995 election was less than 6 years. Table 6.3 places this figure in a comparative context. Though the old Liberal and Nacionalista Parties were revived, they have yet to win more than a handful of seats in any of the post–Marcos elections.

Finally, parties have yet to develop party organizations that "matter," Mainwaring and Scully's third criterion. Parties remain centered around notable individuals and function almost solely as electoral vehicles. As a result, parties are noticeably devoid of any lasting organizational structure. In between elections, parties hibernate, with very little in the way of ongoing connections to party "members." A 1997 study of 10 Filipino parties found that every party considered mass member recruitment a top priority; however, none of the 10 parties were able to produce a membership list, suggesting that "political party memberships ... are as fluid

TABLE 6.3. *Years Since Founding of Parties with 10% of the Lower Chamber Vote, 1996*

Country, Election Year	Average Age
United States, 1996	154
Uruguay, 1994	115
Argentina, 1995	54
Costa Rica, 1994	47
France, 1993	43
Chile, 1993	40
Italy, 1996	39
Venezuela, 1993	29
Thailand, 1996	20
Brazil, 1994	13
Philippines, 1995	6

Sources: Mainwaring (1999); author's calculations.

as the party system itself." (Carlos 1997a, 220) The internal governance structure of parties is also notoriously weak. Members who deviate from the party line (when there is one) are rarely sanctioned. In fact, of the major political parties that were active during the 1980s and 1990s, only one has ever employed a party whip or similar institutions to compel members to toe the party line and protect the party label – Marcos's KBL Party (Kilusang Bagong Lipunan) (Carlos 1997a, 224). Finally, responsibility for and control of financing is very decentralized. Campaign contributions generally flow directly from the donor to candidate (or faction leader), totally bypassing the formal party organization (de Castro, Jr. 1992; Carlos 1997a).

There are a variety of historical, sociological, and institutional explanations for why the Philippines party system developed as it did. To begin with, the characteristics of party system partly reflect the Philippines' experience with colonialism and state building as well as the social structure in place as it transitioned to elected government. A weak central state has been the historical norm in the Philippines. In contrast to much of the rest of Southeast Asia, precolonial Philippines lacked major kingdoms able to exercise control over large areas.[8] The dearth of

[8] The only exceptions to this were the Muslim kingdoms in parts of the southern Philippines.

large political units enabled the Spanish to quickly conquer most areas of the Philippines. However, the new colonial administration was never able to exercise strong and centralized political control over the islands – relying instead on Catholic priests to represent its authority in most areas due to a chronic shortage of men and money (Andaya 1999). At the same time, a new class of large provincial landowners emerged in the Philippines that, in the vacuum of Spanish authority, gradually came to dominate much of provincial life. This land-owning elite, known as the oligarchs, became the patrons atop numerous patron–client networks spread throughout the Philippines (Tancango 1992).

It was into this environment that the United States stepped when it replaced Spain as the colonial power at the beginning of the twentieth century. Several of the U.S. colonial government's decisions had the unintended consequence of hampering the development of a more institutionalized, cohesive, nationally oriented party system (Hutchcroft and Rocamora 2003). First, even though the United States installed democratic institutions in the Philippines, it did very little to build up a strong central administrative bureaucracy. As a result, political and economic power remained spread among the various large land-owning elite throughout the country.

Second, the decentralized and fragmented nature of political life was reproduced at the national level via the early introduction of parties and elections in the Philippines (Hutchcroft and Rocamora 2003). As the political system was thrown open to electoral competition, those in the best position to compete for elected office were the oligarchs. The natural building blocks for their electoral machines and political parties were the pervasive patron–client networks. As a consequence, the oligarchs were able to use elections as a means of acquiring and strengthening political power, first locally, then nationally via congressional elections (Landé 1965; Wurfel 1988; Hutchcroft and Rocamora 2003). Political parties and Congress quickly became the domain of these powerful locally based interests, rather than a forum in which mass interests could be articulated and national policies debated.[9] Conflicts and competition between oligarchs manifested themselves via party switching or intra-party factionalism. In sum, the parties that came to

---

[9] For an analysis of the policy consequences of this arrangement, see Sidel (1996) and Hutchcroft (1998).

dominate the political system were not cohesive parties with national constituencies, but highly fragmented or atomized parties with narrow, particularistic constituencies.[10]

Historical and sociological variables are helpful for understanding the early development of the party system. However, they cannot completely account for why key features of the party system have endured in the Philippines. In fact, many of the sociological and historical factors have varied over time in a way that would seemingly support the emergence of a more institutionalized party system. By the 1960s, traditional patron–client networks were breaking down, beginning first in and around Manila and then spreading to other areas of the Philippines (Wurfel 1988). Likewise, a new class of business elite had emerged to challenge the power of the oligarchs. This business elite (largely Manila-based) had interests that were very different from the traditional landed-elite (Hawes 1992).

One could argue that path dependence might account for the stickiness of the party system in the face of these changes. However, given the political, economic, and social upheaval of the Marcos era, it is not difficult to imagine that new paths were at least possible after his fall from power. The extended presidency of Ferdinand Marcos accelerated the relative decline of the oligarchs as he sought to centralize political and economic authority while empowering a new class of cronies (Hawes 1992).[11] To oust him from power, opposition political parties joined together to back Corazon Aquino for president. They were supported by the mobilized mass of the Filipino populace. Yet this mass mobilization, greater centralization, and the relative decline of the oligarchs did not lead to the creation of large, mass-based national parties. Nor did the coming together of different opposition groups to overthrow Marcos translate into more cohesive parties post-Marcos. Instead, the party system that emerged was similar in most respects to the pre-1972

[10] The fact that the U.S. colonial administration retained the major responsibility for public policy, even after a national elected legislature was in place, did much to facilitate the development of locally focused particularistic parties. It was not until 1934, when the Philippines was able to win Commonwealth status, that the provision of national policies fell to elected politicians. Prior to 1934, national policymaking was the purview of the colonial government, and as a result parties and elected representatives were free to engage in other pursuits (Stauffer 1975).

[11] For an opposing view (i.e., that the reports of oligarchs' deaths were highly exaggerated), see Putzel 1993.

party system. One explanation for the continuity of the party system, despite the significant changes that occurred before and during the Marcos era, is the continuity of key features of the Philippine institutional environment.[12]

Alongside the historical and sociological factors discussed earlier, certain features of the Philippines institutional environment encourage the development of locally focused, noncohesive parties – namely, a powerful presidency and the electoral system. These two features have remained relatively constant across the pre- and postauthoritarian periods and reinforced, and in some cases amplified, the effects of sociological and historical factors.

To begin with, many Filipino scholars blame the establishment of a strong president for the state of the party system (see, e.g., Grossholtz 1964; Wurfel 1988; Banlaoi and Carlos 1996).[13] A powerful presidency undermines party cohesiveness, frees legislators and parties to focus on particularistic concerns (leaving national policies in the hands of the president), and generally discourages the development of a structured party system. This observation is not unique to the Philippines – presidentialism is often associated with weak and noncohesive legislative parties (Lijphart, Rogowski, and Weaver 1993, 322).[14]

In addition to the powerful presidency, the nature of the Philippines' electoral system also helped shape the development of the party system. Specifically, the electoral systems for the House and Senate give candidates strong incentives to pursue a personal strategy while discounting the value of party label. Members of the House of Representatives are

---

[12] The unwillingness of Aquino to capitalize on her popularity to form her own political party or take over the leadership of an existing party also contributed to the return of an unstructured party system.

[13] The pre-1972 Philippines presidency was among the strongest in the world. In the aftermath of the Marcos regime, some of that authority was curtailed, but the president retains an impressive array of both proactive and reactive powers. In Shugart's index of presidential power, the post-1986 presidency rates as "strong" (Shugart 1999).

[14] However, one must be cautious regarding the direction of causality. While a relationship exists between strong presidents and unstructured parties the causal arrows can run both ways. A strong presidency may prevent the rise of a structure party system, but it may also be employed as an institutional antidote in polities with unstructured parties (Shugart 1999). In fact, the effort to institutionalize a powerful executive by the Philippines' first President, Manuel Quezon, was in part a reaction to the perceived shortcomings of the party system (Quezon 1940).

elected from single-seat districts using the plurality rule (SMDP) – a system that is often associated with weak parties and locally focused legislators (Cain, Ferejohn, and Fiorina 1987; Carey and Shugart 1995; Cox and McCubbins 1993).[15] This is certainly the case for the version of SMDP used in the Philippines. Candidates are not required to obtain the nomination or endorsement of a political party in order to run for office. Candidates may run as independents or run under the banner of more than one party.[16] For their part, party officials often lack strong control over nomination and endorsement within their own party. Strong candidates can usually run under the label of their choosing. In some cases, strong/wealthy candidates will use a party's label with or without the party's official endorsement (Wurfel 1988, 96). Districts featuring multiple candidates from a single party (known as "free zones") were more common before martial law (63% of districts), but after martial law free zones were still found in 20% of the districts nationwide (Kasuya 2001a). In such situations, intra-party competition can arise with two or more candidates from the same party running against each other. This lack of party ballot control undermines candidates' incentives to pursue party-centered campaign strategies. In fact, according to Carey and Shugart, the type of electoral system used in the House generates some of the strongest incentives to cultivate a personal vote of any electoral system (Carey and Shugart 1995, 425). This cultivation of a personal vote comes at the expense of the party label and party cohesion and generally requires candidates to focus on narrow constituencies.

The method of electing the Senate has also played a part in the development of an under-institutionalized party system. The Senate

---

[15] The provision for a mixed-member system was included in the 1987 Constitution, but a law fully implementing the measure was not passed until 1995 and not used in an election until 1998. The party list seats make up to 20% of the total House and are allocated using proportional representation. Both political parties and sectoral organizations can compete for the seats, save the five largest parties from the previous election, which are barred from competing. To obtain a seat, parties (or sectoral organizations) must receive at least 2% of the party list votes. For every 2% of the vote, a party is awarded a seat, with an upper limit of three seats in the list tier. During the 1998 elections, only 13 parties passed the 2% threshold and so many party list seats were unfilled. The remaining seats were filled by appointed representatives from groups that fell below the threshold. The rule was subsequently changed to require that unfilled seats be distributed among parties above the 2% threshold, but below the three-seat cap (Hicken and Kasuya 2003).
[16] See the earlier discussion of guest and joint candidacies.

consists of 24 seats, with 12 seats contested every 3 years. Senators are elected from a single nationwide district using the block vote electoral system – the same system used in Thai elections. Each voter casts up to 12 votes – each for a distinct candidate. Seats are awarded to the 12 senators with the highest vote totals. As in the Thai case, the block vote encourages senatorial candidates to eschew party strategies in favor of personal strategies. Senate elections are first and foremost personality contests, and senators generally possess little in the way of party loyalty. Multiple votes allow voters to split their votes among senatorial candidates from different parties – something Filipino voters frequently take advantage of. In every Senate election since 1957, voters have returned candidates from more than one party. (If voters were casting votes on the basis of party label, they would cast all of their votes for candidates from the same party, and all 12 seats would go to a single party.)[17] The vote shares of copartisans also vary widely, another indication that voters split their votes among different parties. In the post-1987 Senate elections, a party's top vote-getter has received as many as 2.7 times the number of votes as other victorious copartisans.[18]

Another contributing factor is the write-in ballot used in Filipino elections. Voters are required to write in the name of each of their chosen candidates for every elected office. Given that local and national elections are synchronized, this can mean that voters must write-in up to 40 names on election day.[19] This cumbersome ballot structure provides voters with ample opportunities to split their votes among many different parties, thus undermining the value of party label. This was not always the case. Shortly after independence, the election code was revised to allow for party voting. Rather than writing individual candidates' names, voters could write in the name of a party and the ballot would be "deemed as a

---

[17] This assumes that all parties present a full slate of senatorial candidates and that voters cast all 12 votes. In reality, the largest parties almost always run a full slate, while many smaller parties present only partial slates. In addition, voters may not cast all of their votes.

[18] Author's calculations from Commission on Elections (1992, 1995, 1998, 2001, 2004).

[19] For this reason, the distribution of sample ballots to voters becomes extremely important. Prior to elections most candidates distribute sample ballots containing their name and the names of candidates for other offices. Tellingly, it is not uncommon for these sample ballots to contain the names of candidates from more than one party. Candidates often include popular candidates from other parties running in other races on their sample ballot in a bid to bolster their own electoral prospects.

Philippines: Term Limits, Aggregation Incentives, No. of Parties 163

vote for each and every one of the official candidates of such party for the respective offices" (Revised Election Code of 1947, Article XI, Section 149, No. 19). A 1951 amendment to the Election Code eliminated the party voting option and, subsequently, split ticket voting became the norm in elections (Wurfel 1988, 94).

To summarize, the Philippine electoral system is one that discourages the development of an institutionalized party system. In the House, SMDP with weak control of nominations undermines the value of party label. Similarly, the Senate's block vote system privileges personal over party strategies. Finally, the write-in ballot gives voters ample opportunity to split their votes between different parties.

6.3 ACCOUNTING FOR CHANGE IN THE FILIPINO PARTY SYSTEM

While in many respects the Philippines' party system today looks similar to the pre–martial law norm, this constancy masks changes in aggregation and aggregation incentives over time. In the last chapter, I discussed the way in which constitutional reforms altered aggregation incentives in Thailand. Constitutional reform also led to change in aggregation incentives in the Philippines. In this section, I explore the way in which aggregation has varied across the Philippines' democratic history, focusing specifically on the pre– and post–martial law party systems. Recall that from 1946 to 1972 the Philippines had regular, democratic elections. President Ferdinand Marcos brought an end to democracy by declaring martial law on September 21, 1972. After 14 years of the Marcos regime, democratic government returned to the Philippines in 1986 in dramatic fashion. After Marcos's attempt to steal the 1986 snap presidential election, millions of Filipinos jammed the streets of EDSA avenue in a show of people's power. For three days, the people stared down Marcos and the military, culminating in the end of the Marcos's dictatorship and a return to democratic government.

Many features of the pre-1972 party system returned along with democracy. The Nacionalista and Liberal Parties were reborn after Marcos, though at only a fraction of their former strength. Many of the individual and family faces prominent during the earlier democratic period reemerged as party leaders after 1986 and, as discussed in the preceding section, post-Marcos political parties were just as weak as

TABLE 6.4. *Aggregation and the Number of Parties before and after Martial Law*

Country (election year)	Average ENP$_{avg}$	Average ENP$_{nat}$	Average I
Philippines I (1946–69)	2.0	2.3	9.8
Philippines II (1992–98)	2.3	3.6	32

Sources: Author's calculations from COMELEC (various years); Hartmann et al. (2001); Kasuya (2001b).

their predecessors. However, at least one characteristic of the earlier democratic period did not return – the stable national two-party system. From 1946 to 1969, the average effective number of national parties (ENP$_{nat}$) was 2.3. Since 1987, ENP$_{nat}$ averages 3.6 (see Table 6.4), reaching a high of just under 5 in the 1992 election.[20] This rise in the number of parties has been the subject of much scholarly attention in the Philippine literature (see for example Kimura 1992; Kasuya 2001b). I will first demonstrate that the rise in the number of parties nationally is primarily the result of deteriorating aggregation post-Marcos. I will then review some of the existing explanations for the rise in the number of parties and argue that they are either incorrect or incomplete. Finally, I will show how changes to the 1987 constitution undermined the incentives to coordinate across districts during concurrent elections.

6.3.1 The Deterioration of Aggregation Post-Marcos

What is the source of the growth in the number of national parties post-Marcos? As Table 6.5 makes clear, this growth is not a result of many more parties winning seats at the district level after 1986. From 1946 to 1969, the average effective number of parties at the district level was 2.0. After 1986, ENP$_{avg}$ increased only slightly to 2.3, an increase of less than 11%.[21] Indeed, a large change in ENP$_{avg}$ would be surprising given that

---

[20] Data are from the 1992, 1995, and 1998 elections. The 1987, 2001, and 2004 elections are excluded due to the lack of comprehensive data on candidate and party vote shares.

[21] ENP$_{avg}$ for the Philippines is actually the average effective number of candidates (ENC$_{avg}$). Because House elections use single-seat districts the ENC$_{avg}$ should be nearly equal to ENP$_{avg}$. The exception is where, due to the Philippines lax nomination requirements, more than one candidate declares for the same party. Where this is the case ENC$_{avg}$ will be slightly higher than ENP$_{avg}$.

TABLE 6.5. ENP_{res}, ENP_{nat}, and ENP_{seat} Compared (Concurrent Elections)

Year	ENP_{res}	ENP_{nat}	ENP_{seat}
1946	2.0	3.3	2.9
1949	2.4	2.4	2.1
1953	1.7	2.6	2.3
1957	3.4	2.1	1.5
1961	2.0	2.0	1.7
1965	2.2	2.3	2.1
1969	1.9	2.1	1.5
Average: 1946–69	2.2	2.4	2.0
1992	5.8	5.0	3.5
1998	4.3	3.1	2.7
2004[a]	3.2	NA	1.7
Average: 1992–98	5.1	4.0	2.6

[a] In 2004, the formal K-4 electoral alliance is counted as a single party.
Sources: Author's calculations from COMELEC (various years); Hartmann et al. (2001); Tehankee (2002).

the electoral rules for the House remained virtually unchanged between the two periods. This small increase in the average size of the local party system cannot account for the 58% increase in the size of the national party system. In short, intra-district coordination failures are not primarily to blame.

Cross-district coordination is another story. Prior to martial law, aggregation between districts was extremely good. The same two parties were the frontrunners in most districts nationwide. Thus the average inflation score was 9.8 – in other words less than 10% of the size of the national party system was due to aggregation failures. This stands in stark contrast to the post-Marcos inflation score of 32 (Table 6.4). Aggregation has clearly declined in the recent democratic period, and it is this failure to coordinate across districts that is primarily responsible for the larger effective number of parties nationally.[22]

[22] Kasuya finds that post-Marcos aggregation failures have been most pronounced between regions (Kasuya 2001b). Before 1972 the *Nationalista* and Liberal Parties were consistently able to garner support across all regions of the country. After 1986, a more regionalized party system emerged, with parties and candidates unable to coordinate across regions. She argues that this reflects the failure of post-Marcos presidential candidates to win cross-regional support. I explain why this failure has occurred later in this chapter.

In the next two sections, I consider why aggregation has deteriorated since 1986. I first review existing explanations for the expansion of the national party system. I then argue that changes to the rules regarding presidential reelection are responsible for the undermining of aggregation incentives and the consequent inflation of the party system.

6.3.2 Existing Explanations

A variety of explanations have been offered in an attempt to explain the inflation of the national party system since 1986. These include a change in the structure of local politics in the Philippines, the decreased importance of the board of elections, and the advent of synchronized local and national elections.[23] A common explanation for both the stability of the two-party system pre-1972 and the rise of multipartism after Marcos is the structure of local politics in the Philippines. Before martial law, bifactionalism at the local level was the norm (Landé 1965, 1971; Wolters 1984; Kimura 1997). As far back as the Spanish colonial period the political elite in each area tended to divide itself into two major factions (Hollnsteiner 1963). This local bifactionalism continued as the norm after independence and prevented the emergence of viable third parties. Each local faction would align itself with one of the two major parties, leaving third parties with no organizational base to rely on at the local level (Landé 1971, 103–4).

Eventually, though, bifactionalism began to break down in the Philippines. This occurred first in urban areas where multifactionalism had begun to displace bifactionalism by the 1960s (Laquian 1966; Nowak and Snyder 1974; Kimura 1997). Bifactionalism continued to deteriorate throughout the Marcos years so that by the time democracy returned multifactionalism was the norm in many localities (Kimura 1992, 49).

Even though the shift from local bifactionalism to multifactionalism is an interesting phenomenon, it cannot fully account for the growth of the national party system. First, by itself bifactionalism *locally* does not necessarily predict bipartism *nationally*. Indeed, it is quite possible to imagine that local factions from different localities might back different sets of parties. In other words, there is no reason to assume, a priori, that

---

[23] The write-in ballot and the plurality rule for presidential elections have also come under fire for causing multipartism (Velasco 1999, 173–4). However, since these two features of the electoral system were the same both before and after Marcos, they cannot explain the growth in the number of parties.

local factions will back the same two parties in every locality. A theory of aggregation, such as the one presented in this book, is needed to explain why actors might have the incentive to coordinate across different localities to produce a national two-party system. Second, the shift toward multifactionalism locally has not been associated with a large increase in the effective number of parties at the district level (ENP_{avg}). If the factional structure of local politics were really driving the growth in the number of parties, one would expect a large increase in ENP_{avg}, and one would also expect the growth of ENP_{avg} to be primarily responsible for the increase in the national effective number of parties (ENP_{nat}). However, as already discussed, this is not the case. ENP_{avg} grew only slightly from 2 to 2.3 and is responsible for only a small portion of the growth of ENP_{nat}. In short, despite the rise of local multifactionalism, intra-district coordination continues to be quite good (as expected given the SMDP electoral system). It is aggregation *across* districts that has broken down.

A second existing explanation for the advent of multipartism since 1986 is the decreased importance of party representation on precinct-level election-monitoring bodies (the Board of Elections Inspectors and Board of Election Canvassers) (Carlos 1997a; Velasco 1999). These bodies consist of four members including one representative from the government party and one from an opposition party (Carlos 1998a; Omnibus Election Code). Before 1972, these party representatives played an active and important role in protecting the votes for their party and monitoring the fairness of the electoral process (Velasco 1999, 173). Candidates were reluctant to join third parties because they would lose the right to party representation on the inspection board (Carlos 1997a, 18). However, the advent of independent electoral watchdog organizations since 1986 has reduced the advantage of having party representation on the official Board of Election Inspectors and Board of Election Canvassers. Thus third parties are no longer deterred from entering (Carlos 1997a, 18). The problem with this argument is the same as the problem with the bifactionalism argument. If the declining importance of party representation on precinct boards is really driving party system growth, then we should see evidence of that growth occurring at the precinct and district levels. But, once again, the source of more national parties post-1986 is primarily poorer aggregation, not more parties winning votes at the local level.

A third explanation for the end of bipartism in the Philippines is the adoption of synchronized local and national elections beginning in 1992.

Before martial law, local and national elections were held in different years. The result was that during national elections local politicos would support national candidates, and national politicians would return the favor when local elections came around. Synchronized elections disturbed this exchange relationship. In the words of one scholar:

> [P]arties are adversely affected, as simultaneous elections weaken party links between national and local candidates. Before 1972, when local and national elections took place at different times, local leaders could devote their full energy to supporting candidates for national office and vice versa: this they cannot do any longer, as they have to fight their own electoral battles during the same period. (Velasco 1999, 173)

It is probably the case that the move to synchronized elections did indeed make electoral coordination between the national and local levels more complicated. However, there is good reason to suspect that this is not the complete answer. The ability and willingness of local candidates to coordinate with national candidates in synchronized elections is itself a function of aggregation incentives. The stronger the aggregation incentives, the more likely candidates are to do what is necessary to overcome the added challenges associated with synchronized elections. To the extent that synchronized elections increase the size of the payoff to coordination, we might actually expect better aggregation during such elections. In fact, there were three instances before 1972 where national and local elections were held at the same time, and in no case did this lead to a proliferation of parties at the national level. In 1947, 1951, and 1971, elections for the Senate were run jointly with local elections. Even though there are important differences between House and Senate elections, it is instructive that the effective number of parties in the Senate was actually lower when elections were synchronized – the average effective number of Senate parties for the 1946–71 period was 2.2 versus 2.0 in 1947, 1.99 in 1951, and 1.99 in 1971.

6.3.3 Presidential Term Limits and Aggregation Incentives

How and why, then, did aggregation incentives change post-Marcos? When democratic government made its return to the Philippines, the rules and institutions in place before martial law were largely re-adopted. Within the national government the distribution of power remained relatively concentrated in the hands of the president.[24] The national government also retained its dominant position over subnational units (though subnational governments did receive new guarantees of budgetary support). In short, the payoff to being the largest party was fairly constant across the two democratic periods.

Nevertheless, even though there was a high degree of institutional continuity before and after martial law, the 1987 Constitution did introduce one important change – a ban on reelection for the president. Before 1972, Philippine presidents were limited to two terms. In the wake of the Marcos dictatorship, the constitution drafters opted to limit presidents to a single term. If the theory outlined in Chapter 2 is correct, the introduction of a reelection ban should boost the effective number of presidential candidates in post-Marcos elections and thereby undermine aggregation incentives and the reductive effect of concurrent elections.

Prior to 1972, incumbent Filipino presidents regularly marshaled the resources and influence of the presidency to back their reelection bids. All but Marcos were unsuccessful in their bid for a second term; nevertheless, the costs associated with challenging a sitting president weeded out all but the most serious of challengers and enabled voters to easily distinguish the frontrunners from the also-rans. This changed with the introduction of the reelection ban. The ban lowered the barriers to entry for presidential contenders and undermined the incentives for sitting presidents to invest in party building. The result has been a large increase in the number of viable presidential candidates.[25] This is clear from a comparison of the effective number of presidential candidates. During the 26 years before martial law, the average effective number of presidential candidates (ENP_{res}) was 2.2. By contrast, the effective number of presidential candidates in the 1992 and 1998 presidential elections was 5.8 and 4.3, respectively (see the ENP_{res} column in Table 6.5). This is consistent with the theory and with the large-N results in Chapter 3. Where there is no incumbent, the effective number of presidential candidates is larger.

---

[24] In a response to the excesses of the Marcos era, a few of the president's powers were curtailed, including the ability to declare a state of emergency and the ability to transfer "saved funds" between governmental departments.

[25] Choi (2001) also draws the connection between term limits and an increase in the effective number of presidential candidates post-Marcos but does not discuss the implications for the legislative party system.

The 2004 presidential election affords a unique opportunity to test the relationship between reelection bans and the number of viable presidential candidates. In 2001, President Joseph Estrada was forced from office less than half-way through his term in the wake of a corruption scandal. The vice-president, Gloria Macapagal Arroyo, took Estrada's place as president for the remainder of his term. Since she was not elected to the office, President Arroyo was eligible to run for her own term as president in the 2004 election. After initially promising she would not run, Arroyo eventually decided to enter the race. In effect, then, the 2004 election was a race with an incumbent president as a candidate, akin to the norm before martial law. If the hypothesis about the effect of incumbency is correct, the presence of an incumbent in the race (albeit a very weak and vulnerable one) should raise the barriers to entry for prospective candidates and make the job of distinguishing between the frontrunners easier, thereby reducing the effective number of candidates. Indeed, this was the case. The effective number of presidential candidates fell to 3.2 in the 2004 election, down from an average of 5.1 in the previous two presidential contests (see the ENP_{res} column in Table 6.5).

To determine whether the increase in ENP_{res} post-Marcos has the hypothesized effect on aggregation, we can compare the total effective number of electoral parties (ENP_{nat}) pre- and post-martial law. As is clear from Table 6.5, the rise the effective number of presidential candidates since 1986 has corresponded with a rise in ENP_{nat}, as hypothesized. Pre–martial law the effective number of electoral parties is 2.4, as opposed to 4.0 after martial law.[26] Comparing the three post-Marcos presidential elections provides additional evidence of a relationship between the number of viable presidential candidates and aggregation incentives. Compare ENP_{res} for the 1992 and 1998 elections. Note that although ENP_{res} for 1998 is quite high (4.3), it is still lower than ENP_{res} for 1992 (5.8). If the theory is correct, fewer viable candidates should translate into better aggregation in 1998. Likewise, in the 2004 election, the effective number of presidential candidates was lower than in either 1992 or 1998 (due to the presence of an incumbent in the race). If the theory is correct, fewer viable candidates should translate into better aggregation in 2004 compared to the previous two elections.

---

[26] Unfortunately, party vote share data are as yet unavailable for 2004 so it is not possible to calculate ENP_{nat}.

Philippines: Term Limits, Aggregation Incentives, No. of Parties   171

Ideally I would measure the extent of aggregation in post-Marcos elections as I have throughout this book – by using party vote share data to calculate the inflation score (I). However, for the 2004 election party vote share, data at both the district level and national level are not yet available, making it impossible to calculate ENP_{avg}, ENP_{nat}, and the inflation score. So in addition to the inflation score for 1992 and 1998, I also use the effective number of legislative parties (ENP_{seat}) as an imperfect proxy for the level of aggregation. ENP_{seat} is calculated in the same way as ENP_{nat} but substitutes party seat shares in place of vote shares. Table 6.5 places the ENP_{seat} and ENP_{nat} side by side. We can see that even though ENP_{seat} is always smaller than ENP_{nat} (as expected), the two almost always move in tandem.[27] Thus, if the theory is correct, we would expect a decrease in the number of presidential candidates (ENP_{res}) to produce improved aggregation and a decline in ENP_{nat} and ENP_{seat}. Table 6.5 demonstrates that the number of electoral and legislative parties does indeed decline as hypothesized – fewer presidential candidates in 1998 and 2004 are associated with fewer parties, whether measured by seat or vote shares.

Figure 6.1 incorporates the post-Marcos data in Table 6.5 with additional information on the effective number of parties at the district level (ENP_{avg}) and the inflation score (I) for 1992 and 1998 (the only years for which the requisite vote share data are available). As expected, the effective number of presidential candidates tracks very closely to the number of parties at the national level. Figure 6.1 demonstrates that we cannot ascribe solely changes in the effective number of parties locally (ENP_{avg}). Looking just at the 1992 and 1998 election for which district-level data are available, we can see that even though ENP_{avg} does drop between the elections, this decline in the average size of the local party systems is not enough to account for the change in ENP_{nat}. ENP_{avg} falls by less than 19%, while the national party system contracts by 38%. Better aggregation accounts for the majority of the decline in the number of parties in 1998. This is reflected in a decline in the inflation score from 45 in 1992 to 28 in 1998.

The upward pressure on the number of viable presidential candidates since the introduction of the reelection ban has also served to undermine the concurrency effect, as hypothesized. In fact, since 1987 the

---

[27] The sole exception is between 1957 and 1961 where ENP_{nat} decreases slightly and ENP_{seat} increases slightly.

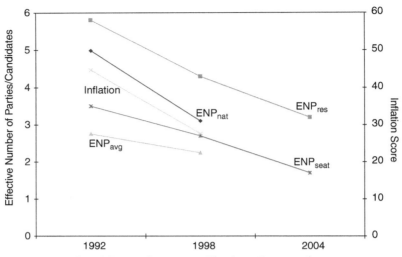

FIGURE 6.1. Post-Marcos Concurrent Elections Compared

Philippines has experienced a *counter*-concurrency effect – midterm elections for the House and Senate produce fewer national parties than do concurrent elections (see Table 6.6). This is understandable in the Philippine context. The payoff to belonging to the president's party is large in both concurrent and mid-term elections, due to the power of the president and the resources she controls. However, the level of uncertainty varies greatly between concurrent and mid-term elections. In concurrent elections, the large number of viable presidential candidates since Marcos reduces the probability that the largest legislative party will also be the party of the president, undermining aggregation. However, the rules allow politicians to switch parties at virtually any time without penalty. As I showed previously, large numbers of politicians at all levels of government take advantage of these rules to switch to the president's party after elections. In other words, uncertainty regarding the presidential frontrunners means that aggregation is both a pre- and post-electoral phenomenon.

The situation is very different in mid-term elections. There is no uncertainty about who the president will be in mid-term elections, thus increasing the probability that the president's party will also be the largest legislative party. As a result, aggregation improves in mid-term elections with a corresponding decrease in the number of national

TABLE 6.6. *Counter-Concurrency in Post-Marcos Philippine Elections*

	Presidential Elections (1992, 1998, 2004[a])	Mid-term Elections (1995, 2001[a])
House		
ENP_{nat}	4.1[b]	2.6
Inflation	36[b]	25
ENP_{seat}	2.6	2.3
Senate		
ENP	3.0	2.0

[a] In 2001 and 2004, formal national electoral alliances (the PPC in 2001 and K-4 in 2004) are counted as a single party.
[b] 2004 election excluded due to lack of data.
Sources: Author's calculations from COMELEC (various years); Hartmann et al. (2001); Tehankee (2002).

parties. Table 6.6 compares aggregation and the number of parties in the three post-Marcos concurrent elections (1992, 1998, 2004) and two midterm elections (1995, 2001).[28] (Once again, the lack of party vote share data requires me to drop the 2001 and 2004 elections from the calculations of the inflation score and ENP_{nat}.) Looking first at aggregation, one can see that inflation is higher during presidential elections years ($I = 36$) than in mid-term elections ($I = 25$). The effective number of electoral parties correspondingly rises in presidential election years ($ENP_{nat} = 4.0$) and falls during mid-term elections ($ENP_{nat} = 2.6$). Of course it is difficult to draw strong inferences from only the 1998 mid-term election, as one is forced to do if we rely solely on the inflation score and ENP_{nat}. However, an analysis of the effective number of legislative parties (ENP_{seat}) in *all* elections reveals a similar pattern – more parties in presidential elections than in mid-term elections. Likewise, Senate elections since 1986 display a similar counter-concurrency pattern.[29] During the presidential election years, the average effective number of parties in the Senate is 3 compared to 2 in mid-term elections. Table 6.6 summarizes the counter-concurrency pattern for both the House and Senate.

[28] The first post-Marcos legislative election in 1987 is excluded due to the lack of reliable information about the distribution of vote and seat shares.
[29] For the Senate, the challenge is not inter-district coordination (aggregation) since all Senators are elected from a single nationwide district.

The counter-concurrency effect described previously is also useful for addressing an as yet undiscussed alternative explanation for the post-Marcos party system – namely, that the inflation of the party system post-Marcos simply reflects the uncertainty among voters, candidates, and parties that is often present in early elections in new democracies. While this argument cannot be dismissed out of hand, there are reasons to think that the shock of a new system is not a sufficient explanation. First, the Philippines had a long history of democratic elections prior to the imposition of martial law – 26 years as an independent state and nearly 40 years as a colony of the United States compared to 14 years of martial law. Thus democratic elections were not novel. Much of the electorate and most of the political elite had participated in the democratic elections prior to martial law. Second, the electoral system the country adopted after the fall of Marcos was familiar. It was the same basic system that had been used throughout the Philippines' electoral history (single-member district plurality for the House and plurality rule for the presidency). Finally, the counter-concurrency effect suggests that even if actors are learning (leading presumably to fewer parties over time), they are also responding to aggregation incentives. When those incentives are the strongest (i.e., in midterm elections), actors coordinate on fewer parties than when aggregation incentives are relatively weaker (i.e., in presidential election years).

To summarize, the switch to a single term limit in 1987 affected aggregation in a manner consistent with the theoretical expectations – namely, the effective number of presidential candidates increased dramatically from what had been the norm prior to martial law. More viable presidential candidates made it difficult for legislative candidates and voters to clearly distinguish the frontrunners from the also-rans and increased the probability that the largest legislative party would not control the executive branch. This undermined the incentive to aggregate across districts, leading to a larger number of more localized/regionalized parties. Finally, the large number of viable presidential candidates offset the effect of concurrent elections on the number of parties. A partial exception to this pattern is the 2004 election where the presence of the an incumbent in the race worked to lower the effective number of candidates, increase aggregation incentives, and lower the number of parties to a level closer to the norm in the pre–martial law period.

6.4 COMPARING AGGREGATION THE NUMBER OF PARTIES IN THE PHILIPPINES AND THAILAND

Returning to the comparison with Thailand that opened this chapter, we see that in many respects the Thai and Philippine party systems are very similar. In both countries, parties tend to be temporary electoral alliances of locally focused politicians. These parties elicit low levels of discipline and cohesion from their members and little loyalty from voters. The two party systems do differ in one important respect, however. Until recently Thailand has been home to many more political parties than the Philippines. What explains this divergence when other aspects of the two-party systems look so alike? One place to begin searching for an explanation is the electoral system. To the extent their electoral systems differ, we would expect the size of their local/district party systems to diverge. And, as local party systems are the building blocks of the national party system, more parties locally would mean more parties nationally, ceteris paribus. So, how do the Thai and Filipino electoral systems differ? Recall that Thailand, prior to the 1997 reforms, used the block vote with district magnitudes of 2 or 3 to elect the House of Representatives. The Philippines, by contrast, has primarily relied on a single member district plurality (SMDP) system throughout its democratic history. Given the difference in district magnitude one would expect the average effective number of parties (ENP_{avg}) to be slightly lower in the Philippines. In fact, this is the case. ENP_{avg} for all postindependence House elections in the Philippines is 2.1 compared to 3.2 in pre-1997 Thailand (see Table 6.7). This difference holds even if we separate pre- and post–martial law elections in the Philippines – the average number of district parties post-Marcos is 2.3 versus 2.0 pre–martial law. However, once Thailand switches to a system where 80% of House seats are filled using SMDP, Thailand's ENP_{avg} falls to the level we observe in the Philippines. In short, some of the differences in the Thai and Philippine party systems can indeed be traced to the different district electoral systems in each country prior to 1997.

Note, however, that the difference between the number of parties in each district is quite modest – on average there are only about 1.2 more parties in each district in pre-reform Thailand compared to the average in all Philippine elections.[30] This is in sharp contrast to the national level

---

[30] If we focus on just post-Marcos elections, the difference is an even smaller 0.9.

TABLE 6.7. *Aggregation in the Philippines and Thailand*

Country (election year)	Average ENP$_{avg}$	Average ENP$_{nat}$	Average *I*
Pre-reform			
Philippines (1946–69)	2.0	2.3	9.8
Thailand (1986–1996)	3.2	7.2	54
Post-reform			
Philippines (1992–98)	2.3	3.6	32
Thailand (2001–2005)	2.4	3.1	23
Combined			
Philippines (1946–69; 1992–98)	2.1	2.6	17
Thailand (1986–2005)	3.0	6.0	45

Sources: Author's calculations from Ministry of Interior, election reports (1986, 1988, 1992a, 1992b, 1995, 1997); COMELEC (various years); Hartmann et al. (2001); Kasuya 2001b.

where there are on average 4.6 more parties in pre-reform Thailand than in the Philippines (7.2 versus 2.6).[31] As these numbers indicate, prior to the recent reforms Thai voters, parties, and candidates did a much poorer job coordinating across districts than did their Filipino counterparts. The poorer aggregation in Thailand is reflected in the inflation scores – the average inflation score for the Philippines is 17 compared to pre-1997 Thailand's 54 (Table 6.7).[32]

6.4.1 Accounting for Aggregation Differences

What explains why aggregation has traditionally been so much better in the Philippines than in Thailand? To begin with, differences in social heterogeneity cannot account for the difference in cross-district coordination. Most measures of social heterogeneity score the Philippines as more diverse than Thailand. For example, the Philippines' score on the ethno-linguistic fractionalization index is 0.84 compared to 0.57 for Thailand (Krain 1997). Similarly, if we look at religious fractionalization the Philippines is also more diverse with a score of 0.29 versus 0.15 for Thailand (Annett 2000).[33] The Philippines' greater social diversity is also

---

[31] Using only post-Marcos elections, the difference is 3.6 parties.
[32] For post-Marcos elections, the inflation score is 32, still much below Thailand's 54.
[33] An exception is Fearon's ethnic fractionalization score based on linguistic diversity, which reports Thailand as more diverse than the Philippines (Fearon 2003).

Philippines: Term Limits, Aggregation Incentives, No. of Parties 177

reinforced by geography with the country's various groups spread out among the country's 7,107 islands. In short, if we look solely at social heterogeneity, we would expect aggregation to be *more* difficult in the Philippines rather than less.

In Chapter 2, I argued that aggregation was primarily a function of (a) the payoff to being the largest party at the national level and (b) the probability that the largest party will be able to capture that payoff. Two factors shape the largest party payoff: the distribution of power between the national and subnational level (vertical centralization) and the distribution of power within the national government (horizontal centralization). Thailand and the Philippines look very similar in terms of vertical centralization. In 1992 (the last year for which reliable data are available for the Philippines), the subnational government's share of expenditures and revenues was 8.7 and 1.9, respectively, in the Philippines versus 8.4 and 1.4 in Thailand (World Bank Group n.d.). In both countries subnational governments are highly dependent on the central government's largesse.[34]

Within the national government, however, power has been relatively more concentrated in the Philippines than in Thailand (again, until the recent Thai reforms). Both countries have bicameral legislatures, but unlike the Thai Senate, which was appointed and somewhat outside of the control of the prime minister, the Philippine Senate is elected and is typically controlled by the president's party. Between 1946 and 2004, the president's party failed to capture at least 50% of the Senate seats only twice. It is important to note that just because the president's party nominally controls the Senate it does not mean that the Senate is not an important veto gate. Filipino parties are notoriously short on discipline and cohesion, and so the president cannot always count on support from his or her party. However, the Philippine president is much better equipped to cobble together a legislative support coalition from across the various veto gates than is the Thai prime minister. As mentioned previously, the Filipino president is very powerful. These powers include proactive powers, such as the ability to shape the legislative agenda, appointment powers, and control over the pork barrel, as well as reactive powers such as line item and package vetoes. Particularly notable is

---

[34] In recent years, subnational governments in the Philippines have received larger shares of government revenues via the International Revenue Allotment (IRA).

the president's control of pork and political appointments – control that the Thai prime minister has historically lacked (Hicken 2005). In short, prior to the Thai reforms, power was more horizontally concentrated in the Philippines than in Thailand, and this generated stronger aggregation incentives.

In addition to the higher aggregation payoff in the Philippines, the probability that the largest party will capture that prize has also been greater. This was particularly true prior to martial law where concurrent presidential and legislative elections typically produced two viable candidates. In effect, this meant that the largest party in the House had a good chance of capturing the executive – giving candidates a strong incentive to coordinate across districts under the banners of the presidential frontrunners. This is in sharp contrast to pre-reform Thailand where it was frequently the case that someone other than the leader of the largest party served as prime minister.

To summarize, aggregation incentives in the Philippines typically outdistanced incentives in pre-reform Thailand. The payoff to aggregation in the Philippines has generally been higher than in pre-reform Thailand due to a greater degree of horizontal centralization and the better likelihood that the largest legislative party would capture the aggregation payoff. Given these stronger aggregation incentives in the Philippines, we would expect both the inflation score and the national effective number of parties to be much lower vis-à-vis pre-reform Thailand, as is the case (Table 6.7).

However, institutional reforms in each country led to a recent reversal of this pattern. As discussed in this chapter, the post-Marcos introduction of a presidential reelection ban in the Philippines caused a proliferation in the effective number of presidential candidates and decreased the chance that the largest legislative party would also control the presidency. The result has been a sharp deterioration in aggregation and an increase in the number of political parties. At the same time, constitutional reform in Thailand increased aggregation incentives causing a dramatic improvement in aggregation and reduction in the number of political parties (see Chapter 5). The combined effect of both sets of reforms is that the 2001–5 Thai party system came to exhibit better cross-district coordination and fewer parties than the Philippines (see Table 6.7).[35]

---

[35] The 2007 Thai Constitution threatens to undermine aggregation incentives.

6.5 CONCLUSION

Like Thailand, the number of national parties in the Philippines reflects both the average size of the district party systems together with the degree of aggregation between those districts. Both periods of Philippine democracy have used SMDP for House elections, resulting in a modest number of parties at the district level. The shift to a multiparty system since Marcos reflects primarily a deterioration of aggregation and aggregation incentives. In the first democratic period, the expected utility of being the largest party in government was high with both a high aggregation payoff and a good chance that the largest legislative party could capture that payoff. When democracy returned in 1986, a new ban on presidential reelection led to an increase in the number of viable presidential candidates, a lower probability of capturing the aggregation payoff, and a corresponding decrease in the incentives to coordinate across districts. This is consistent with the theory outlined in Chapter 2 and the large-N empirical results discussed in Chapter 3.

Together the experiences of the Philippines and Thailand suggest that political institutions have a powerful and predictable effect on aggregation. The rules and institutions in the Philippines were such that for much of its democratic history the expected utility of becoming the largest legislative party was quite high – especially relative to pre-reform Thailand. As a result, cross-district coordination was much more extensive. However, institutional reform in both countries during the 1980s and 1990s has brought about a reversal of this pattern. Cross-district coordination has deteriorated in the Philippines (while improving in Thailand) to the extent that the Philippines now has worse aggregation and more parties than its neighbor.

7

Conclusion

This concluding chapter is divided into two parts. In the first section, I summarize the central arguments and findings. In the second section, I identify some of the questions that still remain to be answered and offer some preliminary thoughts on the implications of various levels of aggregation for policymaking processes and outcomes.

7.1 SUMMARY OF KEY FINDINGS

In this book, I have focused on two dimensions of a country's party system – the number of parties and the degree of the nationalization. I have attempted to broaden the debate beyond the behavior of voters, candidates, and parties *within* electoral districts to include a focus the coordination of such actors *across* districts. I argued that aggregation is a key determinant of both the size of the party system and the degree of nationalization. Thus it is important to understand what factors shape the degree of aggregation.

The causal logic of my argument was grounded in the incentives of party entrepreneurs and candidates for political office. Aggregation is a function of the incentives these actors face to ally across districts under a common party banner. These incentives, in turn, are shaped by (1) the potential payoff for aggregation and (2) the probability of capturing that payoff. The incentives for coordinating across districts increase as the rewards for such coordination rise and the degree of uncertainty about capturing that reward falls.

Conclusion

To the extent the existing literature has explored the determinants of aggregation incentives, it has focused almost exclusively on the influence of the vertical centralization of power within a political system (i.e., the distribution of resources and authority between central and subnational governments). I demonstrated both theoretically and empirically that a high degree of vertical centralization is not sufficient to produce strong aggregation incentives. A focus solely on the distribution of power and resources between national and subnational actors misses a key part of the institutional story. To this vertical dimension I added a second horizontal dimension and showed that horizontal centralization, or the distribution of power within the national government, combines with vertical centralization to affect the size of the aggregation payoff and shape aggregation incentives.

I then explored three of the components of horizontal centralization – bicameralism, party cohesion, and reserve domains. I argued that a second chamber, party factionalism, and the presence of positions or policy areas beyond the reach of elected politicians, each have the effect of dispersing political authority reducing the size of the aggregation payoff any single party is likely to control. The results of the large-N tests revealed substantial support for the bicameralism and reserve domain hypotheses, while party factionalism proved to be an important variable in the Thai case.

In addition to the size of the payoff, both cross-national and country-specific evidence suggested that the probability of capturing that payoff also plays an important role in shaping aggregation incentives. I found that in parliamentary systems aggregation incentives are stronger where the chance of the largest legislative party's capturing the premiership is high, and weaker where there is a high probability that someone other than the leader of the largest party will head the government. As hypothesized, I found that this probability variable interacts with the size of the aggregation payoff to shape coordination incentives. Aggregation is at its worst where a low probability combines with a small aggregation payoff.

In presidential systems, I argued that the probability of capturing executive office is a function of the number of presidential candidates and the proximity of presidential and legislative elections. In line with existing studies, I found that proximate elections lower the number of electoral parties but only where the effective number of presidential candidates is low. A unique contribution of this study was to demonstrate that proximity and the number of presidential candidates also have an effect on *aggregation*. Proximity lowers party system inflation where there are relatively few presidential candidates, and the number of presidential candidates itself has a substantial negative impact on cross-district coordination. The more presidential candidates there are, the more difficult it is for legislative candidates, voters, parties, and donors to identify and coordinate around the frontrunners. The cost is poorer aggregation.

In addition to the large-N quantitative analysis, empirical support for my argument came from the Thai and Philippine case studies. For my analysis of the Thai case, I compiled a unique data set of district-level election results for seven Thai elections since 1986. I discovered that the large number of parties that so characterized the pre-1997 Thai system was primarily a result of poor aggregation. Within individual districts, actors were typically able to coordinate on a small number of parties – in line with what we would expect from Thailand's electoral system. Between districts, however, coordination attempts broke down. I demonstrated that regional differences cannot adequately account for these coordination difficulties – aggregation was in fact worse within regions than it was between them. Instead, poor aggregation reflected the weak linkage present in pre-reform Thailand. Prior to 1997, rampant party factionalism, an appointed Senate, and other reserve domains undermined aggregation incentives. The practice of selecting someone other than the leader of the largest party as premier also reduced the expected utility of aggregation. Given the weak aggregation incentives, cross-district coordination in pre-reform Thailand was poor, and the result was a large number of parties at the national level. By the 1990s, the lingering reserve domains had begun to fade away, and Thailand had adopted a rule that enabled the leader of the largest party to reliably capture the premiership. However, the 1997 constitutional reforms brought even more dramatic changes to the political-institutional environment. The reforms greatly magnified candidates' aggregation incentives. Specifically, the reforms substantially increased the premier's leverage over internal party factions. This increased the potential size of the aggregation payoff resulting in stronger aggregation incentives, better aggregation, fewer parties, and increased nationalization.

For the Philippines, I also used district-level election data to analyze the extent of aggregation in Philippine elections since independence. I found that aggregation was very good in pre–martial law elections but that it deteriorated sharply after the return of democracy in 1986. This deterioration is the primary cause of the demise of the two-party system since Marcos. In the initial democratic period, the expected utility of being the largest party in government was high with both a high aggregation payoff and a good chance that the largest legislative party would capture that payoff. However, when democracy returned in 1986, a new ban on presidential reelection led to an increase in the number of viable presidential candidates, a lower probability that the largest legislative party would also capture the presidency, and a corresponding decrease in the incentives to coordinate across districts. The reelection ban also explains the relatively unusual pattern I observed in post-Marcos elections – namely, poorer aggregation and more parties in concurrent elections, better aggregation and fewer parties in midterm legislative elections.

7.2 UNANSWERED QUESTIONS AND RESEARCH OPPORTUNITIES

The multicountry analysis together with the experiences of the Philippines and Thailand support the claim that political institutions have a powerful and predictable effect on aggregation via their effect on aggregation incentives. However, as always, the questions left unanswered and issues left unresolved present ample opportunities for further research. This book is no exception.

First, how does aggregation actually unfold on the ground? What are the mechanics involved? On the one hand, we might envision aggregation as a bottom-up process, driven mainly by the alliance choices of local candidates or subnational political elite. On the other hand, the recent Thai experience suggests that aggregation might also be a top-down affair – with political entrepreneurs taking the lead in organizing cross-district coordination. This suggests several questions worthy of future research. When aggregation occurs what conditions shape whether it is a top-down or bottom-up process? Does the process of aggregation affect the way in which the resulting parties are organized internally? Is there a relationship between the type of process that predominates and the stability and endurance of cross-district electoral alliances? Does the process by which aggregation occurs affect the likelihood of democratic consolidation? Pursuing answers to these questions is part of my future research agenda and is likely to require the use of multiple methods – from formal modeling of voter, candidate, and elite behavior (see Morelli 2001) to careful fieldwork studying how aggregation unfolds in specific country contexts.

Second, does aggregation influence dimensions of the party system other than nationalization and party system size? For example, aggregation is potentially an important determinant of the degree of party system institutionalization. Mainwaring and Scully (1995) discuss four criteria for party system institutionalization. The last of these criteria deals with party organization and includes the notion that parties should be "territorially comprehensive" (Mainwaring and Scully 1995, 5). Party system institutionalization need not imply that support for parties must be equally distributed across the nation, but it does imply that parties reject strictly local or regional strategies in favor of a more national focus. Party system institutionalization may be weaker, then, where parties fail to move beyond local strongholds and compete across districts or regions nationwide.

Finally, the question of greatest interest to me in terms of a future research agenda is the way in which aggregation affects policymaking – both processes and outcomes. If one is to understand the dynamics of policymaking, it is useful to begin with three sets of questions.

- Who are the actors that make policy decisions?
- What are their interests? (To whom do they respond? What is the nature of their constituency?)
- What are their capabilities? (How able are they to implement their preferred policies? What constraints do they face?)

Aggregation has strong implications for the latter two sets of questions via the affect of aggregation on the number of parties and nationalization. To begin with, there is a clear (though not one-to-one) positive relationship between the number of political parties and the number of actors. The more parties there are in a given party system, the more actors there are likely to be in the policymaking process. As more actors become involved in the policy process, the likelihood that one actor's attempts to change the status quo will be blocked by other actors with different interests increases (Tsebelis 2002).

Conclusion

A good deal of the recent literature on the political economy of policymaking has focused on the number of actors; however, it is not enough to simply count the number of veto players. We need to know something about the interests and incentives of those actors. The broader an actors' constituency is, the stronger will be the incentives to pursue broad, public-regarding policies over those policies targeted to narrow, particularistic interests (Bueno de Mesquita et al. 2003; Hicken, Satyanath, and Sergenti 2005; Hicken and Simmons 2008). Aggregation, through its influence on degree party system nationalization, can have a profound effect on the nature of policy makers' constituencies. Ceteris paribus, the greater the degree of party system nationalization, the broader the constituency to which those parties must respond.

To be more specific, when there is a high degree of aggregation, political competition at the national level occurs between political parties that each have support across most of the regions in the country (as opposed to competition occurring across highly regionalized or localized parties). As a result, debates and conflicts over policies at the national level are more likely to lead to the parties competing to offer comprehensive benefits that affect people spread across most regions of the country. By contrast, when political competition at the national level occurs between parties that represent specific subnational constituencies, the outcomes of policy debates and conflicts lead to two potentially damaging kinds of public policy outcomes: (a) an oversupply of pork-barrel policies resulting from log-rolls across regions that do not benefit the broader population but end up benefiting local political and economic elites and/or (b) an undersupply of nationally focused public goods. Depending on the country, these latter, geographically targeted policy benefits will end up targeting specific ethnic, religious, industrial, linguistic groups, but they will be less comprehensive and all-encompassing than if the parties were nationalized.

Moreover, the degree of nationalization can affect bargaining between and within the executive and legislature. Bargaining involves trades or side payments between different actors – the more actors, the more side payments that must be made in order to pass a given policy. The question then becomes what is being traded? In some cases, bargaining consists of actors bargaining over and trading concessions in national policies. However, bargaining may also take the form of bargaining over, and trades in, pork and particularism. The extent to which actors trade in pork versus public policy is strongly influenced by the degree of nationalization. As argued previously, where the party system is not nationalized, politicians may lack strong incentives to provide national goods/policies. In such a system log-rolling across geographic regions will be rampant, while national policies will be under-supplied. Where the party system is highly nationalized, however, bargaining will tend to be over broader policy, and trades will primarily come in the form of policy concessions (Hicken 2002). My own research agenda includes a closer examination of the implications of aggregation and party system nationalization for policymaking and the propensity to provide needed national public goods.

References

Albritton, Robert B. and Thawilwadee Bureekul. 2002. "Support for Democracy in Thailand." Bangkok: King Prajadhipok's Institute.
Aldrich, John H. 1995. *Why Parties? The Origin and Transformation of Political Parties in America.* Chicago: The University of Chicago Press.
Alesina, Alberto and Nouriel Roubini, with Gerald D. Cohen. 1997. *Political Cycles and the Macroeconomy.* Cambridge, MA: MIT Press.
Amorim-Neto, Octavio and Gary C. Cox. 1997. "Electoral Institutions, Cleavage Structures, and the Number of Parties." *American Journal of Political Science* 41:149–74.
Andaya, Barbara Watson. 1999. "Political Development Between the Sixteenth and Eighteenth Centuries." In *The Cambridge History of Southeast Asia: Volume 1, Part 2, From c. 1500 to c. 1800.* Cambridge: Cambridge University Press.
Anderson, Benedict. 1977. "Withdrawal Symptoms: Social and Cultural Aspects of the October 6 Coup." *Bulletin of Concerned Asian Scholars* 9:3.
  1990. "Murder and Progress in Modern Siam." *New Left Review* 81: 2, 33–48.
Anek Laothamatas. 1989. "From Bureaucratic Polity to Liberal Corporatism: Business Associations and the New Political Economy of Thailand." Ph.D. dissertation, Columbia University.
  1992. *Business Associations and the New Political Economy of Thailand.* Boulder, CO: Westview Press.
  1996. "A Tale of Two Democracies: Conflicting Perceptions of Elections and Democracy." In *The Politics of Elections in Southeast Asia.* R. H. Taylor, ed. New York: Woodrow Wilson Center Press.
Annett, Anthony. 2000. "Societal Fractionalization, Political Stability, and the Size of Government." IMF Working Paper. WP/00/82.
Anusorn Limmanee. 1998. "Thailand." In *Political Party Systems and Democratic Development in East and Southeast Asia. Volume 1: Southeast*

Asia. Wolfgang Sachsenroder and Ulrike E. Frings, eds. Aldershot: Ashgate Publishing.

Arghiros, Daniel. 1995. *Political Structures and Strategies: A Study of Electoral Politics in Contemporary Rural Thailand*. Occasional Paper No. 31. Hull, England: University of Hull, Centre for South-East Asian Studies.

Backer, David and Ken Kollman. 2003. "Electoral Laws Under Extreme Conditions: The Case of Africa." Typescript. University of Michigan. Department of Political Science.

Banlaoi, Rommel C. and Clarita R. Carlos. 1996. *Political Parties in the Philippines: From 1900 to the Present*. Makati: Konrad Adenauer Foundation.

Bartolini, Stefano. 2000. *The Political Mobilization of the European Left, 1860–1980*. Cambridge: Cambridge University Press.

Beck, Nathaniel and Jonathan N. Katz. 1995. "What to do (and not to do) with Time-Series Cross-Section Data." *The American Political Science Review* 89 (3 Sep):634–47.

Beck, Thorsten, George Clarke, Alberto Groff, Philip Keefer, and Patrick Walsh. 2001. "New Tools and Tests in Comparative Political Economy: The Database of Political Institutions." *World Bank Economic Review* 15:1 (165–76).

Bielasiak, Jack. 2002. "The Institutionalization of Electoral and Party Systems in Postcommunist States." *Comparative Politics* 34:189–210.

Blondel, Jean. 1968. "Party Systems and Patterns of Government in Western Democracies." *Canadian Journal of Political Science* 1(2) (June):180–203.

BP (*Bangkok Post*). 1988. "1988 Election Special." July 20, 1988.

   2005. "Sanoh in Open Rebellion." June 9, 2005.

Brambor, Thomas, William Roberts Clark, and Matt Golder. 2005. "Understanding Interaction Models: Improving Empirical Analyses." *Political Analysis* 14(1):63–82.

Brancati, Dawn. 2003. "Design over Conflict: Managing Ethnic Conflict and Secessionism through Decentralization." Ph.D. dissertation, Columbia University.

Bueno de Mesquita, Bruce, Alastair Smith, Randolph M. Siverson, and James D. Morrow. 2003. *The Logic of Political Survival*. Cambridge, MA: MIT Press.

Cain, Bruce E., John Ferejohn, and Morris P. Fiorina. 1987. *The Personal Vote: Constituency Service and Electoral Independence*. Cambridge: Cambridge University Press.

Callahan, William A. 2000. *Pollwatching, Elections and Civil Society in Southeast Asia*. Aldershot: Ashgate Publishing.

   2002. "The Ideology of Vote-Buying and the Democratic Deferral of Political Reform." Paper prepared for delivery at conference entitled, "Trading Political Rights: The Comparative Politics of Vote Buying." Center for International Studies, MIT. August 26–27, 2002.

Campbell, Angus, Philip Converse, Warren Miller, and Donald Stokes. 1960. *The American Voter*. New York: Wiley.

Caramani, Daniele. 2000. *Elections in Western Europe since 1815: Electoral Results by Constituencies*. Oxford: Macmillan.
　2004. *The Nationalization of Elections*. Cambridge: Cambridge University Press.
Carey, John M. 2007. *Carey data archive.* www.dartmouth.edu/~jcarey.
Carey, John M. and Matthew Soberg Shugart. 1995. "Incentives to Cultivate a Personal Vote: A Rank Ordering of Electoral Formulas." *Electoral Studies* 14:14.
Carlos, Clarita R. 1997a. *Dynamics of Political Parties in the Philippines*. Makati: Konrad Adenauer Foundation.
　1997b. *Handbook of Political Parties and Elections in the Philippines*. Makati: Konrad Adenauer Foundation.
　1998a. *History of Electoral Reforms in the Philippines: Pre-Spanish to 1998*. Makati: Konrad Adenauer Foundation.
　1998b. *A Chronicle of the 1998 Elections in the Philippines*. Makati: Konrad Adenauer Foundation.
　1998c. *Selected Election Cases in the Philippines: From the Supreme Court and Electoral Tribunals*. Makati: Konrad Adenauer Foundation.
Carlos, Clarita R. and Rommel C. Banlaoi. 1996. *Elections in the Philippines: From Pre-colonial Period to the Present*. Makati: Konrad Adenauer Foundation.
Carothers, Thomas. 2006. *Confronting the Weakest Link: Aiding Political Parties in New Democracies*. Carnegie Endowment for International Peace.
Ceesay, Ousman. 2005. "NADD Come 2006." *Home of the Mandinmories*. http://gambian.blogspot.com/2005/07/nadd-come-2006.html.
Chaiwat Veeranan. 1992. "Political Roles of the Party Branches: A Case Study of the Democrat Party." MA thesis, Department of Government, Chulalongkorn University [in Thai].
Chambers, Paul W. 2003. "Factions, Parties, Coalition Change, and Cabinet Durability in Thailand: 1979–2001." Ph.D. dissertation, Northern Illinois University.
Chaowana Traimas. 1997. *Phakkanmuang Thai*. (Thai Political Parties). Bangkok: Institute of Public Policy Studies and the Konrad Adenauer Foundation.
Chhibber, Pradeep. 1998. *Democracy without Associations: Transformation of Party Systems and Social Cleavages in India*. Ann Arbor: University of Michigan Press.
Chhibber, Pradeep and Ken Kollman. 1998. "Party Aggregation and the Number of Parties in India and the United States." *American Political Science Review* 92:329–42.
　2004. *The Formation of National Party Systems: Federalism and Party Competition in Canada, Great Britain, India, and the United States*. Princeton, NJ: Princeton University Press.

Chhibber, Pradeep K. and Irfan Nooruddin. 2004. "Do Party Systems Count? The Number of Parties and Government Performance in the Indian States." *Comparative Political Studies* 37(2) (March):152–87.

Choi, Jungug. 2001. "Philippine Democracies Old and New: Elections, Term Limits, and Party Systems." *Asian Survey* 41(3):488–501.

Christensen, Scott et al. 1993. *Thailand: The Institutional and Political Underpinnings of Growth*. Washington, DC: World Bank.

Clark, William Roberts and Matt Golder. 2006. "Rehabilitating Duverger's Theory: Testing the Mechanic and Strategic Modifying Effects of Electoral Laws." *Comparative Political Studies* 39:679–708.

Colomer, Josep M. 2001. *Political Institutions: Democracy and Social Choice*. New York: Oxford University Press.

Commission on Elections (COMELEC). 1992. *Report of the Commission on Elections to the President and Congress of the Republic of the Philippines on the Conduct of the Synchronized National and Local Elections of May 11, 1992*. Manila: Commission on Elections.

1995. *Report of the Commission on Elections to His Excellency President Fidel V. Ramos and to Congress of the Republic of the Philippines on the Conduct of the National and Local Elections of May 8, 1992*. Manila: Commission on Elections.

1998. Election results from the 1998 National and Local Elections. Data on Diskette. Manila: Commission on Elections.

2001. Election results from the 2001 National and Local Elections. http://www.comelec.gov.ph/results_main.html.

2004. Election results from the 2004 National and Local Elections. http://www.comelec.gov.ph/results_main.html

Connors, Michael. 2002. "Framing the 'People's Constitution'." In *Reforming Thai Politics*. Duncan McCargo, ed. Copenhagen: NIAS.

Coppedge, Michael. 1998. "The Dynamics of Latin American Party Systems." *Party Politics* 4(4):547–68.

Corpuz, Onofre D. 1965. *The Philippines*. Englewood Cliffs, NJ: Prentice Hall.

Cox, Gary W. 1997. *Making Votes Count*. Cambridge: Cambridge University Press.

1999. "Electoral Rules and Electoral Coordination." *Annual Review of Political Science* 2:145–61.

Cox, Gary W. and Mathew D. McCubbins. 1993. *Legislative Leviathan*. Berkeley: UC Press.

2001. "The Institutional Determinants of Policy Outcomes." In *Presidents, Parliaments, and Policy*. Stephan Haggard and Mathew D. McCubbins, eds. Cambridge: Cambridge University Press.

Croissant, Aurel and Marei John, eds. 2002. *Electoral Politics in Southeast and East Asia*. Singapore: Friedrich-Ebert-Stiftung, Office for Regional Co-operation in Southeast Asia.

Cutrone, Michael and Nolan McCarty. N.d. "Does Bicameralism Matter?" http://www.princeton.edu/~nmccarty/bicameralism.pdf.

Darling, Frank C. 1971. "Political Parties in Thailand." *Pacific Affairs* 45(2):228–41.
de Castro Jr., Isagani. 1992. "Money and Moguls: Oiling the Campaign Machinery." In *1992 & Beyond: Forces and Issues in Philippine Elections*. Lornal Kalaw-Tirol and Sheila S. Colonel, eds. Quezon City: Philippine Center for Investigative Journalism and Ateneo Center for Social Policy and Public Affairs.
Diamond, Larry. 1988. *Class, Ethnicity, and Democracy in Nigeria: The Failure of the First Republic*. Syracuse, NY: Syracuse University Press.
Diermeier, Daniel and Roger Myerson. 1999. "Bicameralism and its Consequences for Legislative Organization." *American Economic Review* 89(5):1182–96.
Dix, Robert. 1992. "Democratization and the Institutionalization of Latin American Political Parties." *Comparative Political Studies* 24:488–511.
Doner, Richard and Anek Laothamatas. 1994. "Thailand: Economic and Political Gradualism." In *Voting for Reform: Democracy, Political Liberalization, and Economic Adjustment*. Stephan Haggard and Steven Webb, eds. New York: Oxford University Press.
Doner, Richard F. and Ansil Ramsay. 1997. "Competitive Clientelism and Economic Governance: The Case of Thailand." *Business and the State in Developing Countries*. Sylvia Maxfield and Ben Ross Schneider, eds. Ithaca, NY: Cornell University Press.
Downs, Anthony. 1957. *An Economic Theory of Democracy*. New York: Harper and Row.
Druckman, James N. 1996. "Party Factionalism and Cabinet Durability." *Party Politics* 2: 397–407.
Druckman, James N. and Michael F. Thies. 2002. "The Importance of Concurrence: The Impact of Bicameralism on Government Formation and Duration." *American Journal of Political Science* 46(4):760–71.
Dunleavy, Patrick and Francoise Boucek. 2003. "Constructing the Number of Parties." *Party Politics* 9(3):291–315.
Duverger, Maurice. 1954. *Political Parties: Their Organization and Activity in the Modern State*. New York: Wiley.
Epstein, Leon. 1967. *Political Parties in Western Democracies*. New York: Praeger.
Electoral Commission of Thailand. 2005. Results of the 2005 Elections [in Thai.] Electronic file.
ERP KiM Newsletters. 2004. "Kosovo – An Ethnic, Not a Religious Conflict." September 22, 2004.
Fearon, James D. 2003. "Ethnic and Cultural Diversity by Country." *Journal of Economic Growth* 8(2):195–222.
Filippov, Mikhail, Peter Ordershook, and Olga Shvetsova. 1999. "Party Fragmentation and Presidential Elections in Post-Communist Democracies." *Constitutional Political Economy* 10:3–26.

2004. *Designing Federalism: A Theory of Self-Sustainable Federal Institutions*. Cambridge: Cambridge University Press.

Fitzpatrick, John. 2006. "Brazil: Many Parties – Few Ideas." http://www.gringoes.com/articles.asp?ID_Noticia=861.

Franzese, Robert J., Jr. 2002. *Macroeconomic Policies of Developed Democracies*. Cambridge: Cambridge University Press.

2006. "Empirical Strategies for Various Manifestations of Multilevel Data." *Political Analysis* 13(4):430–46.

Golder, Matt. 2005. "Democratic Electoral Systems around the World, 1946–2000" *Electoral Studies* 24(1):103–21.

2006. "Presidential Coattails and Legislative Fragmentation." *American Journal of Political Science* 50(1):34–48.

Golder, Sona Nadenichek. 2006. *The Logic of Pre-electoral Coalition Formation*. Columbus: Ohio State University Press.

Grossholtz, Jean. 1964. *Politics in the Philippines: A Country Study*. Boston: Little, Brown and Company.

Grzymala-Busse, Anna Maria. 2002. *Redeeming the Communist Past: The Regeneration of Communist Parties in East Central Europe*. New York: Cambridge University Press.

Haggard, Stephan. 2000. *The Politics of the Asian Financial Crisis*. Washington, DC: Brookings Institution.

Handley, Paul M. 2006. *The King Never Smiles: A Biography of Thailand's Bhumibol Adulyadej*. New Haven, CT: Yale University Press.

Hartmann, Christof, Graham Hassall, and Soliman M. Santos, Jr. 2001. "Philippines." In *Elections in Asia and the Pacific: A Data Handbook. Volume II: South East Asia, East Asia and the South Pacific*. Dieter Nohlen et al., eds. Oxford: Oxford University Press.

Hawes, Gary. 1992. "Marcos, His Cronies and the Philippines Failure to Develop." In *Southeast Asian Capitalists*. Ruth McVey, ed. Ithaca, NY: Cornell Southeast Asia Program.

Hayden, Joseph. 1950. *The Philippines: A Study of National Development*. New York: McMillan Co.

Heller, William B. 2001. "Political Denials: The Policy Effects of Intercameral Partisan Differences in Bicameral Parliamentary Systems." *Journal of Law, Economics, and Organization* 17(1):34–61.

Henisz, Witold J. 2000. "The Institutional Environment for Economic Growth." *Economics and Politics* 12(1):1–31.

Hewison, Kevin. 2004. "Crafting Thailand's New Social Contract," *The Pacific Review* 17(4):503–22.

Hicken, Allen. 2001. "Parties, Policy and Patronage: Governance and Growth in Thailand." In *Corruption: The Boom and Bust of East Asia*. J. E. L. Campos, ed. Quezon City: Ateneo de Manila Press.

2002. "Parties, Pork and Policy: Policymaking in Developing Democracies." Ph.D. dissertation, University of California, San Diego.

2005. "Constitutional Reform and Budgetary Politics in Thailand." Presented at the annual Midwest Political Science meeting and 2005 Thai Studies Conference. April 2005.
2006. "Party Fabrication: Constitutional Reform and the Rise of Thai Rak Thai." *Journal of East Asian Studies* 2(2):23–46.
2007a. "How Do Rules and Institutions Encourage Vote Buying?" In *Elections for Sale: The Causes, Consequences, and Reform of Vote Buying*. Frederic C. Schaffer, ed. Boulder, CO: Lynne Rienner.
2007b. "How Effective Are Institutional Reforms?" In *Democracy for Sale: The Causes, Consequences, and Reform of Vote Buying* Frederic C. Schaffer, ed. Boulder, CO: Lynne Rienner.
2007c. "The 2007 Thai Constitution: A Return to Politics Past." *Crossroads* 19(1):128–60.
2008. "Developing Democracies in Southeast Asia: Theorizing the Role of Parties and Elections." In *Southeast Asia and Political Science: Theory, Region, and Method*. Erik Kuhonta, Daniel Slater, and Tuong Vu, eds. Stanford, CA: Stanford University Press.
Hicken, Allen and Yuko Kasuya. 2003. "A Guide to the Constitutional Structures and Electoral Systems of Asia." *Electoral Studies* 22(1):121–51.
Hicken, Allen, Shanker Satyanath, and Ernest Sergenti. 2005. "Political Institutions and Economic Performance: The Effects of Accountability and the Dispersal of Power." *American Journal of Political Science* 49(4) (October):497–507.
Hicken, Allen and Joel Simmons. 2008. "The Personal Vote and the Efficacy of Education Spending." *American Journal of Political Science* 52(1) (January):109–24.
Hicken, Allen and Heather Stoll. 2006. "Presidential Power and Presidential Candidates: How Political Institutions Shape Electoral Coordination in Presidential Elections." Presented at the 2006 Annual Meeting of the American Political Science Association, September 2006, Philadelphia, PA.
Hollnsteiner, Mary R. 1963. *The Dynamics of Power in a Philippine Municipality*. Quezon City: Community Development Research Council, University of the Philippines.
Horowitz, Donald. 1985. *Ethnic Groups in Conflict*. Berkeley: University of California Press.
1991. *A Democratic South Africa?: Constitutional Engineering in a Divided Society*. Berkeley: University of California Press.
Hug, Simon. 2001. *Altering Party Systems: Strategic Behavior and the Emergence of New Political Parties in Western Democracies"* Ann Arbor: University of Michigan Press.
Hunsaker, Bryan D. 1997. "Local Capabilities in a Centralized State: The Politics of Thai Municipal Grantsmanship." Ph.D. dissertation, Northern Illinois University.
Hutchcroft, Paul D. 1998. *Booty Capitalism: The Politics of Banking in the Philippines*. Ithaca, NY: Cornell University Press.

Hutchcroft, Paul and Joel Rocamora. 2003. "Strong Demands and Weak Institutions: The Origins and Evolution of the Democratic Deficit in the Philippines." *Journal of East Asian Studies* 3(2) (May–August):259–92.

Ingelhart, Ronald. 1997. *Modernization and Postmodernization*. Princeton, N. J.: Princeton University Press.

Jackson, Matthew and Boaz Moselle. 2002. "Coalition and Party Formation in a Legislative Voting Game." *Journal of Economic Theory* 103:49–87.

Jones, Mark P. 1994. "Presidential Election Laws and Multipartism in Latin America." *Political Research Quarterly* 47(1):41–57.

1997. "Racial Heterogeneity and the Effective Number of Candidates in Majority Runoff Elections: Evidence from Louisiana." *Electoral Studies* 16:349–58.

1999. "Electoral Laws and the Effective Number of Candidates in Presidential Elections." *Journal of Politics* 61(1):171–84.

2000. "Fused Votes." In *International Encyclopedia of Elections*. Richard Rose ed. Washington, DC: CQ Press.

2004. "Electoral Institutions, Social Cleavages, and Candidate Competition in Presidential Elections." *Electoral Studies* 23(1):73–106.

Jones, Mark P. and Scott Mainwaring. 2003. "The Nationalization of Parties and Party Systems." *Party Politics* 9(2):139–66.

Kam, Cindy and Robert J. Franzese. 2007. *Modeling and Interpreting Interactive Hypotheses in Regression Analysis: A Refresher and Some Practical Advice*. Ann Arbor: University of Michigan Press.

Kanok Wongtrangan. 1993. *Phakkanmuang Thai*. (Thai Political Parties). Bangkok: Chulalongkorn Press.

Kasuya, Yuko. 2001a. "Presidential Connection: Parties and Party Systems in the Philippines." Presented at the Annual Meeting of the Association for Asian Studies, Chicago, March 23–25, 2001.

2001b. "Party System Linkage: Explaining its Variation in the Philippine Case." Presented at the 2001 Annual Meeting of the American Political Science Association, San Francisco, August 29–September 1, 2001.

Katz, Richard. 1986. "Intraparty Preference Voting." In *Electoral Laws and Their Political Consequences*. B. Grofman and A. Lijphart, eds. New York: Agathon.

Key, V. O. 1949. *Southern Politics*. New York: Knopf.

Kiewiet, D. Roderick and Mathew D. McCubbins. 1991. *The Logic of Delegation: Congressional Parties and the Appropriations Process*. Chicago: University of Chicago Press.

Kim, Jae-on and Mahn-geum Ohn. 1992. "A Theory of Minor Party Persistence." *Social Forces* 70:575–99.

Kimura, Masataka. 1992. "Philippine Political Parties and the Party System in Transition: Leaders, Factions and Blocs." *Pilipinas* 18 (Spring):43–65.

1997. *Elections and Politics Philippine Style: A Case in Lipa*. Manila: De La Salle University Press.

King, Daniel E. 1996. "*New Political Parties in Thailand: A Case Study of the Palang Dharma Party and the New Aspiration Party.*" Ph.D. dissertation, University of Wisconsin–Madison.
King, Daniel E. and Jim LoGerfo. 1996. "Thailand: Towards Democratic Stability." *Journal of Democracy* 7:1, 102–17.
Kitschelt, Herbert. 1989. *Logics of Party Formation*. Ithaca, NY: Cornell University Press.
Kitschelt, Herbert, Zdenka Mansfeldova, Radoslaw Markowskis, and Gabor Toka. 1999. *Post-Communist Party Systems: Competition, Representation, and Inter-Party Cooperation*. Cambridge: Cambridge University Press.
KPI (King Prajadhipok's Institute). 2003. "Public Opinion Survey on the Performance of the National Assembly, Government, Public Independent Organizations, and Other Issues." Survey Report. http://www.kpi.ac.th/RD/e_pub_open.htm.
Krain, Matthew. 1997. "State-Sponsored Mass Murder: The Onset and Severity of Genocides and Politicides." *Journal of Conflict Resolution* 43:331–60.
Kramol Tongdhamachart. 1982. *Towards a Political Party Theory in Thai Perspective*. Singapore: Maruzen Asia.
Kuezni, Michelle and Gina Lambright. 2000. "Party System Institutionalization and Democratic Consolidation in 32 African Countries." Presented at the Annual Meeting of the American Political Science Association, Atlanta, August 31–September 3, 2000.
Laakso, Marku and Rein Taagepera. 1979. "Effective Number of Parties: A Measure with Application to West Europe." *Comparative Political Studies* 12:3–27.
Landé, Carl H. 1965. *Leaders, Factions and Parties*. New Haven, CT: Southeast Asian Studies, Yale University.
    1971. "Party Politics in the Philippines." In *Six Perspectives on the Philippines*. George M. Guthrie, ed. Manila: Bookmark.
    1996. *Post-Marcos Politics: A Geographic and Statistical Analysis of the 1992 Philippine Elections*. Singapore: Institute of Southeast Asian Studies.
Laquian, Aprodicio A. 1966. *The City in Nation-Building: Politics and Administration in Metropolitan Manila*. Manila: School of Public Administration, University of the Philippines.
Laver, Michael J. and Norman Schofield. 1990. *Multiparty Government: The Politics of Coalition in Europe*. Oxford: Oxford University Press.
Laver Michael and Kenneth Shepsle. 1990. "Coalitions and Cabinet Government." *American Journal of Political Science* 84: 873–90.
Law for the Election of Members of the House of Representatives of 1979 (with 1983 amendments) [in Thai]. 1987. In *The Constitution and Related Laws*. Compiled by Wichitra Funglatta. Bangkok: Thammasat University Press.
LeDuc, Lawrence. 1985. "Partisan Change and Dealignment in Canada, Great Britain, and the United States." *Comparative Politics* 17: 379–98.

Leys, Colin. 1959. "Models, Theories and the Theory of Political Parties." *Political Studies* 7:127–46.
Liang, Dapen. 1970. *Philippine Parties and Politics: A Historical Study of National Experience in Democracy*. San Francisco: The Gladstone Company.
Lijphart, Arend. 1977. *Democracy in Plural Societies: A Comparative Exploration*. New Haven, CT: Yale University Press.
   1994. *Electoral Systems and Party Systems: A Study of Twenty-Seven Democracies, 1945–1990*. Oxford: Oxford University Press.
   1999. *Patterns of Democracy: Government Forms and Performance in Thirty-Six Countries*. New Haven, CT: Yale University Press.
Lijphart, Arend, Ronald Rogowski, and Kent Weaver. 1993. "Separation of Powers and Cleavage Management." In *Do Institutions Matter: Government in the United States and Abroad*. R. Kent Weaver and Bert A. Rockman, eds. Washington, DC: The Brookings Institution.
Likhit Dhiravegin. 1985. *Thai Politics: Selected Aspects of Development and Change*. Bangkok: Tri-Sciences Publishing House.
Lipset, Seymour and Stein Rokkan, eds. 1967. *Party Systems and Voter Alignments: Cross-National Perspectives*. New York: Free Press.
LoGerfo, Jim. 1996. "Attitudes toward Democracy among Bangkok and Rural Northern Thais: The Great Divide." *Asian Survey* 36:9 (September):904–23.
Lovatt, Catherine. 2000. "Miorita: Regional Politics and Instability." *Central Europe Review* 2(2) (17 January 2000). http://www.ce-review.org/00/2/lovatt2.html.
Lupia, Arthur and Mathew McCubbins. 1998. *The Democratic Dilemma: Can Citizens Learn What They Need to Know?* Cambridge: Cambridge University Press.
Machado, K. G. 1978. "Continuity and Change in Philippine Factionalism." In *Factional Politics: Political Parties and Factionalism in Comparative Perspective*. Frank P. Beloni and Dennis C. Belley, eds. Santa Barbara, CA: ABC-CLIO, Inc.
MacIntyre, Andrew J. 1999. "Political Institutions and the Economic Crisis in Thailand and Indonesia." In *The Politics of the Asian Financial Crisis*. T. J. Pempel, ed. Ithaca: Cornell University Press.
   2002. *The Power of Institutions: Political Architecture and Governance*. Ithaca, NY: Cornell University Press.
Mackie, James A. C. 1988. "Economic Growth in the ASEAN Region: The Political Underpinnings." In *Trade and Development Achieving Industrialization in East Asia*. Helen Hughes, ed. Cambridge: Cambridge University Press.
Mainwaring, Scott P. 1999. *Rethinking Party Systems in the Third Wave of Democratization: The Case of Brazil*. Stanford, CA: Stanford University Press.
Mainwaring, Scott and Timothy Scully. 1995. "Introduction." In *Building Democratic Institutions: Party Systems in Latin America*. Scott Mainwaring and Timothy Scully, eds. Stanford, CA: Stanford University Press.

References

Mainwaring, Scott and Matthew Soberg Shugart. 1997. "Conclusion: Presidentialism and the Party System." In *Presidentialism and Democracy in Latin America*. Scott Mainwaring and Matthew Soberg Shugart, eds. Cambridge: Cambridge University Press.

Mangahas, Mahar. 1998. "How the Voters Mix Their Candidates." Social Weather Stations: Social Climate, April 1998. http://www.sws.org.ph/index.htm

Manut Watthanakomen. 1986. *Khomunphunthan phakkanmuang patchuban lae phakkanmuang kap kanluaktang pi 2522–2529*. (Basic Data on Contemporary Political Parties and on Political Parties in the Elections of 1979–1986.) Bangkok: Social Science Association of Thailand.

Manut Watthanakomen et al. 1987. *Kanpramernpreutikam khong prachachon kiewkap khwamniyom phakkanmuan ru bukhon lae batsia khong kanluaktang samachiksaphaphuthaenratsadorn (27 karakatakhom 2529) nay krungthepmahanakorn*. (Evaluation of Public Behavior Concerning the Preference to Elect Party or Individual and the Nullified Ballots of the General Election of Members of Parliament (27 July 1986) in Bangkok Metropolis.) Bangkok: Office of Policy and Planning, Ministry of Interior.

Marshall, Monty G. and Keith Jaggers. 2002. Polity IV Dataset. [Computer file; version p4v2002] College Park, MD: Center for International Development and Conflict Management, University of Maryland.

McCargo, Duncan. 2002. "Thailand's January 2001 General Elections: Vindicating Reform?" In *Reforming Thai Politics*. Duncan McCargo, ed. Copenhagen: NIAS.

2005. "Network Monarch and Legitimacy Crises in Thailand." *The Pacific Review* 18(4):499–519.

2006. "Thaksin and the Resurgence of Violence in the Thai South: Network Monarch Strikes Back?" *Critical Asian Studies* 38(1):39–71.

McCargo, Duncan and Ukrist Pathmanand. 2005. *The Thaksinization of Thailand*. Copenhagen: NIAS.

McVey, Ruth. 2000. "Of Greed and Violence, and Other Signs of Progress." In *Money and Power in Provincial Thailand*. Ruth McVey, ed. Honolulu: University of Hawaii Press.

Ministry of Interior. 1986. *Rainganwichai kanluaktang samachiksaphaphuthaenratsadorn po. so. 2529*. (Research Report on the Elections of Members of the House of Representatives 1986.) Bangkok: Local Administration Department, Ministry of the Interior.

1988. *Rainganwichai kanluaktang samachiksaphaphuthaenratsadorn po. so. 2531*. (Research Report on the Elections of Members of the House of Representatives 1988.) Bangkok: Local Administration Department, Ministry of the Interior.

1992a. *Rainganphon kanluaktang samachiksaphaphuthaenratsadorn 22 Minakhom 2535*. (Report on the Elections of Members of the House of

Representatives, 22 March 1992). Bangkok: Local Administration Department, Ministry of the Interior.

———. 1992b. *Phonkanluaktang samachiksaphaphuthaenratsadorn 13 Kanayon 2535*. (Results of the Elections of Members of the House of Representatives, 13 September 1992). Bangkok: Election Division, Local Administration Department, Ministry of the Interior.

———. 1995. *Khomun sathiti lae phonkanluaktang samachiksaphaphuthaenratsadorn 2 karakatakhom 2538*. (Data, Statistics, and Results of the Elections of Members of the House of Representatives, 2 July 1995.) Bangkok: Local Administration Department, Ministry of the Interior.

———. 1997. *Khomun sathiti lae phonkanluaktang samachiksaphaphuthaenratsadorn 17 prutsachikayon 2539*. (Data, Statistics, and Results of the Elections of Members of the House of Representatives, 17 November 1996.) Bangkok: Local Administration Department, Ministry of the Interior.

Missingham, Bruce. 1997. "Local Bureaucrats, Power and Participation: A Study of Two Village Schools in the Northeast." In *Political Change in Thailand: Democracy and Participation*. Kevin Hewison, ed. London: Routledge.

Morelli, Massimo. 2001. "Party Formation and Policy Outcomes under Different Electoral Systems." Ohio State University. Typescript.

Morgenstern, Scott and Steven Swindle. 2005. "Are Politics Local? An Analysis of Voting Patterns in 23 Democracies." *Comparative Political Studies* 38 (2):143–70.

Moser, R. G. 2001. *Unexpected Outcomes: Electoral Systems, Political Parties, and Representation in Russia*. Pittsburgh: University of Pittsburgh Press.

Mozaffar, Shaheen, James R. Scarritt, and Glen Galaich. 2003. "Electoral Institutions, Ethnopolitical Cleavages and Party Systems in Africa's Emerging Democracies." *American Political Science Review* 97(3):379–90.

Murashima Eiji. 1991. "Democracy and the Development of Political Parties in Thailand: 1932–1945." In *The Making of Modern Thai Political Parties*. Murashima Eiji et al., eds. Tokyo: Institute of Developing Economies, Joint Research Programme Series No. 86, 55–87.

Murashima Eiji, Nakharin Mektrairat, and Somkiat Wanthana, eds. 1991. *The Making of Modern Thai Political Parties*. Tokyo: Institute of Developing Economies, Joint Research Programme Series No. 86.

Murray, David. 1996. "The 1995 National Elections in Thailand: A Step Backward for Democracy?" *Asian Survey* 36(4):361–75.

Napisa Waitoolkiat. 2005. "*Information Costs and Voting in Thailand: Explaining Party- and Candidate-Centered Patterns.*" Ph.D. dissertation, Northern Illinois University.

The Nation. 2006. "No Dictation on the Charter: CNS Chief." 20 December 2006.

Neher, Clark D., ed. 1976. *Modern Thai Politics: From Village to Nation*. Cambridge: Schenkman Publishing Company.

Nelson, Michael H. 1998. *Central Authority and Local Democratization in Thailand*. Studies in Contemporary Thailand No. 6. Bangkok: White Lotus Press.

References

2000. "The Senate Elections of March 4, 2000 (etc., etc.)." *KPI Newsletter* 1 (3):3–7.

2001. "Thailand." In *Elections in Asia and the Pacific: A Data Handbook. Volume II: South East Asia, East Asia and the South Pacific.* Dieter Nohlen et al., eds. Oxford: Oxford University Press.

2002. *Thailand's House Elections of 6 January 2001: A Statistical Report.* KPI Reports No. 2. Nonthaburi, Thailand: Center for the Study of Thai Politics and Democracy, King Prajadhipok Institute.

Nowak, Thomas C. and Kay A. Snyder. 1974. "Economic Concentration and Political Change in the Philippines." In *Political Change in the Philippines: Studies of Local Politics Preceding Martial Law.* Benedict J. Kerkvliet, ed. Hawaii: The University of Hawaii Press.

Ockey, James. 1991. "Business Leaders, Gangsters and the Middle Class." Ph.D. dissertation, Cornell University.

2000. "The Rise of Local Power in Thailand: Provincial Crime, Elections and the Bureaucracy." In *Money and Power in Provincial Thailand.* Ruth McVey, ed. Honolulu: University of Hawaii Press.

2005. "Monarch, Monarchy, Succession and Stability in Thailand." *Asia Pacific Viewpoint* 46(2):115–27.

Ordeshook, Peter C. and Olga Shvetsova. 1994. "Ethnic Heterogeneity, District Magnitude and the Number of Parties." *American Journal of Political Science* 38:100–123.

Painter, Mark. 2005. "Thaksinocracy or Managerialization? Reforming the Thai Bureaucracy," Southeast Asia Research Center Working Paper (May 6, 2005) http://www.cityu.edu.hk/searc/WP.html.

Parichart Siwaraksa, Chaowana Traimas, and Ratha Yayagool. 1997. *Thai Constitutions in Brief.* Bangkok: Institute of Policy Studies.

Party Interviews. 1999. Author interviews with officials from Thai political parties. Bangkok, Thailand. January-June 1999. Anonymity requested.

Party Interviews. 2000. Author interviews with officials from Thai political parties. Bangkok, Thailand. March 2000. Anonymity requested.

Pasuk Phongpaichit and Chris Baker. 1995. *Thailand: Economy and Politics.* Oxford: Oxford University Press.

1997. "Power in Transition: Thailand in the 1990s." In *Political Change in Thailand: Democracy and Participation.* Kevin Hewison, ed. New York: Routledge.

1998. *Thailand's Boom and Bust.* Chiang Mai: Silkworm Books.

2000. "*Chao Sua, Chao Pho, Chao Thi*: Lord's of Thailand's Transition." In *Money and Power in Provincial Thailand.* Ruth McVey, ed. Honolulu: University of Hawaii Press.

Pedersen, Mogens N. 1983. "Changing Patterns of Electoral Volatility in European Party Systems, 1948–1977: Explorations in Explanation." In *Western European Party Systems: Continuity and Change.* Hans Daalder and Peter Mair, eds. Beverly Hills, CA: Sage.

Persson, Torsten and Guido Tabellini. 2000. *Political Economics: Explaining Economic Policy*. Cambridge, MA: MIT Press.

Pisan Suriyamongkol and James F. Guyot. 1986. *The Bureaucratic Polity at Bay*. Public Administration Document, No. 51. Bangkok: Graduate School of Public Administration, NIDA.

Posner, Daniel N. 2004. "Measuring Ethnic Fractionalization in Africa," *American Journal of Political Science* 48(4) (October):849–63.

Powell, G. Bingham. 1982. *Contemporary Democracies: Participation, Stability, and Violence*. Cambridge, MA: Harvard University Press.

  2000. *Elections as Instruments of Democracy*. New Haven, CT: Yale University Press.

Powell, G. B. and Georg Vanberg. 2000. "Election Laws, Disproportionality and Median Correspondence: Implications for Two Visions of Democracy." *British Journal of Political Science* 30(3):383–411.

Preecha Hongkrailuet. 1981. *Phakkanmuang lae banha phakkanmuang thai*. (Political Parties and the Problems of Thai Political Parties.) Bangkok: Thai Watthanaphanit.

Prizzia, Ross. 1985. *Thailand in Transition: The Role of Oppositional Forces*. Asian Studies and Hawaii, No. 32. Hawaii: Center for Asian and Pacific Studies, University of Hawaii Press.

Prudhisan Jumbala. 1998. "Thailand: Constitutional Reform Amidst Economic Crisis." In *Southeast Asian Affairs 1998*. Singapore: ISEAS.

Putzel, James. 1993. "Democratisation and Clan Politics: The 1992 Philippine Elections." Mimeo.

Quezon, Manuel L. 1940. *Addresses of His Excellency Manuel L. Quezon on the Theory of a Partyless Democracy*. Manila: Bureau of Print.

Quimpo, Nathan Gilbert. 2005. "Yellow Pad: Trapo Parties and Corruption." *BusinessWorld*. October 10, 2005.

Reed, Steven R. 1994. "Democracy and the Personal Vote: A Cautionary Tale from Japan." *Electoral Studies* 13:1, 17–28.

Reilly, Benjamin. 2001. *Democracy in Divided Societies: Electoral Engineering for Conflict Management*. New York: Cambridge University Press.

  2006. *Democracy and Diversity: Political Engineering in the Asia-Pacific*. Oxford: Oxford University Press.

Reynolds, Andrew. 1999. *Electoral Systems and Democratization in Southern Africa*. Oxford: Oxford University Press.

Riggs, Fred W. 1966. *Thailand: The Modernization of a Bureaucratic Polity*. Honolulu: East-West Center Press.

Riker, William H. 1982. "The Two-Party System and Duverger's Law: An essay on the History of Political Science." *American Political Science Review* 76:753–66.

Riker, William H. and Peter C. Ordeshook. 1968. "A Theory of the Calculus of Voting." *American Political Science Review* 62:25–42.

Robertson, Philip S. Jr. 1996. "The Rise of the Rural Network Politician: Will Thailand's New Elite Endure." *Asian Survey* 36:9 (September 1996).

References

Rogers, James. 2003. "The Impact of Bicameralism on Legislative Production." *Legislative Studies Quarterly* 28(4):509–28.

Rose, Richard. 1974. *Politics in England: An Interpretation.* Boston: Little Brown.

Samuels, David Julian. 1998. "*Careerism and Its Consequences: Federalism, Elections and Policy-Making in Brazil.*" Unpublished Ph.D. dissertation, University of California, San Diego.

 2002. "Presidentialized Parties: The Separation of Powers and Party Organization and Behavior." *Comparative Political Studies* 35(4):461–83.

 2003. *Careerism and its Consequences: Federalism, Elections, and Policy Making in Brazil.* Cambridge: Cambridge University Press.

Saribo, Vincent Boulekone Viresanial. 2003. "Vincent Chronicle No. 1: Alternative Regime or Constitution Amendment?" March 30, 2003. http://www.news.vu/en/opinion/Chronicles/394.shtml. Accessed March 7, 2007.

Sartori, Giovanni. 1968. "Political Development and Political Engineering." In *Public Policy.* John D. Montgomery and Albert O. Hirschman, eds. Cambridge: Cambridge University Press.

 1976. *Parties and Party Systems: A Framework for Analysis.* Cambridge: Cambridge University Press.

 1986. "The Influence of Electoral Systems: Faulty Laws or Faulty Method?" In *Electoral Laws and Their Political Consequences.* Bernard Grofman and Arend Lijphart, eds. New York: Agathon.

 1994. "Neither Presidentialism nor Parliamentarism." In *The Failure of Presidential Democracy: Comparative Perspectives.* Juan Linz and Arturo Valenzuela, eds. Baltimore: Johns Hopkins University Press.

Schattschneider, Elmer E. 1942. *Party Government.* New York: Farrar and Rinehart.

 1960. *The Semisovereign People: A Realist's View of Democracy in America.* New York: Holt, Rinehart, and Winston.

Schedler, Andreas. 1995. Under- and Overinstitutionalization: Some Ideal Typical Propositions Concerning New and Old Party Systems. Working Paper 213, Kellogg Institute, University of Notre Dame.

Selway, Joel Sawat. n.d. "Crosscutting Cleavages: Theory and Measurement of Social Structure." Working paper, University of Michigan.

Shugart, Matthew Soberg. 1995. "The Electoral Cycle and Institutional Sources of Divided Presidential Government." *American Political Science Review* 89(2) (June):327–43.

 1999. "Presidentialism, Parliamentarism, and Provision of Public Goods in Less-Developed Countries." *Constitutional Political Economy* 10 (1):53–88.

 2001. "Electoral 'efficiency' and the move to mixed-member systems." *Electoral Studies* 20(2) (June):173–93.

Shugart, Matthew S. and John M. Carey. 1992. *Presidents and Assemblies: Constitutional Design and Electoral Dynamics.* Cambridge: Cambridge University Press.

Shugart, Matthew Soberg and Martin P. Wattenberg, eds. 2001. *Mixed-Member Electoral Systems: The Best of Both Worlds?* Oxford: Oxford University Press.

Sidel, John T. 1996. *Capital Coercion and Crime: Bossism in the Philippines.* Stanford: Stanford University Press.

Sombat Chantornvong. 1987. "Kanluaktang kap khwamkhemkhaeng khong phakkanmuang: Khawsangkeet buangton" (The General Election and the Strength of Political Parties: Preliminary Comments). *Warasaan Thammasat* 6(4):77–109.

    1993. *Luaktang wikrit: Panha lae thang ok* (Thai Elections in Crisis: Problems and Solutions). Bangkok: Kobfai.

    1999. Interview with author. Bangkok, Thailand. March 23, 1999.

Somporn Sangchai. 1976. *Coalition Behavior in Modern Thai Politics.* Occasional Paper No. 41. Singapore: Institute of Southeast Asian Studies.

Stauffer, Robert B. 1975. *The Philippine Congress: Causes of Structural Change.* London: Sage Publications.

Stockton, Hans. 2001. "Political Parties, Party Systems, and Democracy in East Asia: Lessons from Latin America." *Comparative Political Studies* 34 (1):94–119.

Stoner-Weiss, Kathryn. 2001. "The Limited Reach of Russia's Party System: Underinstitutionalization in Dual Transition," *Politics and Society* 29 (3):385–414.

Suchit Bunbongkarn. 1999. Interview with author. Bangkok, Thailand. February 25, 1999.

Surin Maisrikrod. 1992. *Thailand's Two General Elections in 1992: Democracy Sustained.* Research Notes and Discussion Paper No. 75. Singapore: Institute of Southeast Asian Studies.

Surin Maisrikrod and Duncan McCargo. 1997. "Electoral Politics: Commercialisation and Exclusion." In *Political Change in Thailand: Democracy and Participation.* Kevin Hewison, ed. London: Routledge.

SWS (Social Weather Stations). 2002. "SWS Survey: National Pride is High, But Satisfaction with Democracy Low." SWS Media Release, July 4, 2002.

Taagepera, Rein and Matthew Soberg Shugart. 1989. *Seats and Votes: The Effects and Determinants of Electoral Systems.* New Haven, CT: Yale University Press.

Tan, Paige Johnson. 2002. "*Streams of Least Resistance: the Institutionalization of Political Parties and Democracy in Indonesia.*" Ph.D. dissertation, University of Virginia.

Tancangco, Luzviminda. 1992. *The Anatomy of Electoral Fraud.* Manila: MLAGM.

Teehankee, Julio. 2002. "Electoral Politics in the Philippines." In *Electoral Politics in Southeast and East Asia.* Aurel Croissant and Marei John, eds. Singapore: Friedrich-Ebert-Stiftung.

Thai Politician. 1999. Interview with Author. Bangkok, Thailand. May 11, 1999.

Tsebelis, George. 1995. "Decision Making in Political Systems: Veto Players in Presidentialism, Parliamentarism, Multicameralism, and Multipartyism." *British Journal of Political Science* 25:289–325.
    2000. "Veto Players and Institutional Analysis." *Governance* 13(4):441–74.
    2002. *Veto Players: How Political Institutions Work*. Princeton: Princeton University Press.
Tsebelis, George and Eduardo Aleman. 2005. "Presidential Conditional Agenda Setting in Latin America." *World Politics* 57(3):396–420.
Tsebelis, George and Jeanette Money. 1997. *Bicameralism*. New York: Cambridge University Press.
Tsebelis George and Tatiana Rizova. 2007. "Presidential Conditional Agenda Setting in the Former Communist Countries." *Comparative Political Studies* 40(10):1155–82.
Valenzuela, Samuel J. 1992. "Democratic Consolidation in Post-Transition Settings: Notion, Process, and Facilitating Conditions." In *Issues in Democratic Consolidation: The New South American Democracies in Comparative Perspective*, Scott Mainwaring, Guillermo O'Donnell, and Samuel J. Valenzuela, eds. Notre, Dame, IN: University of Notre Dame Press.
Vatikiotis, Michael. 1998. "No Quick Fix." In *The Aftershock: How an Economic Earthquake is Rattling Southeast Asia Politics*. Faith Keenan, ed. Hong Kong: Far Eastern Economic Review.
Velasco, Renato. 1999. "Philippines." In *Democracy, Governance, and Economic Performance: East and Southeast Asia*. Ian Marsh, Jean Blondel, and Takashi Inoguchi, eds. New York: UN Press.
Wallack, Jessica Seddon, Alejandra Gaviria, Ugo Panizza, and Ernesto Stein. 2003. "Political Particularism around the World." *World Bank Economic Review* 17(1):133–43.
Wallis, Darren. 2003. "Democratizing a Hegemonic Regime: From Institutionalized Party to Institutionalized Party System in Mexico?" *Democractization* 10(3):15–38.
Wilson, David A. 1962. *Politics in Thailand*. Ithaca: Cornell University Press.
Wolters, Willem. 1984. *Politics, Patronage and Class Conflict in Central Luzon*. Quezon City: New Day Publisher.
World Bank Group. N.d. "Fiscal Decentralization Indicators." http://www1.worldbank.org/publicsector/decentralization/fiscalindicators.htm.
Wurfel, David. 1988. *Filipino Politics: Development and Decay*. Ithaca, NY: Cornell University Press.
WVS (World Values Survey). 2000. http://www.worldvaluessurvey.org/.
    2004. http://www.worldvaluessurvey.org/.

Index

aggregation, 4–6, 10–14
   definition of, 2
   figure, 27
   payoff, 15–16, 33–39
   policymaking implications, 184
   probability of capturing payoff, 16, 39–45
   theory of, 15–17, 27–28, 29–33
Arroyo, Gloria Macapagal, 170

bicameralism, 36, 52
Brambor, Thomas, 61

Carey, John, 53
Carlos, Clarita, 157
centralization,
   horizontal, 16, 27, 35–39, 52
   vertical, 16, 27, 34, 51
Chalerm Yubamrung, 96
Chavalit Yongchaiyudh, 120
Chhibber, Pradeep, 15, 27, 34
Chulalongkorn, 88
Clark, William, 10, 61
coordination, 9–15, 28
   cross-district., *See* aggregation
   within districts, 10, 28
Corazon, 159
Cox, Gary, 10, 15, 28, 40

cross-district coordination., *See* aggregation

Duverger, Maurice, 15
Duverger's law, 10, 43

Estrada, Joseph, 170

Fearon, James, 54
Franzese, Rob, 61

Golder, Matt, 10, 40, 52, 57, 61
Golder, Sona, 30

Handley, Paul, 140

inflation,
   definition of, 13, 47–48
intra-district coordination., *See* coordination, within districts

Kam, Cindy, 61
Kasuya, Yuko, 153, 165
Kollman, Ken, 15, 27, 34

linkage. *See* aggregation

M+1 rule, 10, 43, 102
Magsaysay, Ramon, 152

Mainwaring, Scott, 4, 92, 156
Marcos, Ferdinand, 150, 152
McCargo, Duncan, 140
Mongkut, 88

Ockey, James, 140

Pahonyothin, 88
party factionalism. *See* political parties, cohesion
party system,
    definition of, 3
party system, inflation. *See* inflation
party system, nationalization, 2–3, 6, 8–9
    consequences, 9, 184
party system, number of parties,
    consequences, 7–8, 184
    effective number, definition, 7
Phibun Songkhram, 88
Philippines,
    as a comparative case, 20–24
Philippines, election monitoring, 167
Philippines, electoral system, 160–63
    House of Representatives, 160
    Senate, 161
    write-in ballot, 162
Philippines, party system,
    aggregation, 164–74, 165
    bifactionalism, 166
    characteristics, 152–56
    counter-concurrency effect, 173
    guest candidatures, 154
    history, 150–52
    party platforms, 155
    party switching, 152–53
    post-Marcos, 164
    vote splitting, 154
Philippines, political parties,
    KBL, 157
    LAKAS-NUCD, 152
    Liberal Party, 151, 152, 155, 156

Nacionalista Party, 151, 152, 155, 156
Philippines, presidency, 160
Philippines, term limits, 174
Pinochet, Augusto, 38
political parties,
    party cohesion, 37, 52
    purpose of, 4–6
political party,
    definition of, 3
Prem Tinsulanonda, 118, 122
probability, 16, 39, 65
    operationalization, 65
    parliamentary systems, 44
    presidential systems, 40

Quezon, Manuel, 160
Quimpo, Nathan, 156

Ramos, Fidel, 43
reelection, president, 42–44, 71
reserve domains, 38, 52
Riggs, Fred W., 90

Samuels, David, 40
Sanoh Thienthong, 138
Sarit Thanarat, 88
Sartori, Giovani, 15
Scully, Timothy, 92, 156
Shugart, Matthew Soberg, 4, 8, 10, 40, 53
size of the prize.
    See aggregation payoff
social heterogeneity, 33, 54, 78
strategic coordination, 102
    assumptions, 103
    strategic entry, 102
    strategic voting, 102

Taagepera, Rein, 10
term limits, 42.
    See reelection, president
Thailand,
    as a comparative case, 20–24
Thailand, constitutional history, 114

Index

Thailand, constitutional reform,
 1997, 127–29
 2007, 140–44
 implications, 129–33
 party list, 147
 Senate, 145
Thailand, elections,
 split district returns, 96
 vote buying, 103
Thailand, electoral history, 114
Thailand, electoral system,
 block vote, 100–01
 incentives of block vote, 102–05
Thailand, horizontal centralization, 118
 bicameralism, 118
 party cohesion, 118
 reserve domains, 118
Thailand, monarchy, 119
Thailand, number of parties, 98
 within-district coordination, 100–10
Thailand, party system,
 aggregation, 110–12
 aggregation incentives, 122
 characteristics, 91–94
 history, 88–91
 party cohesion, 138
 regional patterns, 109, 125
 Southern exception, 105, 124
 vote differential, 94

Thailand, political parties,
 Chart Thai, 95, 122, 123
 Democrat Party, 95, 105, 123, 125
 factions, 91
 Muon Chon, 96
 New Aspiration Party, 92, 95, 105, 120, 123, 138
 Palang Dharma, 96, 123, 138
 Palang Prachachon Party, 143
 Prachachon Party, 106
 Thai Rak Thai, 120, 123, 136
Thailand, prime minister selection, 121
Thailand, social heterogeneity, 122
Thailand, vertical centralization, 117
Thaksin Shinawatra, 119
 fall of, 139–40
 rise of, 136–39
Thanom Kittikachorn, 89
turncoatism. *See* Philippines, party system, party switching

Ukrist Pathmanand, 140

volatility, electoral, 93, 154

Wallack, Jessica Seddon, et. al., 53

For EU product safety concerns, contact us at Calle de José Abascal, 56–1º,
28003 Madrid, Spain or eugpsr@cambridge.org.

www.ingramcontent.com/pod-product-compliance
Ingram Content Group UK Ltd.
Pitfield, Milton Keynes, MK11 3LW, UK
UKHW011315060825
461487UK00005B/96